T0291195

The East Asian Negotiator

The East Asian Negotiator

TAN Lee Cheng

Singapore University of Social Sciences, Singapore

LIM Tai Wei

Soka University, Japan

World Scientific

NEW JERSEY · LONDON · SINGAPORE · BEIJING · SHANGHAI · HONG KONG · TAIPEI · CHENNAI · TOKYO

Published by

World Scientific Publishing Co. Pte. Ltd.
5 Toh Tuck Link, Singapore 596224
USA office: 27 Warren Street, Suite 401-402, Hackensack, NJ 07601
UK office: 57 Shelton Street, Covent Garden, London WC2H 9HE

British Library Cataloguing-in-Publication Data
A catalogue record for this book is available from the British Library.

ISBN 978-981-12-8050-4 (hardcover)
ISBN 978-981-12-8051-1 (ebook for institutions)
ISBN 978-981-12-8052-8 (ebook for individuals)

For any available supplementary material, please visit
https://www.worldscientific.com/worldscibooks/10.1142/13520#t=suppl

Desk Editor: Sandhya Venkatesh

Typeset by Stallion Press
Email: enquiries@stallionpress.com

Contents

Introduction

The East Asian Negotiator by Tan Lee Cheng and Lim Tai Wei

Witnessing and experiencing East–West interactions and cross-cultural negotiations as part of her career, Lee Cheng has learnt to appreciate and be open to the plurality and diversity of negotiating styles that East Asia has to offer. In this volume, it is the intention of the authors to share their practical experiences as well as theoretical knowledge with trade professional audiences, business students at colleges, industry practitioners and the general lay readers, to get an idea of these negotiating styles from a cultural relativist perspective.

While many East Asians are becoming more confident in their own culture and ways of doing things, they are simultaneously open to the melding of the east–west ways. Because of this form of cultural hybridization, it is useful to include Tai Wei's multidisciplinary area studies' training, which decodes some of the cultural symbols and contextual language used in such negotiations. He does so keenly with globalization's impact in mind. Due to globalization, western styles of negotiations have constantly engaged closely with negotiation styles in East Asia and the cross-pollination of ideas between the two have resulted in the hybridized negotiation styles in the contemporary setting.

Distilled practical knowledge will be combined with literature review and theoretical readings to share with readers the intricacies as well as theoretician's conceptualizations of East Asian negotiation styles. It is written from the sub-discipline of cross-cultural negotiating styles, adopting some sociological/anthropological perspectives, anecdotes and concepts to discuss this subject matter.

This volume hopes to fill in the gap between theoretical and applied knowledge through the use of theoretical concepts that readers are familiar with from the Western and other English-language textbooks while supplementing them with practitioner-oriented case studies drawn from actual experiences. This prevents the publication from becoming a theory-heavy text. It is also in line with the fact that both authors are teaching in an applied social sciences university's business school.

Our overarching aim is to present an accurate profile of the typical negotiator you are likely to encounter in each of the countries covered in this work. We hope to help you anticipate and understand how this East Asian negotiator will likely behave at the negotiation table. We will also offer suggestions as to how you can have a fruitful and successful negotiation with him or her, in particular, when you are on their turf. To this end, we selected eight broad negotiation themes and concepts to frame our description and discussion of each one of these negotiators. This approach will also enable a meaningful comparison across national boundaries.

The theoretical themes which are discussed in detailed in a separate chapter are:

1. The Environment
2. Culture
3. Communication
4. Negotiation Strategies: Distributive or Integrative
5. Concession-making and Hardball Tactics
6. Role of Women
7. Intermediary/Interpreter
8. Time, Timelines and Timeliness

Asia is so vast that it makes any discussion carrying such a label audacious. In this work, we have selected economies that are significant and representative of the region based on the authors' engagement in the region. These countries are also top trading partners in the Asia-Pacific economies, including CJK (China, Japan, Korea) and the Association of Southeast Asian Nations (ASEAN)10. Together they consist of the world's second and third largest economies and a rising middle economic power as well as probably the world's second most successful economic bloc after the European Union (EU). The population size and GDP of each country (as well as the region in the case of ASEAN) are set out in the following table. Of course, these settings are also where the authors have first-hand experience dealing with their people and cultures and their negotiating styles.

Country (in alphabetical order) CJK and Selected ASEAN10 countries	Population	GDP in USD
China	1.410 billion	23 trillion
Indonesia	277 million	3 trillion
Japan	124 million	5.2 trillion
Korea (South)	51.8 million	2.2 trillion
Malaysia	33.8 million	856 billion
Philippines	114 million	871 billion
Singapore	5.9 million	531 billion
Thailand	69 million	1.2 trillion
Vietnam	104 million	260 billion

Source: CIA, "The World Factbook" dated 12 May 2022 on the CIA website [downloaded on 12 May 2022], available at https://www.cia.gov/the-world-factbook/countries.

Chapterization of the Volume

The volume breaks down the chapters in the following way. It begins with a chapter that sets out the theoretical framework and concepts that will be used to discuss the cultural traits, communication patterns and negotiation styles commonly observed and adopted in each of the countries covered in this book. The country-specific chapters will cover, in alphabetical order, the selected ASEAN countries and their Northeast Asian counterparts (CJK or China, Japan, Korea). In each of these chapters, we will profile the typical negotiator you will likely meet and suggest ways for you to meaningfully engage with them. At the end of each chapter, there is a short quiz to recap some of the key points covered. The following is a short preview of each of the chapters.

The East Asian Negotiator

China. U.S. or Western negotiators often find Northeast Asian (Chinese or Japanese) difficult to read, including interpreting if indeed a deal has been reached, because Northeast Asians tend to conform to the ancient Oriental custom of telling high-level management what they desire to hear rather than the actual facts or reality.[1] Just like other Northeast Asians, Chinese negotiators are unlikely to give an outright denial or rejection of a request. When trying to reject the other party's negotiators, Chinese negotiators used an array of tactics to soften their communication of rejection. Chinese business persons are likely to modify the subject matter, suddenly become quiet, distract and pose another enquiry, use ambiguous expressions and or articulate seemingly positive expressions with indirect negative connections [like *hai bu cuo* ("not bad"), *hai hao* ("seems okay"), and *hai xing* or *hai ke yi* ("seems able to make it")].[2] Reading such verbal signals is included in this chapter.

Indonesia. The Indonesian negotiator is regarded as polite and pleasant externally in their interactions. This demeanor reflects their refinement and high status within Indonesian society. But it also means that their calm exterior will not allow any non-Indonesian negotiator to easily know the Indonesian negotiator's true feelings about the progress of the negotiations. Some may then feel that the negotiation process is leading nowhere and sometimes this can confuse non-Indonesian negotiators about the outcome. This chapter will examine the techniques of the Indonesian negotiator as well as their Tionghua (ethnic Chinese) countrymen and then recommend some coping mechanisms in dealing with the Indonesian negotiator. It can also demystify their negotiating styles and priorities.

Japan. The enigmatic and mystified negotiating culture in Japan is often considered one of the hardest to read for non-natives negotiating with them. The Japanese word for negotiation is "交渉 (Kōshō)". It is written

---

[1] Van Zandt, H. F. (November 1970). "How to Negotiate in Japan." *Magazine/Harvard Business Review (HBR)* [downloaded on 1 January 2022], available at https://hbr.org/1970/11/how-to-negotiate-in-japan.
[2] Graham, J. L. & Lam, N. M. (October 1, 2003). "The Chinese Negotiation." *Harvard Business Review* [downloaded on 1 January 2022], available at https://hbr.org/2003/10/the-chinese-negotiation.

in Kanji and derived from Chinese characters. Culturally, and in terms of semantics, the Japanese word for "negotiation" can also refer to the processes of bargaining and dealing while building relationships or connections. Therefore, the elements of building long-term relations and maintaining the "face" factor for all parties are very important in reaching compromises through the dialogue between two or more parties without burning bridges or embarrassing the disadvantaged party with a view of the possibility of dealing in the future. This is a common feature of many negotiating styles in Northeast Asia. This volume affords the readers an opportunity for comparative studies between Northeast Asian negotiating cultures and styles.

Korea. Korean, like many Asian cultures, is a high-context culture. Inferential skills are necessary to understanding meanings in high-context communication, but such skills are not required in low-context communication. Non-verbal communication therefore plays a larger and more significant role in high-context communication. Simple physical gestures are also important. Greeting with a bow, a handshake and eye contact are well-regarded practices (similar to contemporary Chinese practices whereas the Japanese practice a much more elaborate ritual of bowing only), along with business card exchanges (which are to be received with a respectful head-nodding acknowledgement).[3] This volume peeks into how the two Koreas separated by the Cold War have developed their own negotiating styles.

Malaysia. In building long-term and trustworthy relations with the Malaysian team, showing respect for them is of utmost importance as Malaysian negotiators generally prefer to create strong personal connections first before engaging in business dealings and all Malaysians (regardless of race) prefer to work with familiar and likeable individuals.[4]

---

[3] Wang, Hui-ya Anny. (August 2016). "A study of negotiating strategies in South Korea. *Journal of Literature and Art Studies*, 6(8), 953 [downloaded on 1 January 2022], available at https://pdfs.semanticscholar.org/4b55/963c764aaa41e907835c90ba597ec81acc23.pdf.

[4] Katz, L. (March 2008). "Negotiating International Business — Malaysia." Negotiating International Business — The Negotiator's Reference Guide to 50 Countries Around the World and Mount San Antonio College, p. 1 [downloaded on 1 January 2023], available at https://instruction2.mtsac.edu/rjagodka/BUSM_51_Project/Negotiating/Malaysia.pdf.

This is especially visible in the case of Malaysian ethnic Chinese[5] who tend to place more emphasis on *guanxi* ties with friends, sworn brothers, family members, relatives or trusted subordinates. While there are culture-specific aspects of the Malaysian negotiating styles among its ethnic groups, there are also common features that are equally applicable to all of them. For example, unpleasant conversations with the Malaysian negotiator must be held privately (without public outbursts and indications of being upset), carefully and with great care in order not to disrespect Malaysians.[6] In certain limited contexts, Malaysians may use humor as a tool to reduce tensions and conflicts while downplaying hierarchical gaps and differences.[7] In this chapter, strategies useful for negotiating with multicultural East Asian countries like Malaysia will be covered.

The Philippines. You should always be mindful of the context and atmosphere and understand what the Filipino negotiator is trying to convey to you. Pay attention to the context, gestures and non-verbal signals.[8] The Filipino negotiator will be sensitive to your non-verbal cues such as any change in your tone of voice or subtle gestures. They pride themselves in being able to access your "inner world" and know how you really feel about the negotiation process and any outcome that will follow. When they are able to accurately read your reactions, they take it as a reflection of their emotional intelligence. It assures them that they can deepen their relationship with

---

[5] Hashim, H. M. (2010). "International Negotiation Styles: A Perspective of Malaysian Diplomats." CORE (Connecting Repositories) Research Service, p. 51 [downloaded on 1 January 2023], available at https://core.ac.uk/download/pdf/56361749.pdf.

[6] Katz, L. (March 2008). "Negotiating International Business — Malaysia" dated March 2008 in Negotiating International Business — The Negotiator's Reference Guide to 50 Countries Around the World and Mount San Antonio College, p. 1 [downloaded on 1 January 2023], available at https://instruction2.mtsac.edu/rjagodka/BUSM_51_Project/Negotiating/Malaysia.pdf.

[7] Awang, S., Maros, M., & Ibrahim, N. (May 2012). Malay values in intercultural communication. *International Journal of Social Science and Humanity*, 2(3), 202 [downloaded on 1 January 2023], available at http://www.ijssh.org/papers/96-CH219.pdf.

[8] Katz, L. (2017). "Negotiation International Business — Philippines." Negotiating International Business — The Negotiator's Reference Guide to 50 Countries Around the World [downloaded on 5 January 2023], available at http://www.leadershipcrossroads.com/mat/cou/Philippines.pdf.

you. This empathy is known in their culture as *pakikiramdam*.[9] Therefore, culturally defined atmospherics are something that negotiators would have to feel for in the negotiations. This chapter will examine the non-tangible aspects of the Filipino negotiators' mindset.

Singapore. This chapter will examine how to manage negotiations with Singaporeans in the context of differing interests. In areas where your interests and positions are at odds with those of the Singaporean negotiator, you will still find that their communication style is less direct and that they prefer a more implicit approach to resolving differences. The Singaporean negotiator is always sensitive to surrounding influencing events or happenings, so you should understand their motivation in order to focus on the subject and outcome of your negotiation.[10] They may adopt subtle gestures such as grimacing and shaking of head to convey limitations on their end. Also, laughter may be used to mask embarrassment, disapproval or other feelings of distress. Westerners sometimes observe Singaporeans smiling or laughing at what they might consider inappropriate moments.[11] The chapter, written by Singaporeans, aims to provide some practical insights into the way Singaporean negotiators work.

Thailand. Thai social hierarchy and its impact on negotiation styles is detailed in this chapter. The Thai negotiator expects junior subordinates to follow instructions. In addition to rank, respect for elders is also deeply embedded within Thai social and business culture. Thai negotiating counterparts may even take offence if the non-Thai negotiating party is too young or too junior. The complaint *dek kern pai* (too young) may therefore be levied. Even though company brochures and publicity materials

---

[9] Reyes, J. (2015). Loób and Kapwa: An introduction to a Filipino virtue ethics. *Asian Philosophy*, 25(2), 148–171, doi: 10.1080/09552367.2015.1043173.

[10] Cordeiro, C. M. (2019). Negotiating with managers from Singapore. In M. A. Khan & N. Ebner (Eds.), *The Palgrave Handbook of Cross-Cultural Business Negotiation*. Cham: Palgrave Macmillan. https://doi.org/10.1007/978-3-030-00277-0_16.

[11] Katz, L. (2017). "Negotiation International Business — Singapore." Negotiating International Business — The Negotiator's Reference Guide to 50 Countries Around the World [downloaded on 7 February 2023], available at http://www.leadershipcrossroads.com/mat/cou/Singapore.pdf.

invariably use images of young people, this is only superficial. Decision-making power is still vested with the senior members of the team who may also be elderly. However, the junior or younger members on the team are also treated pleasantly and with courtesy. The Thai understand that ego is important and so will avoid conflict and clashes. Thus, although unequal distribution of power is generally accepted, smooth interpersonal interaction is still the order of the day. This chapter examines the enigmatic Thai negotiator, contextualized in the social norms.

Vietnam. Hierarchy is also important in the case of Vietnam. For example, during negotiations, you should initiate any new discussion or proposal through junior members of the Vietnamese team for them to forward your proposal to someone more senior in the organization. This acknowledges their hierarchy and way of doing things. Frequently, this has to be put in writing to facilitate communication. Junior team members will not offer any comment at all as their task is merely to pass on the message. Especially in a state-owned enterprise (SOE), junior employees will not speak their mind because they fear being seen as "too competent" or worse, arrogant or disrespectful. Although in cities such as Ho Chi Minh and in the IT sectors, many young employees seem outwardly Westernized, hierarchy is still important. And even though decisions are made in groups after reaching consensus, junior members rarely have any dissenting view or liberty to speak up. The final say typically comes from someone with the appropriate authority and rank, with the support of the entire team. This and more negotiating tips will be covered in the chapter.

With this short introduction and chapterization preview, the next chapter launches into the theoretical aspects, which set out the framework for the country-specific discourse based on their negotiating styles.

Bibliography

Awang, S., Maros, M., & Ibrahim, N. (May 2012). Malay values in intercultural communication. *International Journal of Social Science and Humanity*, 2(3) [downloaded on 1 January 2023], available at http://www.ijssh.org/papers/96-CH219.pdf.

CIA. (May 12, 2022). "The World Factbook." CIA website [downloaded on 12 May 2022], available at https://www.cia.gov/the-world-factbook/countries.

Cordeiro, C. M. (2019). Negotiating with managers from Singapore. In M. A. Khan & N. Ebner (Eds.), *The Palgrave Handbook of Cross-Cultural Business Negotiation*. Cham: Palgrave Macmillan. https://doi.org/10.1007/978-3-030-00277-0_16.

Graham, J. L. & Lam, N. M. (October 1, 2003). "The Chinese Negotiation." Harvard Business Review [downloaded on 1 January 2022], available at https://hbr.org/2003/10/the-chinese-negotiation.

Hashim, H. M. (2010). "International Negotiation Styles: A Perspective of Malaysian Diplomats." CORE (Connecting Repositories) research service [downloaded on 1 January 2023], available at https://core.ac.uk/download/pdf/56361749.pdf.

Katz, L. (March 2008). "Negotiating International Business — Malaysia." Negotiating International Business — The Negotiator's Reference Guide to 50 Countries around the World and Mount San Antonio College [downloaded on 1 January 2023], available at https://instruction2.mtsac.edu/rjagodka/BUSM_51_Project/Negotiating/Malaysia.pdf.

Reyes, J. (2015). Loób and Kapwa: An introduction to a Filipino virtue ethics. *Asian Philosophy*, 25(2), 148–171. doi: 10.1080/09552367.2015.1043173.

Van Zandt, H. F. (November 1970). "How to Negotiate in Japan." *Magazine/Harvard Business Review (HBR)* [downloaded on 1 January 2022], available at https://hbr.org/1970/11/how-to-negotiate-in-japan.

Wang, Hui-ya Anny. (August 2016). A study of negotiating strategies in South Korea. *Journal of Literature and Art Studies*, 6(8) [downloaded on 1 January 2022], available at https://pdfs.semanticscholar.org/4b55/963c764aaa41e907835c90ba597ec81acc23.pdf.

Theoretical Matters on Negotiations

Negotiation is a voluntary decision-making process which involves two (or more) parties in an attempt to resolve their opposing interests. We choose to negotiate because we hope for an outcome that exceeds what we are getting without negotiating. Negotiating across borders and cultures has become the norm, facilitated both by increased trade and advances in communication technology. Business executives now find themselves making deals and connections with someone from different nationalities and cultures, whether face-to-face, over zoom or over other electronic exchanges, on a regular if not daily basis.

In each country-specific chapter, we will present the cultural traits, communication patterns and negotiation styles that are commonly observed and adopted in those regions and cultures. Our aim is to provide a granular profile of the typical negotiator you would likely meet in the nine East Asian countries featured in the volume, namely Indonesia, Malaysia, the Philippines, Singapore, Thailand, Vietnam, China, Japan and Korea. Pointers and suggestions are also included to help you achieve a fruitful negotiation session, especially when you are negotiating on their turf. Eight broad negotiation themes and concepts have been selected to frame our analytical discourse:

1. The environment of the negotiation
2. Culture
3. Communication
4. Negotiation strategy: distributive or integrative

5. Concession-making and hardball tactics
6. Role of women
7. Intermediary/interpreter
8. Time, timelines and timeliness

The chapter discussions across the above themes will also provide useful comparisons across national boundaries.

1. The Environment

To varying degrees, the environment in which a negotiator operates affects his or her decision-making. Coming from their culturally high-context background, most East Asian negotiators, consciously or otherwise, take numerous cues from their environment. In each chapter, we will provide a broad overview of the relevant socio-economic environment of the countries covered. This larger environment adds a layer of complexity in international negotiations because there are factors which tend to be beyond the negotiators' control; for example, influences and pressures exerted by external parties such as government, local authorities or business associations. When negotiating with the collectivist East Asian negotiator, even if such parties are not at the table, their impact is often felt. Moreover, in many of the countries covered in this book, fully or partially-owned State-Owned Enterprises operate in various key business sectors. You should thus also be aware of their distinct business culture, if and when negotiating with them.

2. Culture

Dutch social psychologist, Geert Hofstede defined culture as a collective programming of the mind which distinguishes members of one group from another.[1] Culture is a group-level phenomenon; it is learned and not something that one is born with. It affects how we think, behave and communicate. People from different cultures negotiate differently — from how and

[1] Hofstede, Geert. 1980. *Culture's Consequences: International Differences in Work-Related Values*. Beverly Hills: Sage Publications.

why they make the deal; as well as the kind of deal they make. Not understanding or knowing how to bridge these differences will result in unintended or disastrous breakdown in the negotiation or relationship. Because East Asian cultures are collectivist and high-context, culture plays a prominent role in the negotiation process. Of course, culture is not deterministic in every case. Any negotiator can make choices and act contrary to his/her cultural beliefs. In each chapter, we will share selected salient traits of each country's culture and highlight the main operative traits when it comes to business negotiations.

One characteristic shared by the East Asian cultures covered in this book is their collectivist nature. Many of the countries featured in the volume — China, Indonesia, Philippines, Thailand and Vietnam — are among the world's top rice producers.[2] Their long-standing rice farming culture is a huge factor that girds the groupism behavior found there. Rice farmers must get along with one another because irrigation systems require mutual reliance and interdependence.[3] Members of these societies see themselves as being an integral part of larger groups that include the family, the village, the community or sub-groups within. Prioritizing the interests of the group and maintaining pleasant, harmonious relationships are part of their psyche and conditioning. In essence, they are merely being pragmatic because, in their circumstances, survival is a lot harsher without the help of others.

Another significant cultural operator is Confucianism. The philosophy's deep influence in Northeast Asian cultures of China, Japan and Korean are due to historical and political reasons. This influence is also present in various Southeast Asian countries discussed in this book as a result of the Chinese diaspora in those jurisdictions.

The Chinese philosopher, Confucius or *Kong Qiu* was born in China around 551 BCE. This was a period of tumultuous time when China was made up of numerous warring states. To Confucius, harmony is the

---

[2] Wallach, Omri. 2022. "This Is How Much Rice Is Produced around the World — and the Countries That Grow the Most." World Economic Forum. March 9, 2022. https://www. weforum.org/agenda/2022/03/visualizing-the-world-s-biggest-rice-producers/.

[3] Nisbett, Richard E. 2003. *The Geography of Thought: How Asians and Westerners Think Differently — and Why*. New York: Free Press.

highest of all goals. An ideal society should be stable, with minimum conflict or strife so that ordinary people can aspire to the good life. According to his teachings (Analects), harmonious living will be achieved when everyone knows his/her social role and acts accordingly. These roles are to be located within five cardinal relationships in any society, namely: ruler/subject, father/son, husband/wife, older/younger brothers, and between friends.[4] The first four relationships set out vertical social orders — requiring the latter to obey and defer to the former. The hierarchical distance is the greatest as between ruler and subject; and the least as between older and younger brothers. Only the last relationship is horizontal and requires both sides to practice reciprocal respect. However, because of deference to those who are older or more senior in rank, some degree of hierarchy is also observed amongst friends. In all relationships, both parties must observe and carry out complementary obligations towards each other. Everyone should strive to behave virtuously towards the other — treating that other as he or she would like to be treated in a similar situation. Core Confucian virtues are benevolence, righteousness, loyalty, filial piety; and observance of decorum and norms based on one's social position. On a personal level, each person should work hard, acquire knowledge and skills, be patient and persevere in meaningful endeavors. When it comes to enjoyment and pleasure, moderation is key. In each chapter, where relevant, we will elaborate on the role of Confucianism in each culture.

Hofstede's Cultural Dimensions

As culture can be conceptualized as a set of values and norms shared by people in a group, these shared values and norms can function as parameters to help outsiders understand, gauge and respond to a particular culture. Hofstede conducted an extensive research based on data gathered from IBM employees around the world in over 72 countries across 53 cultures over a course of five years. Using statistical analysis of these data, four key parameters referred to as "cultural dimensions" were used to differentiate

---

[4] Hong, Hai. 2019. *The Rule of Culture.* Singapore: Routledge. 16-29

among different cultures[5] in a business environment. In this book, we adopt three of them; namely, power distance, individualism versus collectivism and uncertainty avoidance to expand our discussion on culture.[6] These three dimensions are chosen because they also feature in the GLOBE[7] studies which is a large-scale influential project to understand effect of culture on leadership and organizational behavior covering 62 different national cultures.[8]

- **Power distance**

This dimension describes the extent to which less powerful members of an organization accept the unequal distribution of power. In high power distance cultures, decision-making is concentrated at the top, authority is respected and inequality is tolerated. In low power distance cultures, power and decision-making are more evenly distributed. Put another way — organizations with a high power-distance are hierarchical and closed; those with a lower power-distance have a flatter structure and are more open. Understanding this dimension will help appreciate where power lies and how decision-making will be undertaken by the other

---

[5] Hofstede, Geert. 1980. *Culture's Consequences: International Differences in Work-Related Values.* Beverly Hills: Sage Publications. Hofstede first developed four dimensions: (1) Power Distance, (2) Individualism v Collectivism, (3) Uncertainty Avoidance and (4) Masculinity v Femininity. Two additional dimensions were subsequently added, namely (5) short v long term orientation and (6) "indulgence v restraint". See also Hofstede, G. (1989), (1991).

[6] There are criticisms against Hofstede's model as being limited (since the data essentially comprised responses from IBM employees who do not necessary represent their respective national culture) and the dimensions are too narrow to account for cultures. However, these dimensions are widely recognized and cited especially for cross-cultural studies on work related values.

[7] GLOBE is an acronym for Global Leadership and Organisational Behaviour Effectiveness.

[8] Javidan, Mansour, Peter W. Dorfman, Mary Sully de Luque, and Robert J. House. 2006. "In the Eye of the Beholder: Cross Cultural Lessons in Leadership from Project GLOBE." *Academy of Management Perspectives* 20 (1): 67–90. https://doi.org/10.5465/amp.2006.19873410. This set of studies yielded nine dimensions namely Performance Orientation, Assertiveness, Future Orientation, Humane Orientation, Institutional Collectivism, In-group Collectivism, Gender Egalitarianism, Power Distance, and Uncertainty Avoidance.

negotiator, if they are from a hierarchical culture. You will be able to identify the key members of the other team and understand the relationship dynamics between their members. You will also better appreciate the web of social relations and obligations that are often present in high power-distance cultures.

- **Individualism-Collectivism**

This dimension measures the extent to which a culture places an individual's interests above those of the collective. In individualist cultures, the emphasis is on an individual's autonomy and the protection of his or her rights. A collectivist culture will score low for this index, meaning the emphasis is instead on the individual's social obligations and interdependence between members of that culture. As a result, a negotiator from a collectivist culture will focus on cultivating and sustaining relationships. In contrast, a negotiator from an individualistic culture will tend to emphasise on competency rather than relationship-building. When you negotiate with someone from a collectivist culture, even if you have ticked all the boxes in terms of tangibles, if there are problems with the relationship, it may still be difficult to seal or maintain a deal. International negotiation studies and research often cite this dimension when comparing between cultures.[9] This dimension affects how negotiators frame their goals and interests, as well as their choice of strategy. Many East Asian (especially Northeast Asian) societies are collectivist. Indirect communication and face saving are important to them and they will always be mindful of their social obligations. Knowing how your East Asian counterpart scores on this dimension will guide you in communicating with them, and building and maintaining a relationship with them.

- **Uncertainty Avoidance**

This dimension refers to a negotiator's tolerance for ambiguity or unpredictable situations. Negotiators from cultures with high uncertainty avoidance index prefer stable rules and predictability. This contrasts with negotiators from low uncertainty avoidance cultures, who will be more

---

[9] Bazerman, Max H., Jared R. Curhan, Don A. Moore, and Kathleen L. Valley. 2000. "Negotiation." Annual Review of Psychology 51 (1): 279–314. https://doi.org/10.1146/annurev.psych.51.1.279.

adaptable and more accepting of things that are shifting or ambiguous. An appreciation of the uncertainty avoidance index of your East Asian negotiation partner will help you better understand how they may react to changes or when things do not happen as planned. This dimension may at times serve as an indicator of the East Asian negotiator's propensity to change course or to surprise you during the negotiation.

Below, we have included the tables to show the scores of the countries covered in this book for the three aforesaid dimensions. These scores are obtained, at the time of writing, from a country comparison carried out by the Hofstede Insights Group which is available online.[10] For comparison, the scores of United Kingdom (UK) and United States (US) are also included. We will discuss these dimensions in greater detail in each country chapter.

Power Distance

This dimension describes the extent to which less powerful members of an organization accept the unequal distribution of power. Higher scores reflect more hierarchical societies.

1.	Malaysia	100
2.	Philippines	94
3.	China	80
4.	Indonesia	78
5.	Singapore	74
6.	Vietnam	70
7.	Thailand	64
8.	Korea (South)	60
9.	Japan	54
	United States	40
	United Kingdom	35

---

[10] Hofstede Insights. "Country Comparison" dated 2023 in Hofstede Insights." https://www.hofstede-insights.com/country-comparison/.

Individualism v Collectivism

This dimension measures the extent that a culture places the individual's interests above those of the collective. Lower scores reflect higher collectivistic behaviors.

1.	Indonesia	14
2.	Korea (South)	18
3.	China	20
4.	Singapore	20
5.	Thailand	20
6.	Vietnam	20
7.	Malaysia	26
8.	Philippines	32
9.	Japan	46
	United Kingdom	89
	United States	91

Uncertainty Avoidance

This dimension refers to a negotiator's tolerance for ambiguity or unpredictable situations. Negotiators from cultures with high uncertainty avoidance index prefer stable rules and predictability.

1.	Japan	92
2.	Korea (South)	85
3.	Thailand	64
4.	Indonesia	48
	United States	46
5.	Philippines	44
6.	Malaysia	36
	United Kingdom	35
7.	China	30
8.	Vietnam	30
9.	Singapore	8

3. Communication

At its core, negotiation is a form of interpersonal communication. To be an effective negotiator, we must be skilled in communicating our interests, positions and goals to the other side. At the same time, we must also be able to make sense of these same things that are communicated by the other party. In cross-cultural negotiations, understanding how the East Asian negotiator communicates, the importance of context as well as their use of nonverbal communication can contribute to the efficacy of the negotiation process and help avoid blunders or impropriety.

During negotiation, language operates at two levels; namely, the logical level (e.g. price or payment terms) and the pragmatic level (e.g. use of semantics and style).[11] A skilful negotiator must take in both the logical surface message and the hinted or embedded pragmatic messages. We must listen to what is said, how it is said and be mindful of what is unspoken or inferred. This is especially important in high-context cultures.

There are two broad communication norms.[12] In low-context cultures, communication is direct and explicit so the meaning is clearly contained in the words used or the surface of the message. Low-context communicators tend to "say what they mean and mean what they say". Many Western cultures (e.g. US and UK) are regarded as low-context. Some argue that, because some Westerners (like Americans) are more individualistic and assertive than others, they run into more obstacles during negotiations.[13] In high-context cultures, communication is implicit and the meaning of the message relies on the context surrounding it. The physical setting, the manner in which things are said, and shared understandings are relied upon to convey the key meanings and intentions. Many East Asian cultures covered in this book are high-context. How and when will a high-context communicator say "yes" or "no"? Can these utterances be accepted at face value? Many Asian cultures have been described as being "unstated,

---

[11] Lewicki, Roy J, David M. Saunders, and Bruce Barry. 2021. *Essentials of Negotiation*. 7th ed. McGraw-Hill International. 169-170

[12] Hall, Edward Twitchell. 1976. *Beyond Culture*. New York: Anchor Books.

[13] Graham, John L. and N. Mark Lam, "The Chinese Negotiation" dated 1 October 2003 in Harvard Business Review [downloaded on 1 January 2022], available at https://hbr.org/2003/10/the-chinese-negotiation

implicit and internalised in subtle behavioural patterns".[14] Although it sounds like an old cliché to assert that what is not said is often more important in Asian cultures — their negotiators' information-sharing strategy can be quite implicit and at times, even covet. Looking out for cues is a necessary skillset when negotiating in East Asia.

Frequently, negotiators are focused on "tangibles" such as price, payment terms, delivery schedules and so on. However, an effective negotiator should also be mindful of "intangibles".[15] These refer to underlying psychological factors which influence the negotiating parties, either directly or indirectly, and the list can be long and varied. Examples include needing to trump the other side, to come across as tough or honorable or principled. These "intangibles" can make or break negotiations even if seemingly more important tangible outcomes have been settled. This is because "intangibles" are frequently rooted in a negotiator's personal values and can deeply affect his or her emotions. When negotiating in East Asia, it is vital to understand the intangible factor of "face" during communication.

From a westerner's perspective, the concept of "face" is chiefly about politeness towards another person and respect for his or her autonomy. Thus, to "give face" is to have regard for an individual's desire to be approved and to free from imposition.[16] From that perspective, not giving some "face" to a westerner may not have much adverse impact on the negotiation process. In contrast, not giving "face" in East Asia will frequently jeopardize, scuttle the negotiation or simply introduce unnecessary obstacles. In subsequent chapters, we will elaborate and unpack the specific meaning of "face" in each country. There are distinct differences in the face cultures of the countries covered in this book. Essentially, the concept of "face" in Asia takes into consideration the individual's social role within the community or group to which he or she belongs. Clearly, this social role has its own unique characteristics in each jurisdiction which will be elaborated in the respective chapters.

---

[14] Michael Benoliel. 2013. "Negotiating Successfully in Asia," *Eurasian Journal of Social Sciences*, Eurasian Publications, vol. 1(1), pages 1-18.

[15] Lewicki et al, *Essentials of Negotiation*, 8

[16] Brown and Stephen C Levinson. 1987. *Politeness: Some Universals in Language Usage.* Cambridge University Press.

4. Negotiation Strategies: Distributive or Integrative

Negotiation strategies are commonly grouped into two broad themes — distributive and integrative.[17] The strategy determines our behavior and decision-making process and how we frame our negotiation goals. In this book, we will share our observations and insights into the propensity of each East Asian Negotiator for either distributive or integrative processes. In addition, we will offer some pointers if you decide to pursue either strategy.

Distributive negotiations are commonly described as win-lose negotiations. East Asians often adopt a distributive strategy when they view their goals as being in conflict with those of the other side. Such negotiators consider that resources are fixed and so they will do whatever is necessary to claim the larger reward or gain, at the expense of the other party. Hence, one side "wins" and the other "loses". The key objective is to claim value. Distributive negotiators will jealously guard information about their own position and disclose very little to their counterparts. Distributive negotiation is chiefly about competition. Integrative negotiations are in contrast, win-win negotiations. The two parties' goals are not mutually exclusive, so they work on finding solutions to meet their respective goals and share the reward. Both sides maximize the joint outcomes so both sides "win". The main aim is to create value. Integrative tactics require negotiators to share and exchange information about each other's interests, issues and objectives. Integrative negotiation requires cooperation and collaboration.

A vital difference between the two strategies lies in the parties' attitude towards information sharing. A party who is more open about sharing and exchanging information; or who is more focused on relationship building is probably more inclined to be integrative. Conversely, a party who volunteers little information and who does not appear curious about his counterpart is likely to adopt a distributive stance. Greater information sharing will increase the chances of discovering common interests; which in turn makes integrative outcomes more probable. When dealing with the East Asian Negotiator, if we can gauge their attitude when it comes to the

---

[17] Walton, Richard E, and Robert MacKersie. 1965. *A Behavioral Theory Of Labor Negotiations: An Analysis Of A Social Interaction System*. New York: McGraw-Hill.

handling and provision of information, we can better predict whether we will be engaged in distributive or integrative process.

A more open attitude towards information sharing requires trust. Trust is the willingness to make ourselves vulnerable towards another party despite being uncertain as to their intentions and actions.[18] The challenge is that most cross-cultural negotiations start from a baseline of low or no trust.[19] A further challenge is that societies with a long tradition of Confucian values tend to have low-trust of strangers[20] because social connections are focused on family, relatives or friends (the "in-group"). There is a skepticism against strangers and people from different cultural backgrounds (the "out-group"). In order to achieve an integrative outcome, you will need to know how to gain the trust of your East Asian counterpart.

In reality, most negotiations are frequently a combination of the two strategies. And, even within the same negotiation, there can be distributive and integrative aspects and phases. Negotiations are generally classifiable into three phases: antecedent phase (pre-negotiation stage and preparations), the concurrent phase (ongoing process), and the consequent phase (post-negotiation stage) — negotiation behavior throughout all three phases can affect their outcome.[21]

5. Concession-making and Hardball Tactics

Concession-making is a vital part of negotiation This is the "give-and-take" part of the process when we make changes to our position in response to the other party. Concession-making brings parties closer, narrows the bargaining range and reduces the options available to reach a deal. How we

---

[18] McAllister, D. J. 1995. "Affect- and Cognition-based Trust as Foundations for Interpersonal Cooperation in Organizations." *Academy of Management Journal*, 38 (1), 24–59. https://doi.org/10.5465/256727.

[19] Jang, Sujin, and Roy Chua. 2011. "Building Intercultural Trust at the Negotiating Table." Negotiation Excellence, March, 299–313. https://doi.org/10.1142/9789814343176_0017

[20] Fukuyama, Francis. (1995). *Trust: The social virtues and the creation of prosperity.* New York: Free Press.

[21] Sun, Meihong, "A Comparison of Business Negotiation Behavior between Korea and China" dated December 2009 in International Journal of Business and Management VO. 4 No. 12 [downloaded on 1 January 2022], available at https://pdfs.semanticscholar.org/ccfc/201493ae2e5ced61467653696c4ecb34571d.pdf, p. 212.

make concessions depends on whether the negotiation is distributive or integrative. The type and pattern of concession-making also conveys important signals, whether the negotiation is going to be combative, long-drawn or nearing the end. If concessions are small, it may be indicative that the negotiation is going to take a long time; if the negotiation starts off with a large concession, does it mean there is no much room left? These are all important decisions which have to be made by a negotiator.

Negotiators use hardball tactics[22] essentially to try to extract or gain a concession from the other party. Such tactics aim to pressure the other party to do things he or she would otherwise not do. One example is what is known in many negotiation literature as the "good cop/bad cop" tactic — where members within the same negotiation team alternate between using tough and lenient approaches. Other hardball tactics include "highball/lowball" (using ridiculously high or low starting offers in the hope that the other party will re-evaluate their own openings or position); "intimidation" (faking anger or fear to force a concession); or "bogey" (which is essentially deception e.g. misrepresenting the value or importance of an issue). Hardball tactics, if used, are reserved for distributive negotiations.

In each country-specific chapter, we will highlight some of the concession-making patterns and likely hardball tactics that you will encounter or should avoid using.

6. Role of Women

Women are often viewed as less competent negotiators than men. One oft-cited explanation is that masculine stereotypes are seen as positives. Attributes associated with being effective in negotiation such as "assertive", "rational" and "strong" tend to be seen as being masculine. In contrast, attributes associated with being a weak negotiator, such as "submissive", "emotional" and "weaker" are perceived as female traits.[23] On top of

---

[22] Lewicki, Roy J., David M. Saunders, and Bruce Barry. 2021. *Essentials of Negotiation.* 7th ed. McGraw-Hill International 169-170

[23] Miles, Edward W., and Elizabeth F. Clenney. 2010. "Gender Differences in Negotiation: A Status Characteristics Theory View." *Negotiation and Conflict Management Research* 3 (2): 130–44. https://doi.org/10.1111/j.1750-4716.2010.00054.x.

these generalizations, many East Asian cultures tend to be male-dominated and women frequently play lesser or smaller roles, particularly in the business setting. Does this then mean that if you are a woman negotiator, you will be perceived as being weak or face more obstacles in this part of the world?

In cultures that are influenced by Confucianism, there is a common perception that women occupy a lower status then men. In the five cardinal relationships described by Confucius, women's only role appears to be that of a subservient wife. Moreover, the term used to define the ideal person, junzi (君子), is masculine. A direct reference to women in the teachings (Analects) even warned that "women are difficult to deal with, like petty persons".[24] Despite these generalizations, in Asian culture, *Yang* (commonly translated as masculine forms) is never complete without *Yin* (commonly translated as feminine forms). *Yin* qualities such as being receptive, accepting and intuitive are definitely handy traits when negotiating in this part of the world.

In each country chapter, we will provide an overview of the role of women within that society, their status and particularly, their usual roles in the business setting. This will help prepare female negotiators and explain some behaviors and attitudes that may be encountered. Additionally, if you were negotiating with a female East Asian negotiator, you can have a deeper understanding and additional sensitivity about her environment. For a quick comparison, we set out the relevant countries' ranking in the 2022 Global Gender Gap Report by the World Economic Forum.[25] The countries covered in this book are grouped under the East Asia and the Pacific region which lists 19 countries. In the table below, we provide their regional ranking, as well as their global ranking.

---

[24] Analect 17.25

[25] World Economic Forum. 2022. "Global Gender Gap Report 2022." World Economic Forum. July 13, 2022. https://www.weforum.org/reports/global-gender-gap-report-2022/digest. The Global Gender Gap Index benchmarks the current state and evolution of gender parity across four key dimensions (Economic Participation and Opportunity, Educational Attainment, Health and Survival, and Political Empowerment). It is the longest-standing index which tracks progress towards closing these gaps over time since its inception in 2006.

Global Gender Gap Report 2022 INSIGHT REPORT JULY 2022

EAST ASIA & the PACIFIC	Rank		
Country	Regional (19)	Global (146)	Score
Philippines	2	19	0.783
Singapore	4	49	0.734
Thailand	8	79	0.709
Vietnam	9	83	0.705
Indonesia	10	92	0.697
Korea (South)	12	99	0.689
China	13	102	0.682
Malaysia	14	103	0.681
Japan	19	116	0.650

Source: "Global Gender Gap Report 2022." 2022. World Economic Forum. July 13, 2022. https://www.weforum.org/reports/global-gender-gap-report-2022/digest.

7. Intermediary/Interpreter

In many East Asian cultures, the use of an intermediary is common in negotiation. One reason may be that English is not a common working language or the negotiator on the other side prefers to communicate in their own language. Another practical reason is that an intermediary can serve as a useful bridge and buffer between the negotiator and his/her foreign counterpart. As will be made clear in the subsequent chapters, having some distance between you and an East Asian negotiator is sometimes vital. Finally, another explanation is unfortunately due to the presence of corruptive practices[26] in some parts of this region, and an intermediary is someone

---

[26] A common definition of corruption is the abuse of public power for private gain and includes petty and grand corruption: Kaufmann, Daniel, Aart Kraay, and Massimo Mastruzzi. 2010. "The Worldwide Governance Indicators: Methodology and Analytical Issues." *Hague Journal on the Rule of Law* 3 (02): 220–46. https://doi.org/10.1017/s1876404511200046.

who can help mitigate this and avoid pitfalls. For this topic, we will discuss the level of English proficiency you are likely to encounter in each jurisdiction. Where applicable, we will profile and highlight some of the useful traits you should look out for if you intend to appoint a middle-man in your negotiation, under each chapter.

8. Time, timelines and timeliness

Here, we briefly consider several time-related aspects. It is always useful to understand your counterpart's time sensitivity so that you can appropriately pace the negotiation process and be able to set realistic timelines. If you have an accurate sense of how long the negotiation will take, you will be able to set aside sufficient resources to pursue your goals. And of course, knowing whether punctuality will be keenly observed can help save valuable time and prevent needless offense from being created or taken.

Bibliography

Analect 17.25

Bazerman, M., Curhan, J., Moore, D., & Valley, K. (2000). "Negotiation." *Annual Review of Psychology* 51 (1): 279–314. https://doi.org/10.1146/annurev.psych.51.1.279.

Brown, S. & and Levinson, S. (1987). *Politeness: Some Universals in Language Usage.* Cambridge University Press.

Javidan, M., Dorfman, P., de Luque, M.S., & House, R. (2006). "In the Eye of the Beholder: Cross Cultural Lessons in Leadership from Project GLOBE." *Academy of Management Perspectives* 20 (1): 67–90. https://doi.org/10.5465/amp.2006.19873410.

Fukuyama, F. (1995). *Trust: The social virtues and the creation of prosperity.* New York: Free Press.

Graham, J. & Lam, N.M. "The Chinese Negotiation" dated 1 October 2003 in *Harvard Business Review* [downloaded on 1 January 2022], available at https://hbr.org/2003/10/the-chinese-negotiation

Hall, Edward Twitchell. (1976). *Beyond Culture.* New York: Anchor Books.

Hofstede, Geert. (1980). *Culture's Consequences: International Differences in Work-Related Values.* Beverly Hills: Sage Publications.

Hofstede Insights. "Country Comparison" dated 2023 in Hofstede Insights. https://www.hofstede-insights.com/country-comparison/.

Hong, Hai. (2019). *The Rule of Culture.* Singapore: Routledge. 16-29

Jang, S., & Chua, R. (2011). "Building Intercultural Trust at the Negotiating Table." *Negotiation Excellence,* March, 299–313. https://doi.org/10.1142/9789814343176_0017

Kaufmann, D, Kraay, A., & Mastruzzi, M. (2010). "The Worldwide Governance Indicators: Methodology and Analytical Issues." *Hague Journal on the Rule of Law 3* (2): 220–46. https://doi.org/10.1017/s1876404511200046.

Lewicki, R., Saunders, D., & Barry, B. (2021). *Essentials of Negotiation.* 7th ed. McGraw-Hill International. 169-170

McAllister, D. J. (1995). "Affect- and Cognition-based Trust as Foundations for Interpersonal Cooperation in Organizations." *Academy of Management Journal,* 38 (1), 24–59. https://doi.org/10.5465/256727.

Michael Benoliel. (2013). "Negotiating Successfully in Asia," *Eurasian Journal of Social Sciences,* Eurasian Publications, *1*(1), 1–18.

Miles, E., & Clenney, E. (2010). "Gender Differences in Negotiation: A Status Characteristics Theory View." *Negotiation and Conflict Management Research 3* (2): 130–44. https://doi.org/10.1111/j.1750-4716.2010.00054.x.

Nisbett, Richard E. (2003). *The Geography of Thought: How Asians and Westerners Think Differently— and Why.* New York: Free Press.

Sun, M. (2009) "A Comparison of Business Negotiation Behavior between Korea and China". *International Journal of Business and Management 4* (12): 212[downloaded on 1 January 2022], available at https://pdfs.semanticscholar.org/ccfc/201493ae2e5ced61467653696c4ecb34571d.pdf.

Wallach, O. (2022). "This Is How Much Rice Is Produced around the World — and the Countries That Grow the Most." *World Economic Forum.* March 9, 2022. https://www.weforum.org/agenda/2022/03/visualizing-the-world-s-biggest-rice-producers/

Walton, R., & MacKersie, R. (1965). *A Behavioral Theory Of Labor Negotiations: An Analysis Of A Social Interaction System.* New York: McGraw Hill.

World Economic Forum. (2022). "Global Gender Gap Report 2022." World Economic Forum. July 13, 2022. https://www.weforum.org/reports/global-gender-gap-report-2022/digest.

Chapter 1

The Chinese Negotiator

The rise of China, its economic scale and growing consumption mean that it is now an important and indeed crucial business platform for negotiators to get their deals. Therefore, it is important for stakeholders doing business in China to pick up skills and tips to master the art of the negotiation.

In terms of cultural stereotypes, US business negotiators often perceive Chinese negotiators as inefficient, indirect and even dishonest while the Chinese negotiators stereotype their American counterparts as aggressive, impersonal and excitable, and such cultural stereotypes run deep.[1] But, it also means that those who can overcome such stereotypes can benefit magnificently and be rewarded with good business deals. Some suggest that Chinese society's long-held somewhat semi-xenophobic fears of foreign people, particularly after the Opium Wars, and China's own tumultuous historical past, led to scepticisms about the rule of law and regulations, preferring instead to place their trust on their own family clans and financial health.[2] Even as China's legal system is constantly being revised and updated, some seasoned Western negotiators advise that relevant legal

---

[1] Graham, J. L. & Lam, N. M. (October 1, 2003). "The Chinese Negotiation." *Harvard Business Review* [downloaded on 1 January 2022], available at https://hbr.org/2003/10/the-chinese-negotiation.

[2] *Ibid.*

stipulations, agreements or taxation rules are just a starting platform in the negotiations.[3]

1. The Environment

The macroeconomic environment in which China rises in the 2020s has been highly complicated by a changing world order in which the US–China trade frictions occupy centre-stage. Starting from 2016, the business environment in China was affected by the increasing trade frictions between the Xi and the Trump administrations. From the US perspective, the frictions arose from inequitable bilateral trade conditions among other causes, while the Chinese saw the disagreement as a form of semi-containment on the rise of China. This political–economic disagreement between the two carried over to the corporate environment in many ways. The American politicians and corporate leaders were unhappy with the Joint Venture (JV) condition for their companies entering into China, while some views in China saw the condition as a necessity for a fledgling rising economy to nurture its domestic industries. In their Sinocentric view, this was just as the American industrialists had done when the US developed during its early industrialization era. Given this contentious macro-environment, it becomes even more crucial for negotiators to understand the cultural and corporate environmental nuances when negotiating in China.

Some analysts argue that attending basic training courses before going for a business trip to China, with tips like bringing along business cards, preparing interpretations, articulating in non-wordy sentences, dressing conservatively, may help to guide outsiders through the door and in the early stages of the business negotiations, but not much beyond that in a sustained manner.[4] In fact, some argue that practising only the superficial greeting rituals when carrying out negotiations with Chinese partners may

---

[3] Program on Negotiation (PON) at Harvard Law School. (August 4, 2022). "The Importance of Relationship Building in China When in China, Relationship Building is Critical." Program on Negotiation (PON) at Harvard Law School [downloaded on 4 August 2022], available at https://www.pon.harvard.edu/daily/international-negotiation-daily/negotiation-in-china-the-importance-of-guanxi/.

[4] Graham, J. L. & Lam, N. M. (October 1, 2003). "The Chinese Negotiation." *Harvard Business Review* [downloaded on 1 January 2022], available at https://hbr.org/2003/10/the-chinese-negotiation.

bring about breakdown in relationships frequently after barely getting through the initial gateway in the negotiations due to the failure to comprehend the wider context of Chinese cultural values (that sometimes bewilder the Westerner).[5]

Sometimes, Chinese cultural values even differ between northerners and southerners. A University of Virginia Ph.D. student in cultural psychology and the 'Rice Theory' study's lead author Thomas Talhelm undertook a study at the University of Chicago Booth School of Business on the behavioral traits of Chinese people. He found that the Southern Chinese traditional interdependent rice-farming culture of Southern China has resulted in the Southern Chinese (including those staying outside the cities) being more mutually dependent on each other with less domination over their natural environment compared to the Northern wheat-farming cultural worldview.[6] Mutual dependence often fosters deep trust among groups and people over time.

In the United States and a number of other countries, there is a tendency of trusting others until the occasion arises that breaks that trust, which is in contrast with the Chinese mindset that treats all strangers with suspicion and distrust.[7] Like all other Northeast Asian economies, human relations based on trust and win–win scenarios (mutual benefits) are absolutely essential for the negotiation process. The challenge is that in doing business with the Chinese, trust is often unearnable and depends on *guanxi* relationships to open the door to a business relationship (via transmission rather than earning trust).[8]

Guanxi refers to human relations and/or individuals to whom you can provide favors to and receive reciprocity from qualified individuals that include family predominantly, but also friends, fellow students,

---

[5] *Ibid.*

[6] Sainvilus, M. (April 25, 2018). "Behavioral Differences between Northern vs. Southern Chinese Linked to Wheat vs. Rice Farming, Study Shows." Chicago Booth the University of Chicago Booth School of Business [downloaded on 25 April 2018], available at https://www.chicagobooth.edu/media-relations-and-communications/press-releases/behavioral-differences-between-northern-v-southern-chinese.

[7] Graham, J. L. & Lam, N. M. (October 1, 2003). "The Chinese Negotiation." *Harvard Business Review* [downloaded on 1 January 2022], available at https://hbr.org/2003/10/the-chinese-negotiation.

[8] *Ibid.*

neighbors, fellow alumni, etc. The same principle applies to the overseas ethnic Chinese bamboo network as well. On a comparative scale, despite the fact that the majority of Americans treat acquaintances differentially from strangers, Chinese behavior towards insiders and outsiders appears to be more highly differentiated than the case in the United States and thus, is a major factor in business negotiations.[9]

Another feature of negotiating with all Northeast Asians is not to overly rely on contractual stipulations. A contract symbolically connotes the existence of a business relationship, but does not govern the future shape and format of an evolving relationship. Occidentals frequently err by drawing a long, detailed, unilateral contract in the course of the negotiation and this may intimidate Orientalist Northeast Asians like the Japanese and the Chinese, who may then associate the foreign negotiators as adversaries, therefore it is advisable for contracts to be drawn up jointly by both sides as a statement of negotiated points agreed to.[10] One caveat to lower Chinese dependence on Western-style contracting to regulate business relationship is the fact that times are also changing. Chinese negotiation styles have minor convergence with those of the West, thanks to the business schools offering MBAs that are springing up all over China (including very prestigious ones like the Guanghua School of Management in Beijing's Peking University or PKU) where Western business concepts are being acquired.

2. Culture

Because China is a sub-continental-sized country, there are differences between the Northern and Southern Chinese cultures. Physically, Yangtze River is the dividing line between the two components. The Yangtze River (longest in China) literally splits the country into half from west to east, creating two visible cultural worldviews and separating North–South

---

[9] Program on Negotiation (PON) at Harvard Law School. (August 4, 2022). "The Importance of Relationship Building in China When in China, Relationship Building is Critical." Program on Negotiation (PON) at Harvard Law School [downloaded on 4 August 2022], available at https://www.pon.harvard.edu/daily/international-negotiation-daily/negotiation-in-china-the-importance-of-guanxi/.

[10] Van Zandt, H. F. (November 1970). "How to Negotiate in Japan." *Magazine/Harvard Business Review (HBR)* [downloaded on 1 January 2022], available at https://hbr.org/1970/11/how-to-negotiate-in-japan.

Chinese dialects in China.[11] Even in contemporary Chinese metropolitan urban areas like Beijing and Shanghai, rice–wheat dichotomy in regional agricultural practices continue to influence the behavioral traits of the Southern and Northern Chinese people, and in current revisionist literatures, they may even be as important as the urban–rural dichotomy in that country.[12]

Thomas Talhelm concluded from his study "Moving chairs in Starbucks: Observational studies find rice–wheat cultural differences in daily life in China" published by University of Chicago Booth Business School: "I think people in China have long had a sense that northerners behave differently from southerners. This study suggests a reason why — rice farming — and that those differences are surviving into the modern age."[13] Some cultural differences between Northern and Southern Chinese cultures will be selectively covered in this chapter.

Talhelm's groundbreaking study discovered that the north–south divide in farming practices accounted for differences in Northern and Southern Chinese culture, behaviorial traits and business activities. As a social scientist, Talhelm was engaged in a University of Chicago Booth Business School research on the cultural differentiation between Southern and Northern China while being a resident in Guangzhou, China:

> I noticed little things in people's behavior there (in the south), like people seemed nervous if they accidentally bumped into me in the grocery store. It seemed like people were reserved, focused on avoiding conflict. Then I moved up to Beijing and the north, and I quickly saw that being reserved was certainly not part of the Beijing way of conducting oneself.[14]

---

[11] Talhelm, T. (May 8, 2014). "'Rice Theory' Explains North–South China Cultural Differences, Study Shows." *UVA Today* (University of Virgina News) [downloaded on 1 January 2022], available at https://news.virginia.edu/content/rice-theory-explains-north-south-china-cultural-differences-study-shows.

[12] Sainvilus, M. (April 25, 2018). "Behavioral Differences between Northern vs. Southern Chinese Linked to Wheat vs. Rice Farming, Study Shows." Chicago Booth the University of Chicago Booth School of Business [downloaded on 25 April 2018], available at https://www.chicagobooth.edu/media-relations-and-communications/press-releases/behavioral-differences-between-northern-v-southern-chinese.

[13] *Ibid.*

[14] *Ibid.*

A combined study by Talhelm and his co-authors at Chinese and Michigan universities suggests that Southern Chinese cooperative rice cultivation for generations fostered greater mutual reliance among themselves, while Northern wheat cultivators have practiced autonomous farming techniques over centuries. As Talhelm argued:

> The data suggests that legacies of farming are continuing to affect people in the modern world. It has resulted in two distinct cultural psychologies that mirror the differences between East Asia and the West.[15] [Northern Chinese tend to consume wheat, millet and sorghum in the form of noodles (*miantiao*), baked items (like *bing*, scallion cakes, etc.) or cereal for their diet while Southern Chinese prefer to consume rice for their carbohydrates.]

These shared values and norms of a particular culture function as parameters to help outsiders understand, "gauge" and respond to that culture. For example, Chinese gauge sincerity (*cheng-yi*) of the other parties through ritualistic performances like meeting them several times with high-level delegations to show the sincerity to deal, e.g. in 1995, CEO John F. Smith flew to Beijing three times just to meet with Chinese executives.[16] In Chinese martial arts popular culture, a kung fu (*gongfu* in Hanyu Pinyin) apprentice often seeks his master's guidance by requesting sincerely (kneeling in snow or standing outside the master's entrance in adverse conditions, etc.) at least three times before the master will accept his apprenticeship.

---

[15] Talhelm, T. (May 8, 2014). "'Rice Theory' Explains North–South China Cultural Differences, Study Shows." *UVA Today* (University of Virgina News) [downloaded on 1 January 2022], available at https://news.virginia.edu/content/rice-theory-explains-north-south-china-cultural-differences-study-shows. In this study, Talhelm worked with his Chinese colleagues to carry out psychological research of the thought styles of 1162 Han Chinese college students in northern and southern Chinese counties at the borders of the rice–wheat divide. Research work spanned 6 Chinese cities: Beijing (North China); Fujian (Southeast China); Guangdong (Southern China); Yunnan (Southwestern China); Sichuan (West central China) and Liaoning (Northeast China).

[16] Graham, J. L. & Lam, N. M. (October 1, 2003). "The Chinese Negotiation." *Harvard Business Review* [downloaded on 1 January 2022], available at https://hbr.org/2003/10/the-chinese-negotiation.

China is the birthplace of Confucianism. The philosophy of Confucianism became entrenched in Chinese culture, civilization, worldview, socialization and of course, even in business negotiations. Its influence remains till today. In his key-note speech at the opening of an international commemoration of the 2,565th anniversary (in 2014) of the birth of Confucius, Chinese President Xi Jinping noted that "Confucianism, along with other philosophies and cultures taking shape and growing within China, are records of spiritual experiences, rational thinking and cultural achievements of the nation during its striving to build its home. These cultures have nourished the flourishing Chinese nation."[17] The deep effect of Confucianism will be unpacked in what follows as we discuss the Hofstede dimensions.

Hofstede's Cultural Dimensions

• **Power distance**

In terms of writings on differences in comparative cultural studies, the national culture dimension presented by Hofstede in 1980 is probably the most important analytical framework, featuring the concept of "Power Distance" implying the "acceptance of unequal power distribution in an organization within a society".[18] China's score of 80 is the third highest among countries surveyed in this book. The formality of Chinese society does not fully embrace the casual attitudes of the US, given the existence of Confucian hierarchy and loyalty to superiors and elders (known as *shehui dengji* or social status) so sending negotiators that are too junior to meet with Chinese senior executives is not advisable. It may insult, distress or show disrespect to the Chinese counterpart. Koreans also display this behavioral trait as a comparative reference. Social standing and social capital are also related to the concept of *mianzi* or face.

---

[17] "China Commemorates Confucius with Ceremony." (n.d.). www.china.org.cn. Available at http://www.china.org.cn/china/2014-09/25/content_33608222.htm (Accessed October 31, 2022).

[18] Chang, L.-C. C. (2020). "A comparison of Taiwan and Malaysia in negotiation styles." Universiti Utara Malaysia Course Franchise Business Management (FBPME3023) studoc website [downloaded on 1 Jan 2023], available at https://www.studocu.com/my/document/universiti-utara-malaysia/franchise-business-management/a-comparison-of-taiwan-and-malaysia-in-negotiation-styles/21649420.

It is a good sign when Chinese companies dispatch their high-ranking executives to participate in negotiations, especially in targeted areas, and when this happens, you are well-advised to spot softening of negotiation positions.[19] There are similarities between US and Chinese negotiation cultures in the sense that senior management do have a disproportionate influence on the outcome of the negotiations process. Among traditional companies in the United States, a sizable number of management ideas and decisions originate from the executive suite and are then disseminated from the management in a top-down fashion.[20]

Respect goes beyond being seniority-based, friendship-based and based on positive relationships and has to incorporate *renji hexie* (interpersonal harmonious relationships of equals) and this may mean an extended period of nontask (activities other than the main task of negotiations) sounding to establish camaraderie like extended dining, residential visits, sports events huddling and other non-business activities.[21] *Renji Hexie* (attitude in favor of harmonious interpersonal relationships) can work wonders and tide over shorter-term problems in the negotiation process in view of long-term gains and relationships.[22] All these are social rituals carried out before, during and after the negotiations.

- **Individualism–Collectivism**

China scored 20 on this count, which is the third lowest among countries in this book, out-ranked by South Korea (18) and Indonesia (14). This score does not differentiate between Northern and Southern Chinese. Western (especially American) culture tends to be associated with individualism. Western (and Northern Chinese) wheat cultivation appears to play a part in the formation of individualistic cultures. Wheat cultivation is

[19] Graham, J. L. & Lam, N. M. (October 1, 2003). "The Chinese Negotiation." *Harvard Business Review* [downloaded on 1 January 2022], available at https://hbr.org/2003/10/the-chinese-negotiation.

[20] Van Zandt, H. F. (November 1970). "How to Negotiate in Japan." *Magazine/Harvard Business Review (HBR)* [downloaded on 1 January 2022], available at https://hbr.org/1970/11/how-to-negotiate-in-japan.

[21] Graham, J. L. & Lam, N. M. (October 1, 2003). "The Chinese Negotiation." *Harvard Business Review* [downloaded on 1 January 2022], available at https://hbr.org/2003/10/the-chinese-negotiation.

[22] *Ibid.*

carried out on dry terrains, depending on rainwater for humidity, giving farmers more autonomy and independent-thinking habits.[23]

Millennia of wheat and rice cultivations have affected the behaviors of the Northern and Southern Chinese. In Talhelm's University of Chicago Booth Business School study, researchers shifted classroom chairs around in a way that semi-obstructed the aisles, it was more probable that Northern Chinese participants shifted the chairs to unobstruct the walkway individualistically (thereby altering the environment).[24] It was a behavioral trait that represented individualism. On the other hand, agrarian rice cultivation is often cited as a foundational reason for China's communitarianism, given that 66.6% of the Chinese population continue to reside in the countryside, working on rice or wheat farms (much of it peasant-subsistence farming).[25] Rural life is unkind towards individualism, given that thriving in the countryside often requires community solidarity and living together in harmony while loyalty and conforming to family units and their hierarchical structures provide social safety.[26]

Rice farming is manpower-intensive, necessitating double the time needed from seeding to harvest compared to wheat cultivation, while irrigated rice padis need water resource-sharing and interdependent teamwork in construction/maintenance of dikes/canals (common facilities to all).[27] Rice farming is prevalent in Southern China. Traditional Southern Chinese

---

[23] Talhelm, T. (May 8, 2014). "'Rice Theory' Explains North–South China Cultural Differences, Study Shows." *UVA Today* (University of Virgina News) [downloaded on 1 January 2022], available at https://news.virginia.edu/content/rice-theory-explains-north-south-china-cultural-differences-study-shows.

[24] Sainvilus, M. (April 25, 2018). "Behavioral differences between Northern v. Southern Chinese linked to wheat v. rice farming, study shows." Chicago Booth the University of Chicago Booth School of Business [downloaded on 25 April 2018], available at https://www.chicagobooth.edu/media-relations-and-communications/press-releases/behavioral-differences-between-northern-v-southern-chinese.

[25] Graham, J. L. & Lam, N. M. (October 1, 2003). "The Chinese Negotiation." *Harvard Business Review* [downloaded on 1 January 2022], available at https://hbr.org/2003/10/the-chinese-negotiation.

[26] *Ibid.*

[27] Talhelm, Thomas. (May 8, 2014). "'Rice Theory' Explains North–South China Cultural Differences, Study Shows." *UVA Today* (University of Virgina News) [downloaded on 1 January 2022], available at https://news.virginia.edu/content/rice-theory-explains-north-south-china-cultural-differences-study-shows.

rice peasants had to carry out division of labor and manpower to implement teamwork for irrigation activities (an infrastructure not needed in Northern Chinese wheat cultivation), thereby resulting in interdependent groupist and enmeshed social relationships (rather than autonomous individualistic northerners).[28]

Some observers noticed that even Chinese urbanites retain their agricultural worldview.[29] North–south divides in agrarian mindsets were carried forward into modernity when "rice provide[d] economic incentives to cooperate, and over many generations, those cultures become more interdependent, whereas societies that do not have to depend on each other as much have the freedom of individualism."[30] There are, however, differences in levels of groupist, communitarian and collectivist behaviors even among the Chinese themselves. In his research work "Moving chairs in Starbucks: Observational studies find rice–wheat cultural differences in daily life in China," Talhelm analyzed how among 8964 individuals patronizing Starbucks cafes in six Chinese cities, residents of Southern Chinese cities were less likely to be found sitting in solitude.[31]

In terms of human-originated influence, Confucianism is probably the paramount source of influence on Chinese culture and social behavior. Confucius thinking has enjoyed the resilience of time with 2000 years of history and was the basis for the scholarly exams that determined the

---

[28] Sainvilus, Marielle. (April 25, 2018). "Behavioral Differences between Northern vs. Southern Chinese Linked to Wheat vs. Rice Farming, Study Shows." Chicago Booth the University of Chicago Booth School of Business [downloaded on 25 April 2018], available at https://www.chicagobooth.edu/media-relations-and-communications/press-releases/behavioral-differences-between-northern-v-southern-chinese.

[29] Graham, J. L. & Lam, N. M. (October 1, 2003). "The Chinese Negotiation." Harvard Business Review [downloaded on 1 January 2022], available at https://hbr.org/2003/10/the-chinese-negotiation.

[30] Talhelm, T. (May 8, 2014). "'Rice Theory' Explains North–South China Cultural Differences, Study Shows." *UVA Today* (University of Virgina News) [downloaded on 1 January 2022], available at https://news.virginia.edu/content/rice-theory-explains-north-south-china-cultural-differences-study-shows.

[31] Sainvilus, Marielle. (April 25, 2018). "Behavioral Differences between Northern vs. Southern Chinese Linked to Wheat vs. Rice Farming, Study Shows." Chicago Booth the University of Chicago Booth School of Business [downloaded on 25 April 2018], available at https://www.chicagobooth.edu/media-relations-and-communications/press-releases/behavioral-differences-between-northern-v-southern-chinese.

Chinese power structure and the social hierarchy of the country. The Sage's texts were memorized in a rote learning format and then regurgitated verbatim in rigorous civil service exams. The scores determine the scholastic merit of each examinee to peg them to the appropriate civil service appointments or to deny them entry.

Confucianism also encourages groupthink and conformity. Signs of collective discussions and decision-making among members of the Chinese negotiating team are sometimes a good development in the negotiation process. When Chinese negotiators start huddling and discussing among themselves in Chinese language, it may infer that they are conferencing to make a decision and, if this is followed up by additional meetings, summoning of negotiation intermediaries or additional focused questions, they are all good signs of progress.[32]

The CJK (China, Japan, Korea) groupist and collectivist society means that all members of a unit take collective responsibility for other group members. In the US, studies were carried out to detect the groupist behavior of rice-growing Southern Chinese people.

Observers argue that, because some Westerners (like Americans) are more individualistic and assertive than others, they run into more obstacles during negotiations.[33] American executives and negotiators are primarily driven by profit-making as their end goal for doing business[34] (a stereotypical perception often held by Northeast Asians of their American counterparts). A caveat to the collective nature of Chinese society is that it is not hegemonically uniform in its collectivism. Chinese people residing north of the Yangtze River are considered more individualistic and analytical in contrast to Southern Chinese, who are communitarian, holistic in worldview and exhibit strong loyalty to family and friends.[35]

---

[32] Graham, J. L. & Lam, N. M. (October 1, 2003). "The Chinese Negotiation." *Harvard Business Review* [downloaded on 1 January 2022], available at https://hbr.org/2003/10/the-chinese-negotiation.

[33] *Ibid.*

[34] Van Zandt, H. F. (November 1970). "How to Negotiate in Japan." *Magazine/Harvard Business Review (HBR)* [downloaded on 1 January 2022], available at https://hbr.org/1970/11/how-to-negotiate-in-japan.

[35] Talhelm, T. (May 8, 2014). "'Rice Theory' Explains North–South China Cultural Differences, Study Shows." *UVA Today* (University of Virgina News) [downloaded on 1 January 2022], available at https://news.virginia.edu/content/rice-theory-explains-north-south-china-cultural-differences-study-shows.

3. Communication

Because the Chinese spoken language (or Chinese character-derived Kanji pronunciations in Japanese language as well) is abundant with homonyms, oral verbalized statements are often misunderstood so writing the spoken text down in Chinese or Japanese Kanji characters or in English can prevent miscommunications and misunderstandings.[36]

US or Western negotiators often find Oriental Northeast Asian (Chinese or Japanese) difficult to read, including interpreting if indeed a deal had been reached, because Northeast Asians tend to conform to the ancient Oriental custom of telling high-level management what they desire to hear rather than the actual facts or reality.[37] Just like other Northeast Asians, Chinese negotiators are unlikely to give an outright denial or rejection of a request. When trying to reject the other party's negotiators, Chinese negotiators use an array of tactics to soften their communication of rejection. Chinese business persons are likely to modify the subject matter, suddenly become quiet, distract and pose another enquiry, use ambiguous expressions and or articulate seemingly positive expressions with indirect negative connections [like *hai bu cuo* ("not bad"), *hai hao* ("seems okay"), and *hai xing* or *hai ke yi* ("seems able to make it")].[38]

When Chinese negotiators articulate the words *kan kan* (taking a look) or *yanjiu yanjiu* (studying it further),[39] it typically means that they are rejecting the negotiation proposal indirectly while preserving politeness. In the days before the anti-corruption campaign, a half-jest lore in the Chinese negotiating world was *yanjiu yanjiu* which are homonyms for "cigarettes and alcohol" and which indirectly meant that the negotiators were either asking for a round of lavish drinking and dinner with smoking activities or gifts in these two areas. Regardless of negotiation development, even after the formalities, continuing business communication is

[36] Van Zandt, H. F. (November 1970). "How to Negotiate in Japan." *Magazine/Harvard Business Review (HBR)* [downloaded on 1 January 2022], available at https://hbr.org/1970/11/how-to-negotiate-in-japan.
[37] *Ibid.*
[38] Graham, J. L. & Lam, N. M. (October 1, 2003). "The Chinese Negotiation." *Harvard Business Review* [downloaded on 1 January 2022], available at https://hbr.org/2003/10/the-chinese-negotiation.
[39] *Ibid.*

crucial, particularly on points where the written document is ambivalent. For American negotiators, avoiding slang words is useful in communicating clearly, e.g. "If you will let me have half a 'G' at six bits a piece, it'll be gung ho with me" should be articulated as "I want 500 at 75¢ each."[40]

4. Negotiation Strategies: Distributive or Integrative

Cultural anthropological observations noted that Chinese negotiators tend to pay attention to the means rather than the end goal of the process, as Chinese philosopher Fung Yu-lan argued that Chinese sages differentiated between the "root" (agriculture, a positively favorable component) and "branch" (commerce, a less desired component) of agriculture.[41] The analogy with agriculture, however, may have its own limits as southerners are more communitarian because Southern China has cultivated rice for millennia while Northern China cultivated wheat, and as Thalhelm argued:

> It's easy to think of China as a single culture, but we found that China has very distinct northern and southern psychological cultures and that southern China's history of rice farming can explain why people in southern China are more interdependent than people in the wheat-growing north.[42]

Confucian typically looked upon trade and commerce carried out by merchants with disdain. In terms of social hierarchy, the merchants are considered leeches that profit off other producers and thus follow the Mandarin scholar-gentry officials (intellectual capital propelled into their appointments after arduous exams), peasants (food producers) and artisans (craftsmen) in hierarchy. From this perspective, business dealings are

[40] Van Zandt, H. F. (November 1970). "How to Negotiate in Japan." *Magazine/Harvard Business Review (HBR)* [downloaded on 1 January 2022], available at https://hbr.org/1970/11/how-to-negotiate-in-japan.

[41] Graham, J. L. & Lam, N. M. (October 1, 2003). "The Chinese Negotiation." *Harvard Business Review* [downloaded on 1 January 2022], available at https://hbr.org/2003/10/the-chinese-negotiation.

[42] Talhelm, T. (May 8, 2014). "'Rice Theory' Explains North–South China Cultural Differences, Study Shows." *UVA Today* (University of Virgina News) [downloaded on 1 January 2022], available at https://news.virginia.edu/content/rice-theory-explains-north-south-china-cultural-differences-study-shows.

sometimes perceived as involving little or no trust, or even scruples. The self-fulfilling result is that many Chinese negotiators have a propensity to be distributive (especially when dealing with their fellowmen).

Besides Confucius, another ancient Chinese scholar's work has also had a profound impact on Chinese negotiation style. *The Art of War* is a book on military strategy and tactics written by Sun Tzu around late 400 to early 200 BCE. Chinese negotiators seek inspiration from the military stratagems mentioned in the book with the aim of gaining maximum advantages.[43] Many Chinese can cite the titles of the strategies and use them as idioms e.g. *hiding a knife behind a smile, luring the tiger to leave the mountain,* etc.[44] These strategies cannot be easily classified as being distributive or integrative (despite the names of some the stratagems) — the underlying philosophy is to be flexible and employ the right strategy at the right time and the right place and against the right opponent.[45] Because of the connotations of war and strategies and the fact that many popular idioms associated with *The Art of War* tend to be underpinned by deception — more often than not, the Chinese negotiator may adopt distributive approaches.

A well-known quote from *The Art of War* involves the use of information. It prescribes that knowledge about the opponent and knowledge about yourself will help win every battle; but ignorance about the opponent will severely curtail your winning chances.[46] The Chinese negotiator tends to be circumspect about sharing information. And even when they do share, the way in which the information is delivered, whether verbally or in writing, can make it challenging to understand the key messages. This attitude towards information sharing adds to the challenge if you are aiming for an integrative approach.

Linguistic experts opine that Chinese pictographic writing psychologically inclines Chinese people to look at the holistic, big picture rather than

[43] Jun, C. H. & Chu, J. (2002). 'The art of war' and East Asian negotiating styles. *Willamette Journal of International Law and Dispute Resolution,* 10(1), 161–96. http://www.jstor.org/stable/26211213.

[44] Benoliel, M. (2013). Negotiating successfully in Asia. *Eurasian Journal of Social Sciences,* 1(1), 1–18.

[45] *Ibid.*

[46] *Ibid.*

focusing on the details.[47] Some may then argue that this motivates Chinese negotiators to look at longer-term benefits and macro concerns rather than be bogged down by detailed nitty-gritty stipulations in the contracts or items found in the negotiations. On the other hand, Western negotiators typically desire the contract to state commitments, conditionalities and limitations in specific wordings that cannot be misconstrued.[48] Chinese *zhengti guannian* (holistic thinking) is often contrary to American sequential and individualistic thinking that dissipates complicated negotiation items into manageable issues while Chinese negotiators tend to approach the same items organically and sporadically with no particular order (from the American perspective).[49]

Western understanding concludes that contracts are only valid to a point and, beyond that, Chinese traditions take over in regulating the business relationship. Western negotiators consider Chinese business laws to be underdeveloped compared to the West and therefore guanxi fills in the gaps where legal coverage is wanting, with scholars like Professor Randall Peerenbloom (University of California Los Angeles, UCLA) indicating courts frequently do not implement awards against state-owned enterprises (SOEs) as they are ministerial units under some form of state management.[50] Therefore, there are legal limits to what can be practically enforceable in Chinese contract law.

It is beyond doubt that unless you have established the necessary mutually beneficial relationship or guanxi with the Chinese negotiator, you have

---

[47] Graham, J. L. & Lam, N. M. (October 1, 2003). "The Chinese Negotiation." *Harvard Business Review* [downloaded on 1 January 2022], available at https://hbr.org/2003/10/the-chinese-negotiation.

[48] Van Zandt, H. F. (November 1970). "How to Negotiate in Japan." *Magazine/Harvard Business Review (HBR)* [downloaded on 1 January 2022], available at https://hbr.org/1970/11/how-to-negotiate-in-japan.

[49] Graham, J. L. & Lam, N. M. (October 1, 2003). "The Chinese Negotiation." *Harvard Business Review* [downloaded on 1 January 2022], available at https://hbr.org/2003/10/the-chinese-negotiation.

[50] Program on Negotiation (PON) at Harvard Law School. (August 4, 2022). "The Importance of Relationship Building in China When in China, Relationship Building is Critical." Program on Negotiation (PON) at Harvard Law School [downloaded on 4 August 2022], available at https://www.pon.harvard.edu/daily/international-negotiation-daily/negotiation-in-china-the-importance-of-guanxi/.

very low chances of achieving an integrative process. However, you should be mindful that the Chinese's view of guanxi is ultimately pragmatic and not emotional.[51] Guanxi is primarily an instrument or means to the desired outcome. It is essentially about (present or future) exchange of favors. If the underlying situation or dynamics change, your guanxi will be affected. This is why you should audit guanxi to ensure you still have the requisite level and that it has not been displaced by changes beyond your control. In fact, because it is not emotional, the breaking of any guanxi is not taken too personally in China. The nature of guanxi itself and the challenges surrounding it explain why it is difficult to establish integrative negotiations in China. A positive note though is that guanxi is more dyadic rather than group-based. Therefore, your guanxi can open many doors in China — depending on where the guanxi leads you.

If you adopt a distributive strategy, it is always advisable not to put all the eggs in one basket, especially against the Chinese negotiator. While building up long-term relationships, you should concurrently be building up Plan B BATNAs (Best Alternative to a Negotiated Agreement) as a buffer against Chinese hardballing. Having a reliable option allows you to walk away from the negotiations if need be.[52] BATNAs (best alternative to a negotiated agreements) are activated whenever one's guanxi as an outsider is out-bid by a stronger offer from an insider.[53] Moreover, BATNAs are important for another reason. One tactic (probably not practiced in the West) is *liangshou zhunbei* (two-way prep). This is when the Chinese negotiator initiates negotiations with your rivals or competitors and then

[51] Lee, B. J. & Park, J. H. (2012). East Asians' Social Heterogeneity: Differences in Norms among Chinese, Japanese, and Korean Negotiators. *Negotiation Journal*, 28(4), 429–452. https://doi.org/10.1111/j.1571-9979.2012.00350.x.

[52] PON Staff. (August 15, 2022). "The Negotiation Process in China." PON Harvard [downloaded on 15 August 2022], available at https://www.pon.harvard.edu/daily/international-negotiation-daily/tips-for-navigating-negotiations-in-china/.

[53] Program on Negotiation (PON) at Harvard Law School. (August 4, 2022). "The Importance of Relationship Building in China When in China, Relationship Building is Critical." Program on Negotiation (PON) at Harvard Law School [downloaded on 4 August 2022], available at https://www.pon.harvard.edu/daily/international-negotiation-daily/negotiation-in-china-the-importance-of-guanxi/.

reveals this to you as part of the bargaining pressuring process.[54] Of course, you may choose to do the same. Maintain several guanxi connections and schedule guanxi audits to sustain relations with several connections. This way, when one contact fails to deliver or resigns, other guanxi connections can buffer against the agreement from dissipating.[55] This, of course, requires a lot of work and is usually undertaken if the deal is sizeable or if you have on-going projects in the same field.

5. Concession-making & Hardball Tactics

Saving money or *jiejian* (thriftiness) is considered a virtue in China and mainland Chinese people save nearly four times more household income than Americans and some argue that this gives rise to bargaining and haggling during negotiations.[56] There are other explanations for saving money, e.g. saving up for retirement and age-related expenses due to the lack of social security system for health-related issues, ensuring enough savings for children's education, etc. Most save money up for use during rainy days, or to sustain their retirement. Therefore, it is essential for you to prepare for extended rounds of bargaining, given the strong tendencies of the Chinese negotiator to bargain or haggle aggressively. In preparation, you can draw out a laundry list of concessions or compromises that they might be willing to give up in return for the deal and then patiently horse-trade with each of those items without being under the pressure of the primary negotiations itself.[57]

---

[54] Graham, J. L. & Lam, N. M. (October 1, 2003). "The Chinese Negotiation." *Harvard Business Review* [downloaded on 1 January 2022], available at https://hbr.org/2003/10/the-chinese-negotiation.

[55] Program on Negotiation (PON) at Harvard Law School. (August 4, 2022). "The Importance of Relationship Building in China When in China, Relationship Building is Critical." Program on Negotiation (PON) at Harvard Law School [downloaded on 4 August 2022], available at https://www.pon.harvard.edu/daily/international-negotiation-daily/negotiation-in-china-the-importance-of-guanxi/.

[56] Graham, J L. & Lam, N. M. (October 1, 2003). "The Chinese Negotiation." *Harvard Business Review* [downloaded on 1 January 2022], available at https://hbr.org/2003/10/the-chinese-negotiation.

[57] *Ibid.*

When bargaining, you are well-advised to standby to put all items simultaneously on the table and not necessarily in a rational sequence or in haphazard order as the final settlement is contingent on the whole package being finalized.[58]

In the bargaining process, some Chinese bargaining features and trends may be considered. Chinese negotiators tend to give way on price concessions non-reluctantly and usually only after long negotiations. You must try not to ridicule the initial Chinese low base prices offered or feel insulted at what they perceive as unrealistic counters.[59] Instead of rejecting lowballing offers, it may be useful to rely on guanxi to elicit more favorable price conditions. Guanxi is crucial in negotiating financial and payment decisions as they tend to provide more favorable conditions to insiders more than outsiders.[60]

In theoretical foundations and esoteric conceptualization, concession-making is part and parcel of the ultimate truth. Lao Tzu (a progenitor of the philosophical religion of Taoism based on the universal balance of yin (female and dark forces) and yang (male bright force) encouraged Chinese thinking to seek the mid-way solutions in life, even in negotiations. Therefore, negotiations become rounds of lengthy ritualistic compromises, bargaining that cannot be dismissed summarily and must be concluded up till an equilibrium in the form of a compromise position between two negotiation parties. Negotiations do not proceed with the assumption that there is a gospel deterministic end-point where the enlightened truth lies. Chinese historical, religious and philosophical rhythms tend to be cyclical rather than deterministic like the Judeo-Christian traditions in the West.

In practice, unlike Western (especially American) concessionary gestures, there is no time limit imposed on returning *hui bao* (reciprocal favors and returns) as agricultural conceptualization of time is lengthy and the memories of *hui bao* opportunities and recalls are always reciprocated in the long run. Chinese people and business partners also consider bypassing

[58] *Ibid.*

[59] *Ibid.*

[60] Program on Negotiation (PON) at Harvard Law School. (August 4, 2022). "The Importance of Relationship Building in China When in China, Relationship Building is Critical." Program on Negotiation (PON) at Harvard Law School [downloaded on 4 August 2022], available at https://www.pon.harvard.edu/daily/international-negotiation-daily/negotiation-in-china-the-importance-of-guanxi/.

reciprocity in relationships as discourteous and immoral, condemned with the label *wangen fuyi* (forgetting the source that bestows the favor and then reneges on obligations, justice and loyalty), forever ruining the goodwill for any future business ventures.[61]

Ritualistically, concession is also performance in the symbolic cultural dance of "saving face". In Chinese culture, "saving face" is important and therefore, maintaining relationship with a friendly disposition and practicing self-restraint in emotional discharge without embarrassing the other parties is crucial. East Asian countries (CJK or China, Japan, Korea) regard "saving face" as important, to save face of an important/senior person (some Western business leaders consider this as a form of "special interest" accommodation) is to still be respectful even when not necessarily going through with the negotiation because of economic or political factors.[62]

Western negotiators may meet different intensities of aggression and groupist behavior among the Chinese, especially between the Northern and Southern Chinese. Climate also appears to have an impact on people's behavioral traits as northerners appear more aggressive and independent while southerners have stronger teamwork and communitarian spirit, as explained by Talhelm's study:

> This has sometimes been attributed to different climates — warmer in the south, colder in the north — which certainly affects agriculture, but it appears to be more related to what Chinese people have been growing for thousands of years.[63]

For some scholars, the element of trust reveals a formerly dormant inclination for cooperation hidden by security covers of passive-aggressive behavior and thus trust is a crucial element for developing relationships in

[61] Graham, J. L. & Lam, N. M. (October 1, 2003). "The Chinese Negotiation." *Harvard Business Review* [downloaded on 1 January 2022], available at https://hbr.org/2003/10/the-chinese-negotiation.

[62] Van Zandt, H. F. (November 1970). "How to Negotiate in Japan." *Magazine/Harvard Business Review (HBR)* [downloaded on 1 January 2022], available at https://hbr.org/1970/11/how-to-negotiate-in-japan.

[63] Talhelm, T. (8 May 2014). "'Rice Theory' Explains North–South China Cultural Differences, Study Shows." *UVA Today* (University of Virgina News) [downloaded on 1 January 2022], available at https://news.virginia.edu/content/rice-theory-explains-north-south-china-cultural-differences-study-shows.

negotiations (including cross-cultural ones).[64] Not being poker-faced in negotiations and leaking emotions like anger, frustration or aggression during negotiations can sometimes result in the disruption of *mianzi* dignity of the other party.

Therefore, in this case, even pretend tantrums that are sometimes practiced in the West can lead to negative results,[65] resulting in the loss of face or social capital. As an alternative to hardballing, one can also act dumb strategically (softballing). Some experts opine that it is sometimes strategic to act a little dumb and pose the same question repeatedly to expose flaws in the Chinese negotiators' arguments to compel them to give concessions.[66] However, this may also be challenging given their tendency to depend on group consultation and decision-making processes as well as the all-important priority of preserving *mianzi* (face) and social status (*shehui dengji*).[67]

When Chinese negotiators turn silent tactically, it compels foreign negotiations to reach out by forwarding enquiries or speaking through the intermediary go-between-er and this may occur during pricing discussions when Chinese negotiators are known to deploy weaponized silence against their counterparts (especially impatient American negotiators).[68] Americans often feel puzzled by silence displayed by Northeast Asians (Chinese and Japanese especially) and do not know how to handle it, feeling a loss in trying to comprehend what is going on.[69] Thus, the advice prescribed to negotiators is not to be bothered by

[64] Kim, M.-J., Wang, L., & Park, M.-S. (September 21, 2015). Different levels of trust in global business negotiation: A comparative study about Canadians and Korean perspective on doing business negotiation with Chinese. *International Commerce and Information Review*, 17(3), 158 [downloaded on 1 January 2022], available at https://koreascience.kr/article/JAKO201534164960105.pdf.

[65] Graham, J. L. & Lam, N. M. (October 1, 2003). "The Chinese Negotiation." Harvard Business Review [downloaded on 1 January 2022], available at https://hbr.org/2003/10/the-chinese-negotiation.

[66] *Ibid.*

[67] *Ibid.*

[68] *Ibid.*

[69] Van Zandt, H. F. (November 1970). "How to Negotiate in Japan." *Magazine/Harvard Business Review (HBR)* [downloaded on 1 January 2022], available at https://hbr.org/1970/11/how-to-negotiate-in-japan.

such behavior and stick to concession-haggling as a way to defuse any cold war-like situation.

Playing hardball with Chinese negotiators may also include tactics that are not often employed in the West. Some experts mention that it is also possible to provide Chinese negotiators/customers with market intelligence related to one's rivals as a form of sharing research/education about the market to indicate one's company's track record and performance results.[70] Shared intelligence can be a form of favor gifted to connect with the other party. Whatever techniques the non-Chinese negotiators employ, it is important to remember that any favor received to achieve negotiation success must be reciprocated in the future. Like in all Northeast Asian countries (especially China, Japan, Korea or CJK), reciprocity is an important element of business negotiations, which is an obligation equally applied to business relationships and their accompanying obligations.

6. Role of Women

Northeast Asian societies (specifically China, Japan, Korea or CJK) are male-dominated societies. The number of women in their business leadership positions remains one of the lowest among developed economies. Interestingly, in Chinese socialist lore, Mao had a famous saying that women made up half the sky. In fact, one of the vaunted achievements of the communist revolution was that it removed Confucian feudalism and liberated women to perform the same tasks as men. Women assumed the roles of political leaders, military personnel, business leaders and top cadre members consequently. However, there are some limits to the extent of emancipation, such as rural areas lagging behind urbanites when it came to women's rights or the lack of female leaders at the very top echelons of power in the Chinese Communist Party. In fact, one of the critiques by the West of the makeup of the Politburo Standing Committee or the Politburo's core leaders after the 20th Party Congress was that there were no women among them. Nevertheless, compared to its feudal past, it is clear that improvements were made.

---

[70]Graham, J. L. & Lam, N. M. (October 1, 2003). "The Chinese Negotiation." *Harvard Business Review* [downloaded on 1 January 2022], available at https://hbr.org/2003/10/the-chinese-negotiation.

Based on the 2022 Global Gender Gap Report by the World Economic Forum,[71] China is ranked 13 out of 19 countries in the East Asia and the Pacific region — ahead of only Malaysia and China covered in this book.

Global Gender Gap Report 2022 INSIGHT REPORT JULY 2022			
EAST ASIA & the PACIFIC	**Rank**		
Country	**Regional (19)**	**Global (146)**	**Score**
Philippines	2	19	0.783
Singapore	4	49	0.734
Thailand	8	79	0.709
Vietnam	9	83	0.705
Indonesia	10	92	0.697
Korea (South)	12	99	0.689
China	**13**	**102**	**0.682**
Malaysia	14	103	0.681
Japan	19	116	0.650

China did not share its Labour Force surveys with the International Labour Office (ILO) so it was not included in the 2021 report for G20 countries.[72]

7. Intermediary/Interpreter

Guanxi (human relations) tend to go beyond Western-style networking and dive deep into premium social capital derived from friendships, family clan ties and allied business partnerships. However, guanxi traditionalism is constantly eroded by modernization of business practices though the fundamental strength of guanxi remains in Chinese business decision-

---

[71] Global Gender Gap Report 2022. (July 13, 2022). World Economic Forum. https://www.weforum.org/reports/global-gender-gap-report-2022/digest. The Global Gender Gap Index benchmarks the current state and evolution of gender parity across four key dimensions (Economic Participation and Opportunity, Educational Attainment, Health and Survival, and Political Empowerment). It is the longest-standing index which tracks progress towards closing these gaps over time since its inception in 2006.

[72] International Labour Office. (2021). "Women in managerial and leadership positions in the G20." Available at: https://www.ilo.org/wcmsp5/groups/public/---dgreports/---ddg_p/documents/publication/wcms_762098.pdf.

making. However, guanxi comes with its own set of responsibilities, such as reciprocity (*hui bao* in the Hanyu pinyin Romanized system). Part of the guanxi (human relations) equation is to seek high-level business contacts (especially with those who can have the decision-making authority) and also reach out to negotiators who appear to be flexible and pragmatic.[73]

Negotiations are generally classifiable into three parts: antecedent phase (pre-negotiation stage and preparations), the concurrent phase (ongoing process), and the consequent phase (post-negotiation stage) and negotiation behavior throughout all three phases can affect the outcome.[74] There is much work to be done in the pre-negotiation stage. Like all negotiations, it is recommended for negotiators to carry out detailed research about their company's products and services and create, share and educate awareness among their Chinese negotiation partners while providing details on their company's requirements without being condescending.

In the early phase of the concurrent stage, entertainment activities are seen as very important rituals in the pre-negotiation antecedent phase. Chinese dinners are the most common form of entertainment where alcohol is part of the social rituals. Business negotiations in northern China tend to involve strong liquor like distilled *baijiu* with 52–64% alcohol. Those used to negotiating in the median part of China near the Yangtze River divide may be familiar with alcohols like *Maotai* while those negotiating in southern China may be entertained with wines. Negotiators visiting Western Chinese counterparts may encounter *Xifengjiu* or 'Western Phoenix Alcohol' when translated literally.

Intermediaries would have briefed the non-Chinese negotiators of the cultural features of Chinese drinking rituals. The drinking ritual consists of presenting the alcohols in cups placed on a lazy susan and then a toast (*ganbei*) is held and the non-Chinese guests must finish up their cup with a single or few gulps and then hold up the glass upside-down to indicate they have finished drinking the liquid. If a drop of remaining alcohols drips onto their heads, they would have to consume another cup of the fermented

---

[73] PON Staff. (August 15, 2022). "The Negotiation Process in China." PON Harvard [downloaded on 15 August 2022], available at https://www.pon.harvard.edu/daily/international-negotiation-daily/tips-for-navigating-negotiations-in-china/.

[74] Sun, M. (December 2009). A comparison of business negotiation behavior between Korea and China. *International Journal of Business and Management*, 4(12). [downloaded on 1 January 2022], available at https://pdfs.semanticscholar.org/ccfc/201493ae2e5ced6146765 3696c4ecb34571d.pdf, p. 212.

drink. Drinking on empty stomach is not encouraged and it is best to mentally prepare oneself before attending negotiation dinners, which usually involve much serious drinking.

Using interpretators and constantly clarifying terms that are vague are very useful tools for a successful negotiation. It is advisable to avoid rushing to settle the negotiations within a short time (even when one is on a short business travel schedule, as impatience is seen as a weakness) and mitigate any expectations of a fast deal.[75] In negotiating with Oriental Northeast Asians (China, Japan, Korea or CJK), Americans tend to desire to "get on with it" and conclude the deal when it is down to a few last unsettled points and it is at this point that most mistakes are made by American negotiators,[76] e.g. giving away concessions easily or becoming impatient. The element of time consciousness differs between East Asians and North Americans. North Americans tend to conceptualize time as a finite resource and a highly valuable commodity, much more than Northeast Asian negotiators from Korea or China and this would then affect whether communication styles are straightforward, patiently tolerant of time expended or contextual.[77]

In the initial stages of Chinese negotiations, some practitioners/experts recommend the procedure of "nontask sounding" by building relationship ties with an individual who can be an intermediary with the other negotiating party, e.g. based on personal experiences or hometown links, family connections, school alumni, or business precedents.[78] Initiating guanxi is important for Chinese business negotiations in China, but maintaining an advantage is

[75] Coyner, T. (October 4, 2007). "Korean Concepts of Negotiating." *Korea Times* [downloaded on 4 October 2007], available at http://www.koreatimes.co.kr/www/news/special/2007/10/175_11313.html.

[76] Van Zandt, H. F. (November 1970). "How to Negotiate in Japan." *Magazine/Harvard Business Review (HBR)* [downloaded on 1 January 2022], available at https://hbr.org/1970/11/how-to-negotiate-in-japan.

[77] Kim, M.-J., Wang, L., & Park, M.-S. (September 21, 2015). Different levels of trust in global business negotiation: A comparative study about Canadians and Korean perspective on doing business negotiation with Chinese. *International Commerce and Information Review*, 17(3), 160. [downloaded on 1 January 2022], available at https://koreascience.kr/article/JAKO201534164960105.pdf.

[78] Graham, J. L. and Lam, N. M. (October 1, 2003). "The Chinese Negotiation." *Harvard Business Review* [downloaded on 1 January 2022], available at https://hbr.org/2003/10/the-chinese-negotiation.

just as complex and challenging.[79] A relationship with an intermediary has to be maintained in the long run even after the initial meetings were successfully established through this intermediary.[80] The intermediary often begins the process by bringing up the first negotiation item, steps in when there are differences, interprets the non-verbal communication patterns of the Chinese negotiator and often settles differences and acts as a mediator between the two negotiating parties when there are problems.[81] In all these cases, the *Zhongjian Ren* or intermediary makes all the difference in business deals.

8. Time, Timelines, Timeliness

Chinese negotiators implementing *zhengti guannian* (holistic thinking) often demand lengthy background information with a long list of questioning that can sometimes test the patience of Western negotiators who are used to deterministic linear progression and often assume an end to negotiations after they have completely gone through the list on the stated agenda.[82] A practitioner opined that negotiations in China are complex and require a lengthy period of time to comprehend the motivations, demands and requirements put forward by Chinese negotiating parties.[83] Confucianism and its emphasis on human relationships and their responsibilities mean that the Chinese negotiators expect you to carry out your promises based on guanxi and not on contractual obligations.[84] They can-

---

[79] Program on Negotiation (PON) at Harvard Law School. (August 4, 2022). "The Importance of Relationship Building in China When in China, Relationship Building is Critical." Program on Negotiation (PON) at Harvard Law School [downloaded on 4 August 2022], available at https://www.pon.harvard.edu/daily/international-negotiation-daily/negotiation-in-china-the-importance-of-guanxi/.

[80] Graham, J. L. & Lam, N. M. (October 1, 2003). "The Chinese Negotiation." *Harvard Business Review* [downloaded on 1 January 2022], available at https://hbr.org/2003/10/the-chinese-negotiation.

[81] *Ibid.*

[82] *Ibid.*

[83] PON Staff. (August 15, 2022). "The Negotiation Process in China." *PON Harvard* [downloaded on 15 August 2022], available at https://www.pon.harvard.edu/daily/international-negotiation-daily/tips-for-navigating-negotiations-in-china/

[84] Program on Negotiation (PON) at Harvard Law School. (August 4, 2022). "The Importance of Relationship Building in China When in China, Relationship Building is Critical." Program on Negotiation (PON) at Harvard Law School [downloaded on 4 August 2022], available at https://www.pon.harvard.edu/daily/international-negotiation-daily/negotiation-in-china-the-importance-of-guanxi/.

not comprehend accelerating negotiations to save time because, to them, forging a business relationship without putting in the foundation of *renji hexie* (interpersonal harmonious relationship) is simply discourteous and more important than having the relationship governed by a written text known as the contract.[85]

Even when the demands appear to be onerous and illogical, meeting them halfway can work wonders in building trust and forging a long-term relationship through frequent face-to-face (F2F) conversations/dialogues.[86] The Chinese negotiators tend to exert much effort to provide access to those they have guanxi with, and they place their trust in these individuals to an extent that surpasses the usual limits for Americans.[87] Taking a long-term orientation may mean giving up short-term gains for long-term goals. Some call this the "avoid the gold rush mentality" through a long-term deal that not only benefits the negotiating team but her/his organization as well.[88]

Chiku nailao or the quality of endurance is valued in judging the character of a business partner (instead of appreciating or admiring individual talents like the Americans).[89] This quality of endurance is often displayed during long rounds of relentless negotiations (which can be tiring for Westerners and therefore a weakness for Chinese negotiators to exploit).[90]

---

[85] Graham, J. L. & Lam, N. M. (October 1, 2003). "The Chinese Negotiation." *Harvard Business Review* [downloaded on 1 January 2022], available at https://hbr.org/2003/10/the-chinese-negotiation.

[86] PON Staff. (August 15, 2022). "The Negotiation Process in China." *PON Harvard* [downloaded on 15 August 2022], available at https://www.pon.harvard.edu/daily/international-negotiation-daily/tips-for-navigating-negotiations-in-china/.

[87] Program on Negotiation (PON) at Harvard Law School. (August 4, 2022). "The Importance of Relationship Building in China When in China, Relationship Building is Critical" dated 4 August 2022 in Program on Negotiation (PON) at Harvard Law School [downloaded on 4 August 2022], available at https://www.pon.harvard.edu/daily/international-negotiation-daily/negotiation-in-china-the-importance-of-guanxi/.

[88] PON Staff. (August 15, 2022). "The Negotiation Process in China." *PON Harvard* [downloaded on 15 August 2022], available at https://www.pon.harvard.edu/daily/international-negotiation-daily/tips-for-navigating-negotiations-in-china/.

[89] Graham, J. L. & Lam, N. M. (October 1, 2003). "The Chinese Negotiation." *Harvard Business Review* [downloaded on 1 January 2022], available at https://hbr.org/2003/10/the-chinese-negotiation.

[90] *Ibid.*

Even when the negotiations reached the end of the agenda, the Chinese negotiator may revert back to negotiating the deal as a whole coherent package (sometimes to elicit additional concessions) and this is often considered the most stressful part of the negotiation process for some Westerners[91] and gives the impression to them that 'it ain't over till the fat lady sings.'

When an impasse in the final concluding stages is reached, any dissonance may result in the cold war silent treatment. One possible option in dealing with the strategically weaponized Chinese silence during negotiations is to secure your own management's understanding of the fact that the negotiation is expected to be lengthy and to provide the negotiating team full authority to bide their time while the Chinese negotiators are strategically implementing silent lulls to derail their counterparts' patience.[92] Because time is needed to cultivate guanxi, instant outcomes of negotiations are unlikely and any short-circuiting of the negotiation process can only be done through special guanxi relationships,[93] especially those patiently built up over time as long-term social capital investments.

Bibliography

Graham, J. L. & Lam, N. M. (October 1, 2003). "The Chinese Negotiation." *Harvard Business Review* [downloaded on 1 January 2022], available at https://hbr.org/2003/10/the-chinese-negotiation.

Hofstede Insights. (2022). "Compare Countries." Hofstede Insights [downloaded on 1 January 2022], available at https://www.hofstede-insights.com/product/compare-countries/.

PON Staff. (August 15, 2022). "The Negotiation Process in China." *PON Harvard* [downloaded on 15 August 2022], available at https://www.pon.harvard.edu/daily/international-negotiation-daily/tips-for-navigating-negotiations-in-china/.

Program on Negotiation (PON) at Harvard Law School. (August 4, 2022). "The Importance of Relationship Building in China When in China, Relationship

---

[91] *Ibid.*
[92] *Ibid.*
[93] *Ibid.*

Building is Critical." Program on Negotiation (PON) at Harvard Law School [downloaded on 4 August 2022], available at https://www.pon.harvard.edu/daily/international-negotiation-daily/negotiation-in-china-the-importance-of-guanxi/.

Sainvilus, M. (April 25, 2018). "Behavioral differences between Northern v. Southern Chinese linked to wheat v. rice farming, study shows." Chicago Booth the University of Chicago Booth School of Business [downloaded on 25 April 2018], available at https://www.chicagobooth.edu/media-relations-and-communications/press-releases/behavioral-differences-between-northern-v-southern-chinese.

Talhelm, T. (May 8, 2014). "'Rice Theory' Explains North–South China Cultural Differences, Study Shows." *UVA Today* (University of Virginia News) [downloaded on 1 January 2022], available at https://news.virginia.edu/content/rice-theory-explains-north-south-china-cultural-differences-study-shows.

Van Zandt, H. F. (November 1970). "How to Negotiate in Japan." *Magazine/Harvard Business Review* (HBR) [downloaded on 1 January 2022], available at https://hbr.org/1970/11/how-to-negotiate-in-japan.

China Quiz

1. The American politicians and corporate leaders were unhappy with the _____ condition for their companies entering into China while some views in China saw the condition as a necessity for a fledgling rising economy to nurture its domestic industries. Fill in the blank.
   A. collectivization
   B. command economy
   C. full nationalization
   D. Joint Venture (JV)

2. In the United States, there is a tendency of trusting others until the occasion arises which breaks that trust, which is in contrast with the Chinese mindset that treats all strangers with suspicion and distrust. Is this general tendency true or false?
   A. True
   B. False

3. _____ refers to human relations and/or individuals to whom you can provide favors and receive in reciprocity — qualified individuals that include family predominantly, but also friends, fellow students, neighbors, fellow alumni, etc. Fill in the blank.
   A. Guangong
   B. Guanxi
   C. Guangdong
   D. Guanzhi

4. The overseas ethnic Chinese network is sometimes known as the _____ network. Fill in the blank.
   A. rose
   B. chrysanthemum
   C. bamboo
   D. camelia

5. Another feature of negotiating with all Northeast Asians is not to overly rely on contractual stipulations. Is this general tendency true or false?
   A. True
   B. False

6. Chinese negotiation styles have minor convergence with those of the West, thanks to the business schools offering MBAs that are springing up all over China (including very prestigious ones like Guanghua business school in Beijing's Peking University or PKU) where Western business concepts are being acquired. Is this general tendency true or false?
   A. True
   B. False

7. Since China is a sub-continental-sized country, there are differences between Northern and Southern Chinese cultures. Is this general characterization true or false?
   A. True
   B. False

8. Physically, _____ River is the dividing line between the two components. The _____ River (longest in China) literally splits the country into half from west to east, creating two visible cultural worldviews. Fill in the blanks.
   A. Nile
   B. Han
   C. Moon
   D. Yangtze

9. China is the birthplace of _____. Fill in the blank.
   A. Bahaism
   B. Confucianism.
   C. Shintoism
   D. Judaism

10. In terms of human-originated influence, Confucianism is probably the paramount source of influence on Chinese culture and social behavior. Is this general characterization true or false?
   A. True
   B. False

Answer Bank

   1. D
   2. A
   3. B
   4. C
   5. A
   6. A
   7. A
   8. D
   9. B
   10. A

Chapter 2

The Indonesian Negotiator

1. The Environment

Will the 2036 Olympics be held at Nusantara?[1] It is understandable if you have not yet heard of the city. When Indonesian President Joko Widodo announced the country's bid in late 2022, the planned capital city in East Kalimantan had yet to be built. The name means "archipelago" in Javanese and it is the government's hope that the first phase of completion will be achieved by 2024 when Nusantara will replace Jakarta as its political capital.[2]

Until then, Jakarta remains the political and commercial hub of the largest economy in Southeast Asia and its most populous city.[3] At just over 270 million,[4] Indonesia's population is the fourth largest in the world — after China, India and the United States. The sprawling archipelago is made up of over 16,000 islands including Sumatra, Java, West Timor,

---

[1] Harish, F. (2022). "Indonesia Bids to Host 2036 Olympics in Eventual Capital." *The Jakarta Post*, November 19. Available at https://www.thejakartapost.com/indonesia/2022/11/18/indonesia-bids-to-host-2036-olympics-in-eventual-capital.html.

[2] Mariska, D. (2022). "Nusantara is the Name of Indonesia's New Capital." *TheIndonesia. id*, January 17. Available at https://www.theindonesia.id/news/2022/01/17/164500/nusantara-is-the-name-of-indonesias-new-capital.

[3] World Bank. (April 5, 2022). "The World Bank in Indonesia." World Bank. Available at https://www.worldbank.org/en/country/indonesia/overview.

[4] Badan Pusat Statistik. (2022). "Badan Pusat Statistik." Available at https://www.bps.go.id/indicator/12/1975/1/jumlah-penduduk-pertengahan-tahun.html. (Accessed November 5, 2022). Badan Pusat Statistik (BPS) is the government's statistics agency.

Sulawesi, the Moluccas, parts of Borneo and New Guinea.[5] The country boasts of over 1,300 ethnic groups.[6] Around 85% of its population are Muslim, making Indonesia the largest Muslim-majority state in the world.[7] Indonesia is one of the five founder nations of ASEAN.[8]

When you arrive in Jakarta for your business negotiation, you will immediately feel the buzz and energy of the place. The daily street scene is a hive of activities. The traffic jam in town starts to build up as early as 8 am and lively lunch crowds spill into the eateries and popular food streets. The day is punctuated by loudspeakers broadcasting the *adzan* (call to prayer) five times a day from the city's many, many mosques. Much of this energy can be attributed to demographics. Indonesia has a young population. According to the 2020 national census, the Gen-Z and millennials make up more than half of its citizens.[9] This group plays an essential role in the country's digital technology economy which gave rise to a number of well-known unicorns (technology start-up companies valued at more than US$1 billion) such as Gojek, Tokopedia, Traveloka.[10] In fact, Gojek's founder, Nadiem Makarim, was even named Minister of Education, Culture, Research and Technology in 2019, making history as the youngest cabinet minister ever appointed.

The energetic and vibrant private sector offers a stark contrast to the country's state-owned enterprises sector which is debt-laden and in need of restructuring. In Indonesia, the Ministry of State-Owned Enterprises

---

[5] Sekretariat Kabinet Republik Indonesia. (August 19, 2017). "UN Verifies Names of 16,056 Indonesian Islands." Available at https://setkab.go.id/en/un-verifies-names-of-16056-indonesian-islands/.

[6] World Bank. (April 5, 2022). "The World Bank in Indonesia." World Bank. Available at https://www.worldbank.org/en/country/indonesia/overview.

[7] "Indonesia — The World Factbook," October 26, 2022. Available at https://www.cia.gov/the-world-factbook/countries/indonesia/.

[8] Association of Southeast Asian Nations. (2020). "The Founding of ASEAN." Asean.org. Available at https://asean.org/the-founding-of-asean/. Indonesia, Malaysia, Philippines, Singapore and Thailand are the 5 founding member nations of ASEAN which now includes Brunei, Cambodia, Laos, Myanmar and Vietnam.

[9] Badan Pusat Statistik 2021. Available at https://www.bps.go.id/publication/2021/02/26/938316574c78772f27e9b477/statistik-indonesia-2021.html.

[10] Keoni M. (2021). "Jokowi and the Millennials: Facing the Digital Economy." *RSIS Commentary: The Series*, December, 135–39. https://doi.org/10.1142/9789811232206_0030.

(SOEs) oversees the SOEs or *Badan Usaha Milik Negara* (BUMN).[11] Unfortunately, when SOEs make news headlines, it is generally either about their massive debt problems or corruption at the top. In the case of the national flag carrier, Garuda Indonesia, it was both. Its former chief executive was jailed in 2020 for bribery and money laundering offenses relating to the procurement of aircrafts and engines.[12] Meanwhile, over the course of the pandemic, the listed company's liabilities continued to mount and it eventually restructured its US$10-billion debt in early 2023.[13] When trading of its stocks resumed after the restructuring, its institutional investors started selling them, reflecting the market's bearish outlook.

The Indonesian negotiators are optimistic and ambitious about what you can both achieve at the negotiation table. The country has come a long way since overcoming the Asian financial crisis in the late 1990s. You should not be surprised if Indonesia does become the first Southeast Asian city to host the Olympics.

2. Culture

The largest ethnic group is the Javanese (40%), followed by the Sundanese (15%).[14] The Javanese dominate the country's political and commercial landscape. All seven of Indonesia's presidents since independence in 1945 had Javanese ancestry. They are involved in almost every industry and especially in the SOEs/BUMNs. Besides the capital city of Jakarta, thriving cities such as Surabaya and Bandung are also located on the island of

---

[11] SOEs that are provincial-owned or municipal-owned are known as *Badan Usaha Milik Daerah* (BUMD).

[12] Kahfi, K. (2020). "Former Garuda Boss Sentenced to Eight Years for Bribery, Money Laundering." *The Jakarta Post*, May 9. Available at https://www.thejakartapost.com/news/2020/05/09/former-garuda-boss-sentenced-to-eight-years-for-bribery-money-laundering.html.

[13] *The Jakarta Post*. (January 11, 2023). "Analysis: Garuda Completes Restructuring, Back to Black, Resumes Stock Trading." Available at https://www.thejakartapost.com/opinion/2023/01/11/analysis-garuda-completes-restructuring-back-to-black-resumes-stock-trading.html.

[14] "Indonesia — The World Factbook," October 26, 2022. Available at https://www.cia.gov/the-world-factbook/countries/indonesia/.

Java. Understanding Javanese culture is therefore useful, and perhaps crucial, when doing business and negotiating in Indonesia.

Javanese traditions are patrimonial and hierarchical. They believe that there is a predetermined social order which dictates the rules and norms of behavior. The stratified and class-conscious Javanese society remained intact during three centuries of Dutch administration, which merely inserted the Europeans at the top of the social pinnacle.[15] In the vertical relationship between two persons of unequal status, *hormat* (respect) must be shown. And for relationships between equals, both parties must strive for *rukun* (conflict avoidance) by displaying *sabar* (patience) and practice *gotong royong* (mutual cooperation). These vertical and horizontal relationships, together with associated norms of behavior to promote harmony, share similarities with Confucianism. For the Javanese, in addition to harmony between people, there should also be harmony with the universe. The Javanese practices a syncretic form of Islam which integrates animistic and Hindu elements. Some of them ascribe to mysticism and believe that ancestors and spirits must be respected to maintain total equilibrium. The central underpinning of the Javanese culture to preserve harmony is therefore expansive and extends to all levels and in all respects.[16] Javanese aspire to be equanimous and calm at all times, because this is an embodiment of harmony. There is even disdain for those who cannot keep their cool or show their feelings.

Outwardly, the Javanese negotiator will be unstintingly polite and retain a pleasant countenance throughout. Such a demeanor reflects their refinement and, consequently, high status. You should not be surprised if they come across as superstitious, although this will add a complicated dimension to decision-making. Their calm exterior means you will not easily know the Javanese negotiator's true feelings about your proposals or you. You may find the negotiation process leading you nowhere and sometimes be confused or perplexed about the outcome.

Waves of Chinese migration occurred during the Dutch colonial period. Majority of them can trace their roots to southern China (mainly Fujian and Guangdong provinces) and are from the southern dialect groups

---

[15] van der Kroef, J. M. (1953). Collectivism in Indonesian society. *Social Research, 20*(1), 193–193.

[16] Geertz, H. (1961). *The Javanese Family: A Study of Kinship and Socialization*. New York: Free Press of Glencoe.

(Hokchia, Hokkien/Southern Min, Teochew and Cantonese).[17] During Dutch rule (1816–1941), the Chinese in Dutch Indonesia were inserted as a class to carry out trade and commercial activities and served as intermediaries between the Dutch rulers, Javanese bureaucracy and the commoners. In present-day Indonesia, Chinese Indonesians are sometimes also classified as being either *totok* (to mean "pure") or *peranakan* (to mean "mixed"). *Totoks* celebrate Chinese traditional events, can usually speak Mandarin or Chinese dialects and practice Buddhism or Daoism. *Peranakans* do not observe Chinese festivities, speak mainly Indonesian with little or no Mandarin and/or Chinese dialects and are either Christians or Muslims. Chinese Indonesians made up less than 3% of the country's population at roughly seven million.[18] According to the World Economic Forum (2016), this is the largest Chinese population in the world residing outside of China.[19] Chinese Indonesians or Tionghoa have historically enjoyed business success in Indonesia, and dominate the list of country's richest citizens. There is no official data, but a common assertion is that this ethnic minority group controls 70% of Indonesia's private economy.[20]

The culture of this huge Chinese diaspora shares a lot of similarities with the Chinese negotiators (especially those from the south).[21] Both the *Totoks* and the *Peranakans* embrace Confucian values and respect social order and hierarchy.[22] Confucian virtues such as loyalty and filial piety

---

[17] Arifin, E. N., Sairi Hasbullah, M., & Pramono, A. (2016). Chinese Indonesians: How many, who and where? *Asian Ethnicity*, 18(3), 310–329. https://doi.org/10.1080/14631369.2016.1227236.

[18] *Ibid.*

[19] "Where Are the Largest Chinese Populations Outside of China? | Thailand or Indonesia: Which Country Has the Largest Chinese Population? | By World Economic Forum | Facebook." Available at https://www.facebook.com/worldeconomicforum/videos/where-are-the-largest-chinese-populations-outside-of-china/10153549858561479/ (Accessed November 8, 2022).

[20] Chong, W.-L. Chinese Indonesians in Post-Suharto Indonesia democratisation and ethnic minorities. *Journal of Chinese Overseas*, 17(2), 419–422. https://doi.org/10.1163/17932548-12341451.

[21] See Chapter on "The Chinese Negotiator".

[22] Efferin, S. & Hopper, T. (2007). Management control, culture and ethnicity in a Chinese Indonesian company. *Accounting, Organizations and Society,* 32(3), 223–262. https://doi.org/10.1016/j.aos.2006.03.009.

help engender trust, which sets the foundation for important *guanxi* (connections). The network of *guanxi* within the community gives rise to larger kinship networks. The expansion of these networks beyond national borders to connect with other overseas Chinese business networks in Southeast Asia made them a formidable economic force. This powerful network of overseas Chinese business families is popularly referred to as the Bamboo network[23] or Dragon network.[24] Even though many such businesses are now run by 3rd- or 4th-generation owners, younger Chinese Indonesians still rely on personal networks that are intra-ethnically based; although this is not the only way they do business.[25] For Chinese Indonesians, this heavy reliance on *guanxi* is borne out of necessity as a form of defensive solidarity. In Southeast Asia, ethnic Chinese in Indonesia and Malaysia face a lot of constraints and often feel precarious. This is in contrast to the experience of the Chinese minority in Thailand and the Philippines.[26] During the 30-year reign of Suharto (1967–1998), public and open expressions of Chinese culture through language, religious activities and traditional festivals were outlawed.[27] Ethnic Chinese were strongly encouraged to adopt Indonesian names. Ironically, it was during these times of aggressive assimilation policies that many Chinese conglomerates prospered.[28] These policies were only removed in 2000 when Abdurrahman Wahid (also known as Gus Dur) became the country's fourth President.[29]

Thus, the Tionghua negotiator is careful, circumspect and does not take anything for granted. Compared to the Chinese negotiator, you need to

---

[23] Tanzer, A. (1994). The bamboo network. *Forbes,* 154(2) 138–144.

[24] Susanto, A. B. & Susanto, P. (2013). *The Dragon Network: Inside Stories of the Most Successful Chinese Family Businesses.* Singapore: John Wiley & Sons.

[25] Koning, J. (2007). Chineseness and Chinese Indonesian business practices: A generational and discursive enquiry. *East Asia,* 24(2), 129–52. https://doi.org/10.1007/s12140-007-9011-2.

[26] Susanto, A. B. & Susanto, P. (2013). *The Dragon Network: Inside Stories of the Most Successful Chinese Family Businesses.* Singapore: John Wiley & Sons.

[27] Indonesia. Presidential Instruction No. 14 of 1967. Concerning Chinese Religion, *Beliefs and Customs.* https://www.regulasip.id/book/11041/read.

[28] Susanto, A. B. & Susanto, P. (2013). *The Dragon Network: Inside Stories of the Most Successful Chinese Family Businesses.* Singapore: John Wiley & Sons.

[29] Indonesia. Presidential Decree No. 6 of 2000. Revocation of Presidential Instruction No. 14 of 1967 *Concerning Chinese Religion, Beliefs and Customs.* https://jdih.setkab.go.id/PUUdoc/5371/KP%20NO%206%20TH%202000.pdf.

commit more time and resources to build trust. The elder or senior negotiators among them always try to maintain an outward humility and friendliness when speaking with you. This is one notable Javanese trait that they seem to have picked up. Before they embark on any negotiation with you, they need to be assured of your *cheng-yi* (sincerity). Be prepared for almost endless rounds of meetings and meals as spending more time under different circumstances allows them to gauge your interest and intention. Even when dealing with the younger Chinese Indonesians, these rituals are still practiced, albeit in more trendy settings.

Thus, both Javanese and Indonesian Chinese cultures are hierarchical and lay strong emphasis on harmony and social order.[30]

Hofstede's Cultural Dimensions[31]

- **Power Distance**

Indonesia's national score for this dimension is 78, just below China (80). There is a discernible power structure in the Indonesian society. This is clear from how people address and speak to one another. In Jakarta and the bigger cities on Java island, it is common for the honorific *Bapak/Pak* or *Ibu/bu* to be used in business settings in place of sir/Mr or madam/Ms. *Bapak* translates literally to "father" and *Ibu* means "mother". These are intended to be used for people who are older, but in the business or formal setting they are invariably used simply to show respect; especially if the other person is more senior in age or rank. *Bapak/Ibu* must be obeyed, shown respect and loyalty. In return, they will give protection and help when needed. Crucially, the patriarch must give compliments when due and resolve conflicts. This way, the *Bapak* acknowledges those lower in hierarchy and helps maintain harmony at their level.[32] The emphasis on loyalty, hierarchy and the roles of patriarchal figures in Javanese Bapakism are similar to Confucianism.

---

[30] Efferin, S. & Hopper, T. (2007). Management control, culture and ethnicity in a Chinese Indonesian company. *Accounting, Organizations and Society*, 32(3), 223–262. https://doi.org/10.1016/j.aos.2006.03.009.

[31] The scores here are national scores.

[32] Geertz, H. (1961). *The Javanese Family: A Study of Kinship and Socialization*. New York: Free Press of Glencoe.

- **Individualism–Collectivism**

Indonesia's individualism score at 14 is the lowest among the countries in this book — the second lowest being South Korea (18). The collectivist culture is a product of the patriarchal and hierarchical structures in the country. Because power is concentrated at the top, those lower in social position do not need or want to assume individual responsibility. For the Javanese in particular, there is an overt effort to control individual expression for fear that it would disrupt social harmony.[33] The influence of religions such as Hinduism, Buddhism and Islam, as well as Confucianism, reinforce the overall collectivist structure of the society.[34]

Gotong royong is a long-standing Javanese term which literally means "work together". It is common to see the phrase translated as "mutual assistance". The traditional context conjures up images of villagers who are motivated by the general ethos of reciprocity to mobilize labor to help one another for the common good. This phrase was elevated to state ideology status when it was invoked by the country's first president, Sukarno, during the founding of Indonesia as an independent nation.[35] As a cultural operator, this term has permeated almost all key public discourses. As recent as mid-2022, Indonesia's seventh president, Jokowi, exhorted the country to adopt the *Gotong Royong* strategy in order to face global competition.[36] Everyone is thus a member of the village or community and must work together for the interest of the group. Any disagreement or unhappiness must be resolved by *musyawarah dan mufakat* (consensus building).

In a typical corporate environment, most employees will develop an extensive network among their colleagues, which will also involve their family members. Within the network, there is a communal spirit of returning favors, referred to as *balas budi*. Everyone needs the support of others and the security of being part of a group. Therefore, you should always

---

[33] *Ibid.*

[34] van der Kroef, J. M. (1953). Collectivism in Indonesian society. *Social Research,* 20(1), 193–193.

[35] Bowen, J. R. (1986). On the political construction of tradition: Gotong Royong in Indonesia. *The Journal of Asian Studies,* 45(3), 545–561.

[36] "President J. (June 21, 2022). "'Gotong Royong' Strategy is Key to Facing Global Competition." Sekretariat Kabinet Republik Indonesia. Available at https://setkab.go.id/en/president-jokowi-gotong-royong-strategy-is-key-to-facing-global-competition/.

communicate with the team on the opposite side of the table and not with individual members of the Indonesian team, especially when you introduce a revised offer or make any key changes.

- **Uncertainty Avoidance**

At 48, Indonesia's score is moderate and sits between the highest score from Japan (92) and the lowest score from Singapore (8). Being generally religious, most Indonesians are content to leave matters to higher powers. Moreover, Indonesians are no strangers to natural disasters. The country has the greatest number of volcanoes with over 70 of them active.[37] The populous Java island has experienced numerous earthquakes, and flooding happens quite frequently in Jakarta city. Your Indonesian counterpart probably knows the limitations of human endeavors and will not be easily upset if negotiations deviate from any prescribed norms.

3. Communication

The most prominent feature of Indonesian communication is its indirectness.[38] Meanings are embedded and have to be decoded. For example, both *kami* and *kita* translate literally to "we". However, there is an important difference. *Kami* excludes the addressee and so, if your Indonesian counterpart uses *kami* — the statement is only meant for your information. In contrast, *kita* includes the addressee. When used by your Indonesian counterpart, the statement is meant for your action. Being straightforward and direct is generally considered offensive and crude. A refined person must employ indirect means to find out about the other party's opinions and desires.

In addition, the Javanese speakers frequently consider it necessary to conceal their wishes and intentions so as not to risk disturbing harmony — with people, the environment and even spirits. Whereas many East Asian cultures generally prefer not to reveal their own feelings, the Javanese take this to great extreme.[39] Some would say that this cultural predilection for

---

[37] "Indonesia — The World Factbook," October 26, 2022. Available at https://www.cia.gov/the-world-factbook/countries/indonesia/.
[38] Nadar, F. X. (2012). The prominent characteristics of Javanese culture and their reflections in language use. *Humaniora*, 19(2), 168–174. https://doi.org/10.22146/jh.901.
[39] *Ibid.*

concealment is quintessentially Javanese.[40] Negative feelings such as anger and disappointment are always suppressed; and positive emotions are also downplayed. You frequently have to guess hidden feelings (*rasa*) from their facial expressions as well as other verbal or non-verbal cues provided. The Javanese believe that such concealment will protect their own peace of mind and equanimity. Especially towards someone who is of higher status or someone who is a stranger, the Javanese feel compelled to be respectfully polite even to the extent of suppressing their true feelings out of deference. This is regarded as being appropriately shy (*sungkan*). This *sungkan* culture means that they will tell you what (they think) you want to hear, even if they know it is untrue. On a more critical note, this is sometimes seen as being irresponsible or even hypocritical.

All these create a lot of uncertainty when you communicate with the Indonesian negotiator. They will not reject or refuse your offers outright because saying "no" is to create conflict, which they want to avoid. To maintain an open atmosphere, you should also refrain from turning down their requests directly. In the same vein, getting them to say "yes" is also a tedious exercise. Because your Indonesian counterpart's reflex is to hide their genuine desire, they will not be quick to say yes to your offer of a favor or kind gesture until after you have persisted for a third or fourth time. However, over time, once you are more familiar with their speaking patterns, you will gain confidence in reading their signals. The key is to commit more time and effort so that you can better understand each other.

In Indonesia, meetings and negotiations may take place in formal settings (offices or meeting rooms) or less formal settings (restaurants or residences). More often than not, the communicative pattern can become more nuanced when the atmosphere and setting is more informal. If you notice that there is a change in the composition of the negotiation team, with the inclusion of more senior members or family — and usually involving less people — this is where important relationship building can take place. Gaining the trust and approval of this select team is critical to achieving a successful integrative outcome. The Indonesian negotiators much prefer to form alliances with those they can co-opt rather than confront. During such occasions, the Indonesian negotiator will use more deferential language

---

[40] Borsuk, R. & Chng, N. (2014). A Javanese "King" and his Cukong. In *Liem Sioe Liong's Salim Group: The Business Pillar of Suharto's Indonesia* (pp. 1–20). Singapore: ISEAS Publishing. https://doi.org/10.1355/9789814459594-003.

when addressing you as this reflects their respect for your high status. They may also politely ask about your family and background in order to enhance the private and personal connection with you. By reciprocating and contributing to this harmony in the business relationship, you will be giving "face" or showing deference to your Indonesian host.[41]

4. Negotiation Strategies: Distributive or Integrative

In 2019, Indonesia's National Cyber and Crypto Agency (BSSN) chose the Chinese Technology company Huawei as its cybersecurity partner. BSSN signed a memorandum of understanding (MOU) with Huawei's subsidiary in Indonesia to provide training for its government officials and civil servants as part of the country's cybersecurity capacity building.[42] Huawei's story in Indonesia is a stark contrast to its experience in US, UK and Australia — where the Chinese suppliers of ICT Infrastructure have been excluded or banned because they are perceived as a national security threat. The top global think tank, The Carnegie Endowment for International Peace, investigated into this unusual phenomenon and interviewed the actors involved to produce a detailed research paper (the "Carnegie Paper").[43] Huawei's experience in Indonesia provides instructive insights as to how to negotiate using both distributive and integrative strategies in Indonesia.

The Indonesian negotiators are adept at distributive and contingency bargaining.[44] According to the Carnegie Paper, it is widely accepted that

---

[41] Gray, N. (2012). "Parantara : The Javanese Way of Managing Business Relationships in Indonesia." [PDF] *Semantic Scholar*. Available at https://www.semanticscholar.org/paper/Parantara-%3A-The-Javanese-Way-of-Managing-Business-Gray/4e9e2a0120a6ce6f9fded34821c06f8dae501328?p2df

[42] Yudha, P. (October 29, 2019). "BSSN dan Huawei Kerja Sama Kembangkan SDM untuk Keamanan Siber," [BSSN and Huawei Cooperate to Develop Human Resources for Cybersecurity], Kompas. Available at https://tekno.kompas.com/read/2019/10/29/15460047/bssn-dan-huawei-kerja-sama-kembangkan-sdm-untuk-keamanan-siber

[43] Most of the information in this segment is taken from Priyandita,G., van der Kley,D., & Herscovitch,B. (n.d.). "Localization and China's Tech Success in Indonesia." Carnegie Endowment for International Peace. Available at https://carnegieendowment.org/2022/07/11/localization-and-china-s-tech-success-in-indonesia-pub-87477.

[44] Katz, L. (2017). "Negotiating International Business — Indonesia." Negotiating International Business — The Negotiator's Reference Guide to 50 Countries around the World [downloaded on 1 January 2022], available at http://www.leadershipcrossroads.com/mat/cou/Indonesia.pdf.

Huawei consistently offers lower prices than its competitors. In this case, Huawei likely outpriced its competitors by up to 30%.[45] The differential comprised financing options supported by Chinese state-owned banks, direct maintenance add-ons and high level of technical support committed by Huawei. These competitive terms reflect Huawei's strong desire to win over the Indonesia business, but they are equally indicative of the Indonesian buyer's distributive skills at the negotiation table. When in Indonesia, a large part of your negotiation, particularly the concurrent phase (ongoing process),[46] will be dominated by distributive bargaining. During this phase, the discussion will mainly relate to tangibles such as price, product specifications and other terms and conditions. If you are negotiating as a seller, you need to prepare yourself for intensive and pro-longed bargaining sessions. The Indonesian buyer, especially if they are from larger or government enterprises, frequently takes the view that they have the upper hand. A team may be assembled to specifically handle the hard haggling. The Indonesians often adopt the "Buyer is King" mentality. In a social environment, the Javanese are generally reserved, but when it comes to bargaining, they are animated and may play by a different set of rules. For a Javanese buyer, a good price must always be at the lowest end of what you are quoting everyone else.[47] If your Indonesian counterpart is also negotiating with others, you definitely need to uncover what kind of offers your competitors are making.

If the tables are turned and you are negotiating with an Indonesian seller, you may have a hard time trying to figure out what is their bottom-line or resistance price. This is because during the initial stage, the opening stance and offers made by the Indonesian negotiator may be confusing and hard to reconcile. They will want to test the level of your information gathering and watch your reactions to the offers made by them. If this is the first time you are negotiating with them, they will take the opportunity to size you up.

---

[45] Priyandita, G., van der Kley, D., & Herscovitch, B. (n.d.) "Localization and China's Tech Success in Indonesia." Carnegie Endowment for International Peace. https://carnegieen dowment.org/2022/07/11/localization-and-china-s-tech-success-in-indonesia-pub-87477.

[46] Negotiations are generally classifiable into three parts: antecedent phase (pre-negotiation stage and preparations), the concurrent phase (ongoing process), and the consequent phase (post-negotiation stage) — See Theoretical Chapter under Negotiation Strategies: Distributive or Integrative.

[47] Alexander, J. & Alexander, P. (1987). Striking a Bargain in Javanese markets. *Man,* 22(1), 42–68. https://doi.org/10.2307/2802963.

If the Indonesian negotiator's offers are generally out of your range and you are sticking to your resistance point — they will be too polite to bring the negotiation to a swift end. Mostly, they will patiently wait for you to come back with an improved offer. Because this can be time-consuming and protracted, you need an exit plan to know when to walk away.

After most or all of the tangibles such as price and other material terms are settled, the integrative chapter to the negotiation will follow. This is the relationship-building aspect of the negotiation which must take place before any agreement or deal can be finalized — even if all the tangibles have been negotiated. The Indonesian negotiator always prefers a win–win deal and this means a deal with someone they can trust and a relationship that will bring gains to both sides.

The Indonesian negotiators are tight-lipped so there will not be much information sharing. Key information is controlled and retained by the decision-makers and the selected few high up in the hierarchy. There is usually not much paper trail, and important decisions tend to be relayed verbally. This is even more so for family-owned businesses as decisions are often made during social gatherings among trusted members and not recorded.[48] Even if you do close a deal, your Indonesian negotiator will appreciate discretion on your part in not disclosing much about the terms to others. Information sharing — which is needed for an integrative process — is not a strong feature of negotiation in Indonesia. To play your part to secure an effective integrative outcome, you need to find coalitions.

To achieve an integrative outcome with your Indonesian counterpart, you must know that they are always part of a larger network within their collectivist society. As they negotiate with you, you will potentially become a node in their network. To position yourself in an advantageous position, you should find and link up with other nodes in their network. Thoroughly assess the presence of any potential coalition(s), their strength and how you can capture their support for your own benefit.[49] If you can skilfully embed yourself in your Indonesian counterpart's network, they will see this as a win for both of you. Of course, if you can also bring in a network of your own to the table, it will be an added bonus.

---

[48] Weidenbaum, M. (1998). The bamboo network: Asia's family-run conglomerates. *Strategy+Business*. Available at https://www.strategy-business.com/article/9702.
[49] Lewicki, R. J., Saunders, D. M., & Barry, B. (2021). *Essentials of Negotiation* (7th edn.). McGraw-Hill International Edition, p. 270.

Initially, Huawei built centers to train and develop its Indonesian work-force skills for their own needs. Then in 2011, Huawei launched an annual program known as "Seeds for the Future" to give ICT (Information and Communication Technology) training, scholarships and internships for Indonesian students.[50] Later in 2017, Huawei expanded their outreach and launched training ICT programs for several top Indonesian universities including the leading Bandung Institute of Technology to provide training in internet protocols.[51] Through this, Huawei located influential coalitions within the ICT community. The Chinese company recognized that their business counterparts and the Indonesia government have a deeper interest and need — which is to urgently scale up their technology capacity and human capital. By forming the coalitions with the universities, Huawei demonstrated a broad commitment to help meet those interests and needs. Being able to identify and satisfy your counterpart's interests is a critical step in integrative processes because these interests are what motivate them.[52] This helps to entrench the Chinese company within Indonesia's technology eco-system. As Indonesia's cybersecurity provider of choice, Huawei placed themselves in an enviable position in Indonesia's colossal market. Huawei Indonesia enjoyed steady growth in revenues from 2016 to 2020 with an average of 14% annually.[53] This is a definite case of win–win for all parties concerned.

Coalitions can have significant effects on the negotiation process and outcome.[54] This is especially true when you need to achieve a successful integrative outcome in Indonesia and build long-term relationships. You

[50] "Program Huawei Seeds for the Future Ajak Mahasiswa Terbaik Indonesia Belajar Inovasi Teknologi di Tiongkok," [Huawei Seeds for the Future Program Invites the Best Indonesian Students to Study Technological Innovation in China], Daily Social Newswire, December 10, 2015. Available at https://dailysocial.id/wire/program-huawei-seeds-for-the-future-ajak-mahasiswa-terbaik-indonesia-belajar-inovasi-teknologi-di-tiongkok.

[51] "Huawei Brings Digital Economy-Based Training and Wealth to State Colleges," *China Daily*, May 15, 2017. Available at https://web.archive.org/web/20200417065638/https://www.chinadaily.com.cn/cndy/2017-05/15/content_29345046.htm.

[52] Lewicki, R. J., Saunders, D. M., & Barry, B. (2021). *Essentials of Negotiation* (7th edn.). McGraw-Hill International Edition, p. 270.

[53] "Huawei's Indonesian Presence Goes beyond Business: CEO." (2021). Jakarta Globe, November 26. Available at https://jakartaglobe.id/tech/huaweis-indonesian-presence-goes-beyond-business-ceo/.

[54] Lewicki, R. J., Saunders, D. M., & Barry, B. (2021). *Essentials of Negotiation*, 7th ed. McGraw-Hill International Edition. 67.

should proactively seek out coalitions and manage them. It takes considerable time and effort, but will lead to meaningful payoffs, in particular during the implementation stage. There may also be situations where you need to also look out for coalition(s) that are against you. For example, when negotiating with Chinese Indonesian family-owned businesses, even if the top decision-makers are satisfied with the negotiation, lack of buy-in from other key members of their team may work against you. When you are building coalitions, you should remember that business people will accord you more respect and attention if you are of a high status. In addition to age, credentials and your network, even small details such as your choice of hotel, transportation and the way you speak or listen will affect your standing.[55]

Even though the Indonesian negotiators do not often reveal much and are adept at concealing their intentions, they are single-minded about their own needs and will not be distracted or give in to peer pressure. They are prepared to trust their own deep instincts. Authors of the Carnegie paper, "Localization and China's Tech Success in Indonesia", interviewed many government employees and asked about warnings that Huawei may pose security threats.[56] The Indonesian attitude is encapsulated in one reply which is quoted in the paper: "If we're constantly afraid, our development will stagnate."[57] The Indonesians know that the single biggest hurdle to their flourishing digital economy is a lack of cybersecurity talent and technology.[58] If you patiently uncover the Indonesian negotiators' underlying interests and needs, they will not hesitate to reinforce their relationship with you.

---

[55] Katz, L. (2017). "Negotiating International Business — Indonesia." Negotiating International Business — The Negotiator's Reference Guide to 50 Countries Around the World [downloaded on 1 January 2022], available at http://www.leadershipcrossroads.com/mat/cou/Indonesia.pdf.

[56] Priyandita, G., van der Kley, D., & Herscovitch, B. (n.d.). "Localization and China's Tech Success in Indonesia." Carnegie Endowment for International Peace. https://carnegieendowment.org/2022/07/11/localization-and-china-s-tech-success-in-indonesia-pub-87477.

[57] Ibid.

[58] Indonesia has a shortage of information technology (IT) expertise and tech-savvy entrepreneurs. An Australian government report noted, "Indonesia has only 278 IT workers per 1 million people, compared to Malaysia (1,834) and India (1,159)." Australian Trade and Investment Commission, "Digital Technology to Indonesia: Trends and Opportunities," Australian Trade and Investment Commission. Available at https://www.austrade.gov.au/australian/export/export-markets/countries/indonesia/industries.

5. Concession-making and Hardball Tactics

The Indonesian negotiators make very tight concessions. They, and in particular the Javanese, believe that a skilled negotiator should make progress in only small and slow increments.[59] And then when you do accept their concessions and reciprocate with yours — they may even turn around and jokingly retract what they had offered. This to-and-fro is usually their way of enjoying the haggling process and they do not mean to renege. You will soon get used to these side antics once you progress further into the negotiation. The Indonesian negotiators are clear as to their goals so do not underestimate them or be distracted by their bargaining habits. Be firm with your own concessions and be clear with what has been agreed upon. As for the Chinese Indonesian, their concession-making pattern is similar with those of the Chinese negotiators.[60] They are price-conscious and always exercise financial prudence when it comes to business.[61] As the negotiation process can be protracted, it is difficult to know how much more concessions you can get out of your counterpart. Moreover, the Indonesian negotiators, especially if Javanese or Tionghua, are skilled at masking their resistance points. They can be quite inscrutable if negotiations seem to be stalling or if no new concessions are forthcoming, you need to evaluate whether alternatives are being considered or if this is a sign that they are no longer interested. Perhaps more than the other East Asian cultures, the Indonesian negotiators enjoy concession-making as they see it as an important plank of relationship-building. Beyond your immediate negotiation with them, they also see generalized reciprocity as involving both a general obligation and the idea of an eventual return. The return is "not stipulated by time, quantity, or quality: the expectation of reciprocity is indefinite".[62] Whether or not your negotiations result in an eventual agreement, if you have demonstrated genuine goodwill and established trust with your Indonesian negotiator, their door is generally

---

[59] Alexander, J. & Alexander, P. (1987). Striking a Bargain in Javanese markets. *Man*, 22(1), 42–68. https://doi.org/10.2307/2802963.

[60] See Chapter on "The Chinese Negotiator."

[61] Efferin, S. & Hopper, T. (2007). Management control, culture and ethnicity in a Chinese Indonesian company. *Accounting, Organizations and Society*, 32(3), 223–262. https://doi.org/10.1016/j.aos.2006.03.009.

[62] Bowen, J. R. (1986). On the political construction of tradition: Gotong Royong in Indonesia. *The Journal of Asian Studies*, 45(3), 545–561.

open when the next opportunity arises. It is crucial to not burn bridges in Indonesia.

During the distributive phase of the negotiation, the Indonesian negotiators believe that deception is part and parcel of the haggling process.[63] They do not expect you to be honest and will not begrudge you over exaggerated claims since they will do the same to you. Thus, a common hardball tactic you may encounter is the use of a bogey — pretending that a low priority item is important so that it can be traded for another concession. In some instances, this may go on for some time and will be frustrating if you are constantly having to edit drafts of offers sent to them. Remember that composure and patience (*sabar*) must always be maintained so do not embarrass anyone and you must avoid all emotional outbursts.

Because they prize restraint, the Indonesian negotiators will rarely use hardball tactics that require strong show of emotion such as intimidation or other aggressive behavior. Rather than to try to subdue you, their standard reaction is to befriend you. In any case, it is quite difficult to openly upset your Indonesian counterpart. Suharto was the country's longest-serving president who held on to power with an iron grip for 30 years until he was toppled in 1998. Aptly nicknamed "The Smiling General", he was always remembered as being soft-spoken and composed.[64]

The Indonesian negotiator may negotiate in a team or individually. There may be several negotiations going on concurrently and both in formal and informal settings. Even so, they will not use "good cop, bad cop" routines. Everyone on the Indonesian team works as part of their *gotong royong* (cooperation among members) strategy for the interest of the group, so they will maintain a united front. As a result, you should also not bother with any "good cop, bad cop" hardball tactics. First, they have a hierarchical culture so they will respect and prefer to believe those on your team with higher status. Second, they will expect your side to reach consensus among yourselves because *runkan* (conflict avoidance) must be maintained at all times. In a nutshell, such a tactic will have no effect.

---

[63] Alexander, J. & Alexander, P. (1987). Striking a Bargain in Javanese markets. *Man*, 22(1), 42–68. https://doi.org/10.2307/2802963.

[64] Borsuk, R. & Chng, N. (2014). 1. A Javanese "King" and His Cukong. In *Liem Sioe Liong's Salim Group: The Business Pillar of Suharto's Indonesia* (pp. 1–20). Singapore: ISEAS Publishing. https://doi.org/10.1355/9789814459594-003.

6. Role of Women

The country's fifth president (2001–2004) was a woman. Megawati Sukarnoputri, daughter of the first president, was the first woman to hold the post. At the time of writing this chapter, Megawati heads the largest political party in Indonesia and remains an influential figure in Indonesian politics.[65] Meanwhile, Sri Mulyani Indrawati is serving her second term as the Minister of Finance of the largest economy in Southeast Asia. She previously held the same post from 2005 to 2010 until she was appointed Managing Director of the World Bank. Over in Yogyakarta, its Sultan appears to be lining up his eldest daughter to succeed him in the royal court. When the country gained independence, the Indonesian government allowed the Yogyakarta Javanese monarchy to keep its power, out of gratitude for their role in fighting the colonial Dutch rulers. The Javanese royal rule stretches back to the 16th century. In 2015, Sultan Hamengkubuwono X passed a decree to bestow the title *Mangkubumi* (meaning The One Who Holds the Earth) onto his daughter.[66] Until then, the title had been reserved only for male heirs.

Despite these prominent examples, women's career progression is still impacted by gender bias and by the country's deep-seated patriarchal culture.[67] Indonesia has a male-dominated corporate culture. Leadership positions are generally reserved for men who are perceived to be more competent, whereas women are placed in supervisory and middle-management positions. Even in middle management roles, women are over-represented in support functions such as administration and human resources.[68] Strategic management positions that lead to decision-making typically fall to their male colleagues. This phenomenon is known as "glass walls".[69] Further, many married women choose not to climb the corporate ladder as the task of balancing work and home largely falls on

---

[65] Megawati heads the Indonesian Democratic Party (Partai Demokrasi Indonesia; PDI).

[66] *BBC News*. (June 1, 2018). "Sultan of Yogyakarta: A Feminist Revolution in an Ancient Kingdom," sec. Asia. Available at https://www.bbc.com/news/world-asia-43806210.

[67] "The Gender Gap in Indonesia's Corporate World." (n.d.). *The ASEAN Post*. Available at https://theaseanpost.com/article/gender-gap-indonesias-corporate-world.

[68] "Leading to Success: The Business Case for Women in Business and Management in Indonesia." (July 13, 2020). www.ilo.org. Available at https://www.ilo.org/jakarta/what-wedo/publications/WCMS_750802/lang--en/index.htm.

[69] *Ibid.*

them, rather than their husbands. Even the Yogyakarta Sultan's feminist gesture is not accepted by his siblings who are openly outraged and threaten to evict their royal niece when the time comes.[70]

Based on the 2022 Global Gender Gap Report by the World Economic Forum (see the following table), Indonesia is ranked 10th in the East Asia and Pacific region and 92nd globally, out of 146 countries.[71]

Global Gender Gap Report 2022 INSIGHT REPORT JULY 2022			
EAST ASIA & the PACIFIC	Rank		
Country	Regional (19)	Global (146)	Score
Philippines	2	19	0.783
Singapore	4	49	0.734
Thailand	8	79	0.709
Vietnam	9	83	0.705
Indonesia	**10**	**92**	**0.697**
Korea (South)	12	99	0.689
China	13	102	0.682
Malaysia	14	103	0.681
Japan	19	116	0.650

Source: "Global Gender Gap Report 2022." World Economic Forum. July 13, 2022. https://www.weforum.org/reports/global-gender-gap-report-2022/digest.

If you are a woman negotiating in Indonesia, you will probably face some gender stereotypes stemming from the hierarchical structures and patriarchy. Even if you are addressed as Ibu (or Bu for short), you may nevertheless feel that you are not being taken seriously enough by your (male) Indonesian counterpart. In such situations, you must always maintain a calm demeanor. Remain firm and be very clear as to when and under

---

[70] *BBC News*. (June 1, 2018). "Sultan of Yogyakarta: A Feminist Revolution in an Ancient Kingdom," sec. Asia. Available at https://www.bbc.com/news/world-asia-43806210.

[71] "Global Gender Gap Report 2022." (July 13, 2022). World Economic Forum. Available at https://www.weforum.org/reports/global-gender-gap-report-2022/digest. The Global Gender Gap Index benchmarks the current state and evolution of gender parity across four key dimensions (Economic Participation and Opportunity, Educational Attainment, Health and Survival, and Political Empowerment). It is the longest-standing index which tracks progress towards closing these gaps over time since its inception in 2006.

what conditions you should walk away from the negotiation table. For the Javanese, and also the Chinese Indonesian businessmen, academic titles, government or military titles are regarded as significant social symbols.[72] You should therefore highlight these credentials when introducing yourself. Generally, the Indonesians admire people who speak well and in gentle tones; therefore, you should not behave too assertively or act masculine as this will backfire. Even if you have a strong Best Alternative To a Negotiated Agreement (BATNA) and feel empowered, you should not immediately try to claim value from the table. Aggressive openings and stances will collapse the negotiation. When negotiating in Indonesia, being patient and polite will serve you well, whether you are a woman or a man.

7. Intermediary/Interpreter

The official language is Bahasa Indonesia (which is very similar to Malay). However, this is still the second language of most people, who would still speak their own ethnic or regional language such as Javanese or Sundanese. English proficiency is low. The 2022 English Proficiency Index ranked Indonesia 81st out of 111 countries.[73] Indonesia is the only country in Southeast Asia that has not made English a compulsory language at elementary level. In the cities, business is conducted in Indonesian or Javanese. Many young Indonesians return from overseas studies and can speak English, but it is not common. Therefore, having an intermediary or interpreter to bridge the language issue is necessary if you do not speak Bahasa Indonesia.

However, there is another cultural reason for you to appoint an intermediary when negotiating in Indonesia. The Javanese term for intermediary is *perantara* (bridge). It is common to hear that this is the Javanese way of doing business because without proper introductions, you cannot even get through the reception.[74]

[72] Nadar, F. X. (August 8, 2012). "The Prominent Characteristics of Javanese Culture and Their Reflections in Language Use." Available at https://jurnal.ugm.ac.id/jurnal-humaniora/article/view/901.

[73] EF EPI 2022 — EF English Proficiency Index. Available at https://www.ef.com/wwen/epi/. (Accessed March 31, 2023).

[74] Gray, N. (2012). "Parantara: The Javanese Way of Managing Business Relationships in Indonesia." [PDF] *Semantic Scholar*. Available at https://pdfs.semanticscholar.org/4e9e/2a0120a6ce6f9fded34821c06f8dae501328.pdf?_ga=2.185200041.1807965529.1517384107-49518897.1517384107.

There are some obvious advantages to having a *perantara*. First, given the reliance on kinship network in Indonesia, a well-placed intermediary certainly helps with trust building during the early stages of negotiation, shorter waiting time for appointments, more expedient introductions and even going to the right place to hold the negotiations. It will validate the other party's intelligence-gathering process about you and your intentions. Second, the intermediary will add to your social "status" because having a respected introducer and middleman fits in with the Indonesian hierarchical culture. With the (right) *perantara*, your team will scale up the vertical power structure. This puts your Indonesian counterpart at ease instead of them trying to figure out where to fit you in and how to communicate with you. Third, and most importantly, because the Indonesian negotiator prefers more indirect communication, having a buffer between the two parties will ironically facilitate some communication. During the concurrent phase (ongoing process), conflicts and disagreements will arise and need to be resolved in order to take the negotiation to the next level. However, this requires both sides to be honest about their own needs and interests, and to explain what is not working out and why. The Indonesian negotiator's deep need to appear unruffled and conceal their disagreement makes it almost impossible for them to say these to you directly. Quite often, impasse follows at this point. The *perantara* and his network will act as an "unofficial" or back channel to receive and transmit the difficult conversations.[75] This way, the Indonesian negotiator is not seen as telling you what is wrong — that conversation is taken offline, almost in a parallel universe. Outwardly, you should also play your part to keep up the harmonious relationship and relay your feedback through the intermediary. Some might find this tedious and hypocritical. However, it can also be thought of as a form of risk management — various options and alternatives can be explored without risking the relationship.

However, you should note that though the *perantara* can help introduce you and act as a conduit for difficult communication, they generally operate in the background. Even if present at some discussions and meals, they are rarely directly involved in the negotiations.[76] You should therefore exercise some judgement as to when and whether to involve them as your negotiation progresses. More importantly, you should clarify what the *perantara* expects from you in return for their involvement.

---

[75] *Ibid.*
[76] *Ibid.*

Transparency International's Corruption Perception Index ranked Indonesia 110 out of 180 countries in 2022.[77] Indonesia thus fares worse than the other countries covered in this book, except for the Philippines (at 116th place).[78] Indonesians are familiar with the acronym "KKN" which stands for corruption (*korupsi*), collusion (*kolusi*) and nepotism (*nepotisme*). Clientelism in the form of patronage politics and vote buying and other forms of *quid pro quo* among politicians, bureaucrats and businesses was rampant during President Suharto's long reign (1967–1998).[79] After Suharto's fall, in 2003, a government agency was established to investigate and prosecute cases of corruption. This is the Corruption Eradication Commission (Komisi Pemberantasan Korupsi, abbreviated as KPK). However, after more than two decades, opinion remains divided as to whether KPK has been effective. Even though President Jokowi himself enjoys a graft-free reputation, his administration faced many challenges and also criticism in its effort to tackle corruption. Clientelist practices permeate and are embeded quite deeply in shared norms within the Indonesian society.

When negotiating in Indonesia, you will soon understand the importance of a personal network and hierarchical social relationships. However, the relationship exchanges that go on can be complex and worrying. You should tread carefully and have all the important conversations with the potential *perantara* before involving them.

8. Time, Timelines and Timeliness

You will keep hearing the words *jam karet* (rubber or stretchable time). Unfortunately, arriving late for meetings and appointments is part of the business culture. It is understandable for your Indonesian counterpart to be delayed because traffic congestions are horrific in cities such as Jakarta. However, traffic conditions cannot explain all missed timelines. Typically, you will receive some light excuse for the lack of timeliness, but do not be

---

[77] Transparency.org. (January 31, 2023). "2022 Corruption Perceptions Index — Explore Indonesia's Results." Available at https://www.transparency.org/en/cpi/2022.

[78] *Ibid.*

[79] Aspinall, E. & Berenschot, W. (2019). Conclusion: Clientelism and the search for good governance. In *Democracy for Sale* (pp. 249–262). New York: Cornell University Press.

upset if they come up more often than you like. Not only the bosses tend to keep you waiting, but even the middle and junior members of the team are rarely punctual.

Given their culture to communicate indirectly, you need to set aside more time for discussions and tasks. During the fasting month of *Ramadan*, working hours will be shorter as the employees will be allowed to leave office earlier to break their fast. Also, some offices may also give slightly more time for Friday noon prayers.

Bibliography

Alexander, J. & Alexander, P. (1987). Striking a Bargain in Javanese markets. *Man,* 22(1), 42–68. https://doi.org/10.2307/2802963.

Arifin, Evi Nurvidya, M. Sairi Hasbullah, and Agus Pramono. 2016. "Chinese Indonesians: How Many, Who and Where?" Asian Ethnicity. 18 (3): 310–29. https://doi.org/10.1080/14631369.2016.1227236.

Aspinall, E. & Berenschot, W. (2019). Conclusion: Clientelism and the search for good governance. In *Democracy for Sale* (pp. 249–262). New York: Cornell University Press.

Association of Southeast Asian Nations. (2020). "The Founding of ASEAN." Asean.org. Available at https://asean.org/the-founding-of-asean/.

Badan Pusat Statistik. (2021). Available at https://www.bps.go.id/publication/202 1/02/26/938316574c78772f27e9b477/statistik-indonesia-2021.html.

Badan Pusat Statistik. "Badan Pusat Statistik." Available at https://www.bps. go.id/indicator/12/1975/1/jumlah-penduduk-pertengahan-tahun.html. (Accessed November 5, 2022). Badan Pusat Statistik (BPS) is the government's statistics agency.

BBC News. (June 1, 2018). "Sultan of Yogyakarta: A Feminist Revolution in an Ancient Kingdom." sec. Asia. Available at https://www.bbc.com/news/world-asia-43806210.

Borsuk, R. & Chng, N. (2014). A Javanese "King" and His Cukong. In *Liem Sioe Liong's Salim Group: The Business Pillar of Suharto's Indonesia* (pp. 1–20). Singapore: ISEAS Publishing. https://doi.org/10.1355/9789814459594-003.

Bowen, J. R. (1986). On the political construction of tradition: Gotong Royong in Indonesia. *The Journal of Asian Studies,* 45(3), 545–561.

China Daily. (2017). "Huawei Brings Digital Economy-Based Training and Wealth to State Colleges," *China Daily*, May 15. Available at https://web.archive.org/web/20200417065638/https://www.chinadaily.com.cn/cndy/2017-05/15/content_29345046.htm.

Chong, W.-L. (2021). Chinese Indonesians in post-Suharto Indonesia democratisation and ethnic minorities. *Journal of Chinese Overseas,* 17(2), 419–422. https://doi.org/10.1163/17932548-12341451.

CIA. (October 26, 2022). "Indonesia — The World Factbook." Available at https://www.cia.gov/the-world-factbook/countries/indonesia/.

EF English Proficiency Index. Available at https://www.ef.com/wwen/epi/. (Accessed March 31, 2023).

Efferin, S. & Hopper, T. (2007). Management control, culture and ethnicity in a Chinese Indonesian Company. *Accounting, Organizations and Society,* 32(3), 223–262. https://doi.org/10.1016/j.aos.2006.03.009.

"Global Gender Gap Report 2022." (July 13, 2022). World Economic Forum. Available at https://www.weforum.org/reports/global-gender-gap-report-2022/digest.

Geertz, H. (1961). *The Javanese Family: A Study of Kinship and Socialization.* New York: Free Press of Glencoe.

Gray, N. (2012). "Parantara: The Javanese Way of Managing Business Relationships in Indonesia." [PDF] *Semantic Scholar.* Available at https://pdfs.semanticscholar.org/4e9e/2a0120a6ce6f9fded34821c06f8dae501328.pdf?_ga=2.185200041.1807965529.1517384107-49518897.1517384107.

Harish, F. (2022). "Indonesia Bids to Host 2036 Olympics in Eventual Capital." *The Jakarta Post,* November 19. Available at https://www.thejakartapost.com/indonesia/2022/11/18/indonesia-bids-to-host-2036-olympics-in-eventual-capital.html.

Indonesia. Presidential Decree No. 6 of 2000. *Revocation of Presidential Instruction No. 14 of 1967 Concerning Chinese Religion, Beliefs and Customs.* https://jdih.setkab.go.id/PUUdoc/5371/KP%20NO%206%20TH%202000.pdf

Indonesia. Presidential Instruction No. 14 of 1967. *Concerning Chinese Religion, Beliefs and Customs.* https://www.regulasip.id/book/11041/read.

International Labour Organization. (July 13, 2020). "Leading to Success: The Business Case for Women in Business and Management in Indonesia." www.ilo.org. Available at https://www.ilo.org/jakarta/whatwedo/publications/WCMS_750802/lang--en/index.htm.

Jakarta Globe. (November 26, 2021). "Huawei's Indonesian Presence Goes beyond Business: CEO." Jakarta Globe. Available at https://jakartaglobe.id/tech/huaweis-indonesian-presence-goes-beyond-business-ceo/.

Kahfi, K. (2020). "Former Garuda Boss Sentenced to Eight Years for Bribery, Money Laundering." *The Jakarta Post,* May 9. Available at https://www.thejakartapost.com/news/2020/05/09/former-garuda-boss-sentenced-to-eight-years-for-bribery-money-laundering.html.

Katz, L. (2017). "Negotiating International Business — Indonesia" Negotiating International Business — The Negotiator's Reference Guide to 50 Countries Around the World [downloaded on 1 January 2022], available at http://www.leadershipcrossroads.com/mat/cou/Indonesia.pdf.

Koning, J. (2007). Chineseness and Chinese Indonesian Business Practices: A Generational and Discursive Enquiry. *East Asia*, 24(2), 129–152. https://doi.org/10.1007/s12140-007-9011-2.

Lewicki, R J., Saunders, D. M., & Barry, B. (2021). *Essentials of Negotiation* (7th edn.). New York: McGraw-Hill International Edition.

Mariska, D. (January 17, 2022). "Nusantara Is the Name of Indonesia's New Capital." *TheIndonesia.id*, available at https://www.theindonesia.id/news/2022/01/17/164500/nusantara-is-the-name-of-indonesias-new-capital.

Marzuki, K. (December 2021). Jokowi and the Millennials: Facing the digital economy. *RSIS Commentary: The Series*, 135–139. https://doi.org/10.1142/9789811232206_0030.

Nadar, F. X. (2012). The prominent characteristics of javanese culture and their reflections in language use. *Humaniora*, 19(2), 168–174. https://doi.org/10.22146/jh.901.

"President Jokowi: 'Gotong Royong' Strategy is Key to Facing Global Competition." (June 21, 2022). Sekretariat Kabinet Republik Indonesia. Available at https://setkab.go.id/en/president-jokowi-gotong-royong-strategy-is-key-to-facing-global-competition/.

"Program Huawei Seeds for the Future Ajak Mahasiswa Terbaik Indonesia Belajar Inovasi Teknologi di Tiongkok," [Huawei Seeds for the Future Program Invites the Best Indonesian Students to Study Technological Innovation in China], Daily Social Newswire, December 10, 2015. Available at https://dailysocial.id/wire/program-huawei-seeds-for-the-future-ajak-mahasiswa-terbaik-indonesia-belajar-inovasi-teknologi-di-tiongkok.

Pratomo, Y. (October 29, 2019). "BSSN dan Huawei Kerja Sama Kembangkan SDM untuk Keamanan Siber," [BSSN and Huawei Cooperate to Develop Human Resources for Cybersecurity], Kompas. Available at https://tekno.kompas.com/read/2019/10/29/15460047/bssn-dan-huawei-kerja-sama-kembangkan-sdm-untuk-keamanan-siber.

Priyandita, G., van der Kley, D., & Herscovitch, B. (n.d.). "Localization and China's Tech Success in Indonesia." Carnegie Endowment for International Peace. Available at https://carnegieendowment.org/2022/07/11/localization-and-china-s-tech-success-in-indonesia-pub-87477.

Sekretariat Kabinet Republik Indonesia. (August 19, 2017). "UN Verifies Names of 16,056 Indonesian Islands," available at https://setkab.go.id/en/un-verifies-names-of-16056-indonesian-islands/.

Susanto, A. B. & Susanto, P. (2013). *The Dragon Network: Inside Stories of the Most Successful Chinese Family Businesses.* Singapore: John Wiley & Sons.

Tanzer, A. (1994). The bamboo network. *Forbes,* 154(2), 138–144.

The ASEAN Post. (n.d). "The Gender Gap in Indonesia's Corporate World." *The ASEAN Post.* Available at https://theaseanpost.com/article/gender-gap-indonesias-corporate-world.

The Jakarta Post. (n.d.). "Analysis: Garuda Completes Restructuring, Back to Black, Resumes Stock Trading," January 11, 2023. Available at https://www.thejakartapost.com/opinion/2023/01/11/analysis-garuda-completes-restructuring-back-to-black-resumes-stock-trading.html.

Transparency.org. (January 31, 2023). "2022 Corruption Perceptions Index — Explore Philippines's Results." Available at https://www.transparency.org/en/cpi/2022.

van der Kroef, J. M. (1953). Collectivism in Indonesian society. *Social Research,* 20(1), 193.

Weidenbaum, M. (1998). "The Bamboo Network: Asia's Family-Run Conglomerates." *Strategy+Business.* Available at https://www.strategy-business.com/article/9702.

World Bank. (April 5, 2022). "The World Bank in Indonesia." World Bank. Available at https://www.worldbank.org/en/country/indonesia/overview.

World Economic Forum. "Where Are the Largest Chinese Populations Outside of China? | Thailand or Indonesia: Which Country Has the Largest Chinese Population? | By World Economic Forum | Facebook." Available at https://www.facebook.com/worldeconomicforum/videos/where-are-the-largest-chinese-populations-outside-of-china/10153549858561479/. (Accessed November 8, 2022).

Indonesia Quiz

1. The largest ethnic group in Indonesia is the _____ which makes up approximately 40% of its population.
   A. Sundanese
   B. Minang
   C. Javanese
   D. Bugis

2. In Javanese society, between two persons of unequal status, *hormat* must be shown; and between two persons of equal status, both parties must strive for *runkun*. What are the respective meanings of these two terms?
   A. patience and conflict avoidance
   B. hierarchy and patience
   C. respect and patience
   D. respect and conflict avoidance

3. Some Chinese Indonesians or *Tionghuas* do not speak Mandarin or observe Chinese festivities and are either Christians or Muslims. As a result, they do not embrace Confucian values. Is this general characterization true or false?
   A. True
   B. False

4. Indonesia is a highly collectivist culture and, especially among the Javanese, there is an overt effort to control individual expression in order to preserve social harmony. Is this general characterization true or false?
   A. True
   B. False

5. Communication is typically indirect and being appropriately shy requires the Indonesian negotiators to suppress their true feelings out of deference, so you may be told what you want to hear even if it is untrue. This "shy" culture is also known within their society as _____. Fill in the blank.
   A. Songkran culture
   B. Sungkan culture
   C. Sabar culture
   D. Krengjai culture

6. One effective way to give "face" to your Indonesian negotiator is to share information about your family and personal background so as to enhance private and personal connection. Is this general characterization true or false?
   A. True
   B. False

7. When negotiating in Indonesia, the concurrent phrase (on-going process) will first be dominated by _____. Fill in the blank.
   A. concession-making during which small and slow increments will be made
   B. hardball tactics during which intimidation and aggressive behavior will be displayed
   C. integrative negotiation during which relationship building must take place before bargaining on price and product specification
   D. distributive bargaining during which tangibles such as price and product specifications will be discussed

8. The Indonesian negotiators generally enjoy concession-making because they see this as _____. Fill in the blank.
   A. good opportunity to practice deception
   B. necessary part of distributive bargaining
   C. an important plank of relationship building
   D. an effective way to test your resistance point

9. If you are a woman negotiating in Indonesia, you may face some gender stereotypes due to the patriarchal structures in the society. You should therefore be aggressive and behave assertively to claim value. Is this general characterization true or false?
   A. True
   B. False

10. Having an intermediary who speaks Bahasa Indonesia can help bridge the language barrier. Additionally, the right intermediary or *perantara* can also _____. Fill in the blank.
    A. help with trust building
    B. add to your status
    C. act as a communication buffer between you and your Indonesian counterpart
    D. all of the above

Answer Bank

1. C
2. D
3. B
4. A
5. B
6. A
7. D
8. C
9. B
10. D

Chapter 3

The Japanese Negotiator

The Japanese word for negotiation is '交渉 (Kōshō)'. It is written in Kanji and derived from Chinese characters. Culturally and in terms of semantics, the Japanese word for 'negotiation' can also refer to the processes of bargaining and dealing while building relationships or connections. Therefore, the elements of building long-term relations and maintaining the 'face' factor for all parties are very important in reaching compromises through the dialogue between two or more parties without burning bridges or embarrassing the disadvantageous party with a view of the possibility of dealing in the future. This is a common feature of many negotiating styles in Northeast Asia.

1. The Environment[1]

Let us introduce you to 32 year-old Haruki Yamamoto. He is a salaryman. You would have seen him depicted in Japanese pop culture, with his ubiquitous dark suit, catching the early train to work and the very late train back home. He joined the company right after graduation and aspires to work for the same employer till he retires. Yamamoto-san works extremely long hours in exchange for the hope of a lifetime employment. (This is an example straight from the Showa-era. It is less relevant in the Heisei (8 Jan 1989 to 30 Apr 2019) or Reiwa period (current) where long hours or aspirations for lifetime employment (LTE) system is no longer tenable or

---

[1] This is more for a Showa-era firm or a traditional company in the contemporary period.

possible in many cases. In the late Heisei and Reiwa periods, there is greater emphasis among state economic agencies and the corporate world to encourage greater work–life balance.)

The typical Japanese corporation, like its society, is hierarchically organized so everyone knows his/her position within the company and in relation to each other. This hierarchical structure determines career paths, sitting arrangements and speaking order in meetings and how a person should behave and be treated. (This still applies to many companies although the more progressive or Westernized ones, especially those in the tech industry, fast retailing industry or highly globalized structures no longer adhere to hierarchical structures as much as before). Yamamoto is a team leader in charge of a group of younger employees. He reports to his Section Manager, a position he aspires to take over in a few years' time. Promotion and status is based on seniority.

Understanding their hierarchical structure can help improve your working relationship with the Japanese. More importantly, it will let you know how to interact with the team of negotiators that Yamamoto belongs to. This is because the Japanese invariably negotiate in teams, and not alone. As a result, there is an expectation that you will also bring along a team whose members are of similar status and hierarchy as theirs. When visiting a Japanese company, it is typical that a senior management ranking member will be in the welcoming party (usually directorial level), but they may not be the deal-makers and decision-makers, a function they will leave to other internal departments who have the onus to deal appropriately with the guests in negotiations.[2]

We can consider using Yamamoto to illustrate some of the "Japanese" traits in the following paragraphs.

Yamamoto-san represents the traditional Showa-era (1945 to 1989) mould of Japanese corporate behavior. The concepts of (benevolent) hierarchy are visible in the seating arrangement, although the open office concept connotes a more egalitarian imagery understanding of this hierarchical structure. When the Japanese negotiators huddle together to consider their non-Japanese negotiators' terms and conditions, everyone is

---

[2] Van Zandt, Howard F. "How to Negotiate in Japan" dated November 1970 in Magazine/ *Harvard Business Review* (HBR) [downloaded on 1 January 2022], available at https://hbr. org/1970/11/how-to-negotiate-in-japan.

expected to contribute to and given a fair share of opinion-making due to the very strong consensus-seeking culture guiding Japanese corporate and social behaviors.

2. Culture

Reaching out to each other's culture can involve an act as simple as the ritual of giving a gift. American or Western negotiators can do well to gift US-made inexpensive souvenirs to their negotiating partners as a token of friendship. There are other ways of reaching out in a more esoteric manner. For example, one strategy to try to bridge cultural differences is developing cultural empathy. Business leaders in Japan advise Westerners in the country to empathize with the Japanese mind and appreciate the little details in life that are sometimes missed by American expatriates (some couched this as showing kindness and emotional sensitivity).[3] Japanese value and place substantial efforts in forging good interpersonal relationships as the optimal emotional foundation for business-making, allowing for emotions to guide parts of the negotiation process.[4]

It is also important to known that there are regional cultural differences, too. The Kinki region (the old feudal stronghold, now known as Kansai) in western Japan includes the Hyogo, Mie, Nara, Shiga and Wakayama prefectures and the metropolitan prefectures of Osaka, Kyoto and Kobe (sometimes synonymously known as Kansai).[5] Humor is part of Kansai people's daily routine. They believe that smiling and laughing help to lighten the atmosphere and loosen up, but caution is taken not to adopt the same assumption when interacting with Kanto-ites. This is something experienced in everyday business lives of executives, as detailed by Nara native Teruko Nishiguchi (aged 30):

> At the office, my Osaka (Kansai) colleague made fun of another colleague from Chiba (Kanto) who is bald. He joked, 'Where is your hair? So bald!' and that shocked the bald guy. Kansai people's words sound

---

[3] *Ibid.*

[4] *Ibid.*

[5] Richie, S. "East and West: Differences between the Kanto and Kansai regions" dated 15 June 2019 in WorkInJapan.today [downloaded on 15 June 2019], available at https://workinjapan.today/culture/east-and-west-differences-between-the-kanto-and-kansai-regions/.

harsh sometimes, but they aren't meant to be. If I fall down the stairs, it's embarrassing, I want people to laugh at me so at least we can have fun. But I think Kanto people are too uptight to acknowledge their embarrassment.[6]

There may be strong attempts on the part of Yamamoto-san and his team at conflict avoidance. Therefore, during the negotiations, incidences of clearly articulated rejection on their part of your terms and conditions will be rare in order to maintain the harmony of the discussions/dialogue. There may be collective attempts to achieve conflict avoidance, with expectations of reciprocity in this process from you.

There will be skilful attempts at preserving 'face'. Even if you are or appear to be getting the shorter end of the stick in the bargaining and negotiations process, Yamamoto-san and his team will continue to avoid making you feel you had lost all grounds in the negotiation process. Power distance is avoided in this context.

While every attempt is made to ensure accomplishment of preparatory work leading to certainty and lack of surprises during the negotiations, unexpected issues are considered natural and may be resolved with a dependence on the long-term nature of the relationship and an avoidance of litigative or conflictual relationships. Japanese negotiators do not like power plays and reach for conciliation whenever they can. Litigation is avoided because a court judge making a ruling is itself symbolically a raw display of power and the ruling will result in one party suffering a detriment or losing face.[7]

Japan's relationship to Confucianism is different from that of China, Korea and Vietnam. This may explain its score in terms of power distance and individualism being in a different tier from those. Some opine that the Confucian social stratification found in China, Vietnam and Korea is based on the hierarchical order of scholar gentry officials right at the very top followed by farmers, artisans and then merchants (in that order). The

---

[6] Lau, V. "Kansai vs. Kanto: Japan's most bitter regional feud" dated 29 April 2015 in CNN [downloaded on 1 January 2022], available at https://edition.cnn.com/travel/article/discover-japan-kansai-vs-kanto/index.html.

[7] Van Zandt, Howard F. "How to Negotiate in Japan" dated November 1970 in Magazine/ *Harvard Business Review* (HBR) [downloaded on 1 January 2022], available at https://hbr.org/1970/11/how-to-negotiate-in-japan.

scholar gentry officials attained their positions by virtue of arduous meritocratic academic tests. Japan has the same social order except for the top elite stratum which are occupied by the warrior class (the samurais) instead of scholar gentry officials. Therefore, the hierarchical order may be more rationalized and disciplined, given military officials follow a stronger command structure that requires more conformity and compliance with practical decisions made within the group rather than engaging in scholarly debates when engaging in a decision-making process.

Hofstede's Cultural Dimensions

- **Power Distance**

At a score of 54, Japan's Power Distance is the lowest among the countries covered in this book. Japanese negotiators greatly disliked power plays and viewed them with strong negativity. Even senior leaders and negotiators are expected to be consensus builders rather than alpha leaders in the negotiations. Even at the apex of Japan's political structure, the Prime Minister (PM) is not expected to be an alpha leader but a consensus builder negotiating between different political *habatsu* factions to reach the agreement that takes into account everyone's view and try to strike a compromise as a final decision.

Consensus building is extremely important in Japan's group-oriented business culture. In Japan, business proposals and ideas often emanate from bottom up and then emerge as a group decision through consensus.[8] The Japanese consensual decision-making mechanism *ringi* is predicated upon a voluntary consensus with a documentation known as *ringisho* that contains briefing information and/or recommendations from the management that is then disseminated throughout the hierarchy to all relevant stakeholders who then have a chance to look at the proposal and provide their agreement/inputs. Decisions are then made this way by the group collectively, after obtaining everyone's buy-in. The *ringisho* used to be a written document in a binder that all team members had to read and then affix their signatures to. However, in the digital world, it may be an online document which team members can register digitally as having read.

---

[8] *Ibid.*

Despite the egalitarian approach to obtain inputs from all team members, a final authority is needed to approve of the final collective decision after obtaining consensus. The final decision is still made by someone with the necessary authority and status. It is typically the president (the *torishimariyakukaicho*) of the *kaisha* company, who with his personal vermilion seal will legally seal the deal after a whole team of negotiators have concluded it. [In Japan, the *hanko* seal instead or in addition to the signature is needed to make agreements legally valid.] The team's support for the decision dissipates the responsibility of one single person. Due to this groupism, when negotiating, therefore, it is important to not focus only on a single person, but the entire Japanese team must be convinced and this is attributed to the Buddhist influence known as *shujo no on* (obligation owed to the entire universe when one attains success due to the help of others instead of pretending one's singular intellect or efforts).[9] In this way, Japanese shun Prima donnas in their teams. Typically, Prima donnas like those in baseball teams who have a flair to show off individual talents and skills are compelled to go overseas to play for more individualistic American teams.

- **Individualism–Collectivism**

Japan scores the highest in Individualism (46) among the countries discussed in this book, although this is still below the halfway mark and is low compared with UK (89) and US (91). Perhaps a contemporary case study to understand Japan's communitarian groupism vis-à-vis the more Western individualistic culture is the Japanese management of the COVID-19 pandemic. Japan did not have to go through any lockdowns during the pandemic and yet did a remarkable job containing the pandemic. It may be possible that the collectivist nature of the country played a role in this aspect. Due to the postwar Japanese US-imposed constitution, the authorities had no unambiguous power to lock down the country during the COVID-19 pandemic. Instead, the authorities dispensed advisory and the tight communitarian groupism of Japanese society, their strong homogeneity (both perceived and real) as well as the shame culture (peer pressure to follow the group) resulted in moderately impressive results for the liberal democratic country that had no compulsory lockdowns for its people. The

---

[9] *Ibid.*

number of deaths was the lowest when compared to the developed economies and the vaccination rate was among the highest.

Japan usually prioritizes employment opportunities as a goal for its companies/country rather than profit-making. That is why the Japanese name for 'companies' is 'kaisha', flipping the characters for 'shakai' which means society. Therefore, the company is a microcosm of society, looking after the welfare of society rather than profiteering. Some argue that wheat-growing northern Chinese and Westerners were more individualistic and analytical while rice-cultivating southern Chinese, Vietnamese, Japanese and Korean were mutually reliant on each other, with a holistic worldview and strong loyalty to friends, as psychological tests indicated.[10]

The Japanese civilization and society defined themselves as the 'wa' people. The essence of the meaning of 'wa' refers to constant/consistent consensus-seeking ways to maintain harmony within Japanese society and the avoidance of conflicts. Therefore, sociologists and anthropologists often describe Japanese social relations as reflecting groupism, communitarianism and cohesion. The Japanese proverb *deru kugi wa utareru* ("The nail that sticks out must be hammered down", which has become an American proverb, too) describes the proclivity for making decisions as a group so that no one single person can be faulted for making an outstanding risky error and be struck down like a nail. Similarly, in business negotiations, they prefer to work as a group rather than as individuals. There is strong reliance on each other within the team. Each team member is given an important role to play. Thus, all Japanese negotiation team members may have to reach a consensus on important decisions and items in the negotiation. You must convince the entire team of Japanese negotiators in order to achieve strong success in the negotiation process.

The Japanese view of outsiders is clearly defined in their concepts of the 'in' (uchi) and 'out' (soto) groups. What constitutes the 'in' and 'out' groups is contextual and situation based. When one is in a section team, the sectional colleagues would be the 'in' group while their colleagues from other sections within the division would be the 'out' group. But, when all

---

[10] Talhelm, T. "'Rice Theory' Explains North–South China Cultural Differences, Study Shows" dated 8 May 2014 in UVA Today (University of Virgina News) [downloaded on 1 January 2022], available at https://news.virginia.edu/content/rice-theory-explains-north-south-china-cultural-differences-study-shows.

sections get together to work with another division, then the entire division's sections would be the 'in' group while the external divisions become the 'out' group. Japanese have a strong sense of loyalty. This comes from the *senpai–kohai* traditions where the seniors (*senpai*) take care of their juniors (*kohai*) in exchange for their *kohai*'s loyalty. This applies to all social structures and betrayals of trust are viewed very negatively in Japanese society. Therefore, mid-career changes are comparatively rarer and can be viewed with suspicion by other companies.

- **Uncertainty Avoidance**

At 92, Japan's score is the highest among the countries covered in this book. From its score in all three dimensions, it can be seen that Japan is an outlier among the East Asian countries. As the country faces constant threats from natural disasters such as earthquakes and typhoons, preparedness and strict adherence to precautions is part of its national DNA. There is a strong preference for predictability and certainty.

3. Communication

When negotiating, some experts argue that the speakers themselves have the responsibility to not use long sentences, double negatives, negative words (replace them with positive terms if possible), slang words, superfluous words or generalities.[11] The Japanese prefer to have detailed explanations of every item (including new product offerings and concepts) in visual presentation format to back up verbal narratives, thus samples, models, photographs, maps, sketches, diagrams, catalogues, pamphlets, books, leaflets, blueprints, printed materials, photos, etc. are important (especially in the Japanese language).[12]

Japan, like many Asian cultures, is a high-context culture. Inferential skills are necessary to understand meanings in high-context communication, but such skills are not required in low-context communication. Non-verbal communication therefore plays a larger and more significant role in high-context communication. There are experts that recommend

---

[11] Van Zandt, Howard F. "How to Negotiate in Japan" dated November 1970 in Magazine/ *Harvard Business Review* (HBR) [downloaded on 1 January 2022], available at https://hbr. org/1970/11/how-to-negotiate-in-japan.
[12] *Ibid.*

the greater use of body language in communicating with high-context cultures like the Japanese. Non-Japanese can be expressive utilizing movements of hands, eyes, lips, shoulders, head and other non-verbal forms of communication to reinforce verbal communication.[13]

Personal feelings are not revealed during any social events, including negotiations. Therefore, the non-Japanese team of negotiators may also have to restrain their tendencies to inject feelings and intentions into the negotiations unless they are crucial for the process itself. Revealing true feelings may also inadvertently project the image of arrogance or markers of an undesirable human relationship (*ningen kankei*).

Rejection is often expressed in ambiguous, indirect and/or polite terms to preserve long-term relationships, even if the deal falls through. As respected sociologist Professor Chie Nakane of Tokyo University articulated: "Expression of no is virtually never used outside of completely reciprocal relationships, and from superior to inferior. You rarely receive a no from a Japanese; even when he means no he would use yes in the verbal form."[14] Physically, Japanese body language for rejection is typically a hissing sound with air sucked through the gaps of their teeth, a turn of the head to 30 to 40 degrees and then sometimes articulating the words "chot-tone" while appearing to lean back in a ponderous manner. Sometimes, the body language for rejection is in the form of drawing air through his mouth and then articulate "sah" (a lexicon-less word) and if foreigners cannot read body language like this, they may be misled in their conclusion of the negotiations.[15]

Arguments are to be avoided at all cost. Silence is usually the ultimate response if the disagreement becomes too acute. A speedy retort or response in a debate is often not expected or even desired. Japanese avoid arguments at all costs and will desist from retorting, arguing or even discussing even if she/he feels they are correct and prefer to keep quiet rather than retort/respond as it happens in European culture. This trait is visible right from childhood.[16] When a breakdown or pause in the negotiation

---

[13] *Ibid.* Hall, E.T. (1976). *Beyond Culture*, Anchor, Garden City, N.Y.

[14] Van Zandt, Howard F. "How to Negotiate in Japan" dated November 1970 in Magazine/ *Harvard Business Review* (HBR) [downloaded on 1 January 2022], available at https://hbr. org/1970/11/how-to-negotiate-in-japan.

[15] *Ibid.*

[16] *Ibid.*

occurs, Japanese negotiators tend to stay silent without feeling the pressure to articulate disagreements and may even avoid responding to an enquiry, which may make American negotiators feel worried and compelled to say something or give a concession to kick-start the process again.[17]

Maintaining pleasantness throughout the negotiations is desirable. Japanese negotiators tend to size up the personalities of the people they are dealing with. They like to feel comfortable with the parties they are dealing/partnering/working with, emotionally and in terms of teamwork. Personalities matter a lot to the Japanese. Only under the most deprived circumstances will they consider doing business with a party that they find unpleasant or arrogant and so, if there are hints during the negotiations that the Western negotiator might be arrogant, unreasonable or reluctant to provide adequate technical support, Japanese negotiators may not sign (and *hanko* stamp) on the final contract.[18] Even among the Japanese, pride can be a source of harmless tensions. To Kanto-ites, Kansai-ans appear boisterous, emotional and proud of their linguistic and expressive cultures, resistant to speaking standardized Japanese (*hyojungo*) while being judgemental about non-Kansai-ans attempting the Kansai dialect.[19] Regardless of regional locations in Japan, many follow the social ritual of drinking/dining. The act of *nemawabushi* or act of establishing personal relations through social events such as after-negotiations dinners/drinks can help build up relationships to avoid tensions. Very often, these activities are carried out in *izakaya*s (drinking pubs that double up as restaurants).

It is helpful to bear in mind sub-regional cultural traits, too. Kansai people tend to be stereotyped as being more proactively extroverted and humorous and are often animated and funny, in contrast to the more impersonal, colder and complex Kanto people and their thinking. Some Kanto denizens like Akira Nagao (37 years old) opined: "It's true that some people are cold, but I think most of us are just shy. Sometimes I want to talk, but it's really hard to talk to strangers because I'm shy."[20] Saitama local Akiharu Katsuta (41 years old) rationalizes Kanto standoffishness in

[17] *Ibid.*

[18] *Ibid.*

[19] Lau, V. "Kansai vs. Kanto: Japan's most bitter regional feud" dated 29 April 2015 in CNN [downloaded on 1 January 2022], available at https://edition.cnn.com/travel/article/discover-japan-kansai-vs-kanto/index.html.

[20] *Ibid.*

the following manner: "I think some people just work in Tokyo and don't have friends. Maybe they want to talk to people, but they don't have anyone to talk to."[21]

4. Negotiation Strategies: Distributive or Integrative

There is high expectation of Yamamoto-san and his team to be far more integrative. This is due to the long-term orientation of Japanese business relationships, the tendency to avoid conflicts/tensions in any relationships and the constant consensus-seeking preferences in human relations (*ningenkankei*). *Ningenkankei*, friendship and good human relations are extremely important in Japan. Once you have accumulated private social capital and old friendships (the longer, the better), you can enjoy access to insights and intermediary roles in negotiations. The renowned and highly regarded sociologist Professor Chie Nakane explained:

> [[Despite] The more good friends a man has, the more secure he feels. There are degrees of friendship, however] The relative strength of the human bond tends to increase in proportion to the length and intensity of actual contact. The reason the newcomer in any Japanese group is placed at the very bottom of the hierarchy is that he has the shortest period of contact. This is a primary condition of the seniority system, which dominates Japan. Therefore, the placement of an individual in a social group is governed by the length of the individual's contact with the group. In other words, the actual contact itself becomes the individual's private social capital. ...[22]

Another reason that will contribute to an integrative outcome is the Japanese's approach to information-sharing. The Japanese will prepare meticulously for negotiations and are typically armed with organized information and data which will be shared with their entire team (*ringisho* system). Internally, all questions and possible scenarios would be discussed ahead of the negotiation. Therefore, if you politely request for

---

[21] *Ibid.*

[22] Van Zandt, Howard F. "How to Negotiate in Japan" dated November 1970 in Magazine/ *Harvard Business Review* (HBR) [downloaded on 1 January 2022], available at https://hbr. org/1970/11/how-to-negotiate-in-japan.

information from the Japanese negotiator, you are likely to receive disclosure that is generally more open than most of the countries covered in this book. They in fact welcome queries and joint investigations of such information in order to take the negotiation to a greater level. Also, the Japanese negotiator's comparatively low power distance score (54) motivates them to seek for information from the other party[23] and this encourages information exchange.

Nevertheless, you should also be prepared for distributive behavior when negotiating with the Japanese. Japanese negotiators will try their maximum to conceal their true positions. This is a process known as *tatemae*. Following the concept of *tatemae* (adopting external interface or front when interacting with strangers), the Japanese hide their true sentiments and intentions, thus foreign negotiators may never see this side of their Japanese counterparts. Although personal feelings play a significant role in Japanese behavior, a stranger from overseas may never realize it (conforming to the ancient Japanese proverb *No aru taka wa tsume wo kakusu* or "A capable hawk hides his talons"). Northeast Asians tend to view negotiators yapping away about their capabilities negatively and perhaps as being arrogant.

Kanto people tend to be even more careful of strangers than Kansai counterparts. Even giving way on elevators is differentiable between western and eastern Japanese people. Kanto individuals tend to stand towards the left due to their samurai past. In the pre-modern era, the Kanto were ruled by samurai warrior class who were trainned to bear left when coming across strangers in case they need to draw their katana swords for battle.[24]

One article suggests that Japanese negotiators are more likely to use distributive tactics when compared with Chinese and South Korean negotiators.[25] This could be true in certain contexts. Chinese culturally

[23] Lee, Brett, J. & Park, J. H. (2012). East Asians' Social Heterogeneity: Differences in Norms among Chinese, Japanese, and Korean Negotiators. *Negotiation Journal*, 28(4), 429–452. https://doi.org/10.1111/j.1571-9979.2012.00350.x.

[24] Lau, V. "Kansai vs. Kanto: Japan's most bitter regional feud" dated 29 April 2015 in CNN [downloaded on 1 January 2022], available at https://edition.cnn.com/travel/article/discover-japan-kansai-vs-kanto/index.html.

[25] Lee, Brett, J. & Park, J. H. (2012). East Asians' Social Heterogeneity: Differences in Norms among Chinese, Japanese, and Korean Negotiators. *Negotiation Journal*, 28(4), 429–452. https://doi.org/10.1111/j.1571-9979.2012.00350.x.

may be considered to be the most individualistic of the three (CJK or China, Japan, Korea) and their negotiation styles vary from region to region. Thus, they are most likely to be comparatively more distributive than the other two (Koreans and Japanese).

5. Concession-Making and Hardball Tactics

Japanese terminology for internalized comprehension, a eureka moment which all parties attain simultaneously, is *kan* (a form of emotional attunement) and, from this point onwards, it is considered that a decision will be made in the negotiation in the context of a blossoming relationship.[26]

Even when there is a breakdown in negotiations and Japanese negotiators stop communicating, you are advised to maintain open channels of communication in the absence of official meetings. Meanwhile you can investigate familiar lower-ranking executives (the "inside friends") to find out the reasons for the stalemate and perhaps even solicit solutions to overcome the pause. The "inside friends" may even sometimes suggest solutions to resolve the outstanding issues from the interest of their own companies while the senior executives may sometimes mobilize the naysayers in private luncheons to explain their opposition to the foreign negotiators.[27] Even after practicing all these pointers,[28] concessions may not come easily and negotiators will need to wait patiently to receive them from the Japanese party.

Japanese are experts in conciliation. Thus, concession-making is usually pegged at the path of least resistance where both parties to a negotiation can benefit from the final deal. There is also a strong sense of reciprocity. Thus, when you are provided with concessions, you ought to reciprocate, especially when asked by the Japanese negotiator.

[26] Van Zandt, Howard F. "How to Negotiate in Japan" dated November 1970 in Magazine/ *Harvard Business Review* (HBR) [downloaded on 1 January 2022], available at https://hbr.org/1970/11/how-to-negotiate-in-japan.
[27] *Ibid.*
[28] Katz, L. "Negotiating International Business — Japan" dated 2017 in Negotiating International Business — The Negotiator's Reference Guide to 50 Countries Around the World [downloaded on 1 January 2022], available at http://www.leadershipcrossroads.com/mat/cou/Japan.pdf. Co-author in this volume Tan notes: It is also my experience that my Japanese clients are usually very careful and meticulous about the concessions I am allowed to make on their behalf.

Sometimes, concessions are made based on the 'face' factor rather than business necessity or economic rationality, to prevent a disagreement from breaking the overall harmony of the relationship.

In the case of multinational firms' negotiations, sometimes, the Japanese authorities (state or semi-state entities) may be important stakeholders in the negotiation. Therefore, non-Japanese negotiators may find it useful to understand how industry–state relations tend to be complementary, consensually cooperative and harmonious and not disregarding the needs of the local or national authorities. To keep human relations (*ningen kankei*) strong, when either side asks for concessions in the name of long-term friendship and relationship, it may be useful to reciprocate for building up long-term trust. The more concessions both parties can provide each other, with the passage of time, the stronger the trust. Emotional or empathetic responses are often appreciated in offering concessions in such cases rather than relying on cold hard facts.

After contracting, you should not consider it to be the end of the process. The Japanese negotiator will reconcile differences in such a way that both sides do not appear to have given involuntary concessions. They will come up with an appropriate strategy to fit the negotiation agenda and therefore prefer some flexibility in agreements rather than clearly defined ones, particularly in items like prices and quantities.[29] Pricing therefore is typically the trickiest part of the deal-making. [There are regional differences, too. Kansai was historically a mercantile rice-trading region (especially pre-modern Osaka city) and it was vital for them to conserve their hard-earned finances and valuables, so many Kansai-ans and Osakans tend to be more financially conscious in business activities.[30] So much so that sometimes elderly Osakans greet each other by saying *mokarimakka* ('are you making money nowadays?')]

The same principles apply to the implementation stage that both parties continue the modus operandi of strong post-contractual communications,

---

[29] Van Zandt, Howard F. "How to Negotiate in Japan" dated November 1970 in Magazine/ *Harvard Business Review* (HBR) [downloaded on 1 January 2022], available at https://hbr. org/1970/11/how-to-negotiate-in-japan.

[30] Lau, V. "Kansai vs. Kanto: Japan's most bitter regional feud" dated 29 April 2015 in CNN [downloaded on 1 January 2022], available at https://edition.cnn.com/travel/article/ discover-japan-kansai-vs-kanto/index.html.

emotional support, concession-making and consensus-building instead of turning to litigation to resolve disputes, disagreements or unexpected circumstances. Contract commitment is not absolute but the start of a dialogue to meet the needs of both parties. Concessions are a constant feature of post-negotiation phases.

Even among the Japanese themselves (to be even more specific, among the western Japanese people), there are subtle sub-cultural differences, too. Osaka business reps tend to be "pushy, over-familiar but kind salesmen" compared to their Kyoto counterparts who appear "amiable, but you never know what they are really thinking", and while the former are rougher, with grittier linguistic mannerisms, the latter speak a softer refined dialect (even though in both cases they are technically speaking in Kansai *ben* or dialect).[31]

For some scholars, the element of trust can uncover dormant inclinations for cooperation hitherto hidden under the security covers of defensive-aggressive behavior and thus trust is a crucial element for developing relationships in negotiations (including cross-cultural ones) by eliminating such fronts.[32] For some scholars, the element of trust reveals the dormant inclination for cooperation that was previously hidden under security covers of defensive-aggressive behavior and thus trust is a crucial element for developing relationships in negotiations (including cross-cultural ones).[33]

Yamamoto-san and team will react negatively if you adopt hardball tactics. If your team has an alpha member who is dramatic, exercises power plays and plays hardball, it is likely to impact negatively on the negotiations. Japanese shun dictatorial attitudes and methods of negotiations. The Japanese negotiator prefers a low-pressure sales pitch and displays of sincerity so you may wish to incrementally construct your case to the Japanese

---

[31] Richie, S. "East and West: Differences between the Kanto and Kansai regions" dated 15 June 2019 in WorkInJapan.today [downloaded on 15 June 2019], available at https://workinjapan.today/culture/east-and-west-differences-between-the-kanto-and-kansai-regions/.

[32] Kim, Mie-Jung, Liyuan Wang and Moon-Suh Park, "Different Levels of Trust in Global Business Negotiation: A Comparative Study about Canadians and Korean Perspective on Doing Business Negotiation with Chinese" dated 21 September 2015 in International Commerce and Information Review Volume 17, Number 3 [downloaded on 1 January 2022], available at https://koreascience.kr/article/JAKO201534164960105.pdf, p. 158.

[33] *Ibid.*

negotiators. Use soft language and avoid extravagant claims while providing the leeway for the Japanese to make enquiries by not articulating one's position in one long narrative.[34] Such efforts on your part to reach broad consensus with the Japanese would be greatly appreciated. Once consensus is achieved by the team, rarely will any single member from the Japanese team scuttle the deal.

Sincerity and honesty on your part will be greatly appreciated because they smoothen the way for a long-term relationship.[35] This sometimes may even go to the extent of admitting competitors' strengths to show one's frank and honest assessments of their business capabilities. Such behavior rather than hardball steamrolling over the Japanese negotiators are likely to yield more results. Low-pressure sales presentation or marketing without making bold claims are preferred over slick marketing that overly raises expectations. Japanese prefer negotiating presentations that are objective, fact-based and present the cost–benefit analysis.

6. Role of Women

Japan is a male-dominated society. The number of women in its business leadership positions remains one of the lowest among developed economies. According to the International Labour Office (ILO), Japan's share of women in senior and middle management roles in 2019 was 14.5% as compared with 40.7% in the United States, 37.1% in Singapore and 35.5% in Australia.[36] The Japanese government set a target to increase the percentage of women managers in private corporations to 30% by 2025.[37] As of 2019, this figure is only 18.9%.[38] Based on the 2022 Global Gender

---

[34] Van Zandt, Howard F. "How to Negotiate in Japan" dated November 1970 in Magazine/ *Harvard Business Review* (HBR) [downloaded on 1 January 2022], available at https://hbr. org/1970/11/how-to-negotiate-in-japan.

[35] *Ibid.*

[36] International Labour Office. "Women in managerial and leadership positions in the G20", (2021), at: https://www.ilo.org/wcmsp5/groups/public/---dgreports/---ddg_p/documents/ publication/wcms_762098.pdf.

[37] One of the Japanese government initiatives to promote equal opportunities and women's participation and advancement in the workplace is the Fifth Basic Plan for Gender Equality: https://www.gender.go.jp/english_contents/about_danjo/whitepaper/pdf/5th_bpg.pdf.

[38] *Ibid.*

Gap Report by the World Economic Forum,[39] Japan is ranked last out of 19 countries in the East Asia and the Pacific region — below all of the other countries covered in this book.

Global Gender Gap Report 2022 INSIGHT REPORT JULY 2022

EAST ASIA & the PACIFIC	Rank		
Country	Regional (19)	Global (146)	Score
Philippines	2	19	0.783
Singapore	4	49	0.734
Thailand	8	79	0.709
Vietnam	9	83	0.705
Indonesia	10	92	0.697
Korea (South)	12	99	0.689
China	13	102	0.682
Malaysia	14	103	0.681
Japan	**19**	**116**	**0.650**

Source: World Economic Forum (WEF), "Global Gender Gap Report 2022 INSIGHT REPORT JULY 2022" dated 13 July 2022 in World Economic Forum website [downloaded on 13 July 2022], available at https://www.weforum.org/reports/global-gender-gap-report-2022/.

Despite the low ranking, Japan has seen the status of its women improving over the past years. The resignation of the Tokyo Olympics Chief, Mr Yoshiro Mori, after making sexist remarks[40] and being replaced by Ms Seiko Hashimoto reflects this trend.

---

[39] "Global Gender Gap Report 2022." 2022. World Economic Forum. July 13, 2022. https://www.weforum.org/reports/global-gender-gap-report-2022/digest. The Global Gender Gap Index benchmarks the current state and evolution of gender parity across four key dimensions (Economic Participation and Opportunity, Educational Attainment, Health and Survival, and Political Empowerment). It is the longest-standing index which tracks progress towards closing these gaps over time since its inception in 2006.

[40] "Ex-Tokyo Olympics Chief Again Criticized for Sexist Comment | the Asahi Shimbun: Breaking News, Japan News and Analysis." n.d. The Asahi Shimbun. Accessed October 31, 2022. https://www.asahi.com/ajw/articles/14309141.

Paddock & Kray advised that women negotiators should avoid falling into the trap of self-handicapping, instead they should direct their efforts towards careful preparation and go into negotiation with a strong Best Alternative To a Negotiated Agreement (BATNA). While building up long-term relationships, practitioners have advised concurrently building up Plan B, or BATNAs, as a buffer against negotiation failures and having a reliable option that gives Western/foreign negotiators an alternative plan.[41] BATNAs are activated whenever one is out-bid by a superior rival.[42]

However, the authors advised that women negotiators should not act like men or they will face backlash. Some argue that female lawyer nego-tiators (like all other professionals, e.g. doctors, accountants, architects, dentists) are often addressed honorifically as *sensei*s and are given a higher social status compared with normal salaried women (*sarari-uman*) or O.L.s (Office Ladies). It may be that higher status or respect is accorded to women lawyers due to their occupational role. Also, women lawyers are seen to be soliciting and advocating on behalf of a client, which is consist-ent with gender stereotypes for women to show a high concern for others as nurturers and empathetic figures.

The co-author of this volume recounted her experiences negotiating in Japan which were all done when she was a lawyer and she can confirm that she did not experience any gender stereotype. This volume's co-author was even included in the social events (except maybe not the "special ones" that she defined as night entertainment or *mizu shobai*, e.g. hostess clubs). *Mizu shobai* activities were common during the post-war Showa period (1945 to 1989) but fizzled out by the Heisei period (8 Jan 1989 to 30 Apr 2019) after the economic bubble burst and company entertainment budgets were slashed. There were also generational changes as Heisei salaried men execu-tives (*sarariman*) preferred to have a better work–life balance and shunned late drinking activities (especially *mizu shobai* hostess club activities).

---

[41] PON Staff, "The Negotiation Process in China" dated 15 August 2022 in PON Harvard [downloaded on 15 August 2022], available at https://www.pon.harvard.edu/daily/international-negotiation-daily/tips-for-navigating-negotiations-in-china/.

[42] Program on Negotiation (PON) at Harvard Law School, "The Importance of Relationship Building in China When in China, Relationship Building is Critical" dated 4 August 2022 in Program on Negotiation (PON) at Harvard Law School [downloaded on 4 August 2022], available at https://www.pon.harvard.edu/daily/international-negotiation-daily/negotiation-in-china-the-importance-of-guanxi/.

Since Equal Employment Opportunity Law (EEOL, some publications use the word 'Act' instead of 'Law') 1985 (some publications use the date 1986, the implementation year, rather than the legislation year), discrimination against women were disrupted. Women follow all the same rules of negotiations as men. If women executives choose a managerial track, they would observe the same level and procedures of business negotiations as their male counterparts. There are no gender differences. Some scholars argue that non-Japanese female negotiators who are Westerners may even sometimes have an advantage over male negotiators as they are seen as confident individuals who can articulate their preferences conspicuously compared to the Japanese women or even men. This may be a stereotype rather than a universal feature.

7. Intermediary/Interpreter

It is advisable that you get your executives prepared with detailed explanations of the negotiation or business activities, carry out research of Japan related to the negotiations and get interpreters/translators who are culturally tuned into Japan ready. This is important as there are subtle linguistic differences to take note of. The translators/interpreters hired for negotiations may be aware of subtle linguistic dialect differences. Kanto native Shigeru Kaneko (aged 55) explained this point dramatically:

> I remember riding the train in Osaka and on the window was a sign that read: 'Be careful of cutting your finger'. I thought maybe there were a lot of gangs in Kansai. But later I found out the real meaning: 'Be careful of getting your fingers stuck when the door shuts.' They used a word I've never seen in Kanto.[43]

Sincerity is indicated in preparedness that a negotiator has when preparing her/his presentation in textual form and then responding precisely when challenged in order not to lose face (social standing). Japanese negotiators like data, especially tranches of data, nearer the tail end of negotiations for internal use, submission of documentation to state agencies and also to

---

[43] Lau, V. "Kansai vs. Kanto: Japan's most bitter regional feud" dated 29 April 2015 in CNN [downloaded on 1 January 2022], available at https://edition.cnn.com/travel/article/discover-japan-kansai-vs-kanto/index.html.

keep the supporting data for records in case the project meets any challenges in the future and there is a need to refer back to the original rationale in approving the project.[44]

Before beginning the negotiations, you should go through the subject matter with the interpreter and provide her/him with a duplicate text of the discussion, articulate the points well, not using difficult words, put on an affable front, discuss important points by rephrasing/reiterating, leave time for the translator to do her/his job while taking notes. It is useful to double check numbers in aggregates of 10 000 (Japanese counting system) while writing them down for clarity (being careful of numbers that run over one billion), allow the translator access to a dictionary, leave ample time for the translator to clear mistranslations without interruptions, avoid half-translated text, patiently allowing the translator to articulate.[45]

During the negotiations, it is advisable to pen down the main points discussed for verification of comprehension, while allowing the interpreter rest-time from fatigue and stress, rotate translators if there are two or more to prevent fatigue, and try not to suspect mistranslations even if the translated text appears shorter than the original utterance (due to long-windedness, e.g.).[46] When the translator errs, some experts advised negotiators to show understanding due to the impossibility of not making errors, given the complexities and dissimilarities of Japanese and Western languages and another advice is to provide ample time for the Japanese to articulate their side of the narrative and consult with the translator every time there is a roadblock in communication.[47]

Another key explanation for using a Japan whisperer is that the use of an intermediary provides a necessary bridge and buffer between the negotiator and his/her foreign counterpart. Negotiations are generally classifiable into three parts: antecedent phase (pre-negotiation stage and preparations), the concurrent phase (ongoing process), and the consequent phase (post-negotiation stage) and negotiation behavior throughout all three phases can

[44] Van Zandt, Howard F. "How to Negotiate in Japan" dated November 1970 in Magazine/ *Harvard Business Review* (HBR) [downloaded on 1 January 2022], available at https://hbr.org/1970/11/how-to-negotiate-in-japan.

[45] *Ibid.*

[46] *Ibid.*

[47] *Ibid.*

affect their outcome.⁴⁸ Entertainment activities are seen as very important rituals in the pre-negotiation antecedent phase. Entertainment is often seen as a good platform to de-stress from the negotiation, enhance goodwill and practise *naniwabushi* (forging good personal human relations with an individual from the other party who can respond to a favor when you make the request).⁴⁹ In entertaining Japanese clients in dining activities, it helps to do research first or even ask the Japanese counterparts about their culinary preferences. Even within Japan, it may be useful to note that Kanto cuisines are stronger in taste than Kansai dishes, which are subtly and lightly flavored goods, e.g. products like fermented natto soybeans with a pungent smell enjoyed in Kanto are less appreciated by Kansai individuals.⁵⁰

Japan is a high-context culture. Some scholars characterize Japanese negotiators as having high emotional sensitivity. The towering intellectual and sociologist Professor Chie Nakane of Tokyo University noted after many years of researching on Europeans, Indians and Americans that Japanese are as probably emotional as the Italians but the difference is that Japanese emotions are outwardly manifested towards others while the Italians self-reflect on their own emotions.⁵¹ However, at the same time, Japanese hide their true intentions and feelings from others, leading to the need to decipher emotional outreaches from Japanese negotiators when conversing with them. Showing emotional resonance to Japanese negotiating counterparts or business partners can be done with as simple an act as appreciating a handcrafted gift from a Japanese business partner.

⁴⁸ Sun, Meihong. "A Comparison of Business Negotiation Behavior between Korea and China" dated December 2009 in International Journal of Business and Management VO. 4 No. 12 [downloaded on 1 January 2022], available at https://pdfs.semanticscholar.org/ccfc/201493ae2e5ced61467653696c4ecb34571d.pdf, p. 212.
⁴⁹ Van Zandt, Howard F. "How to Negotiate in Japan" dated November 1970 in Magazine/ *Harvard Business Review* (HBR) [downloaded on 1 January 2022], available at https://hbr.org/1970/11/how-to-negotiate-in-japan.
⁵⁰ Lau, Virgina. "Kansai vs. Kanto: Japan's most bitter regional feud" dated 29 April 2015 in CNN [downloaded on 1 January 2022], available at https://edition.cnn.com/travel/article/discover-japan-kansai-vs-kanto/index.html.
⁵¹ Van Zandt, Howard F. "How to Negotiate in Japan" dated November 1970 in Magazine/ *Harvard Business Review* (HBR) [downloaded on 1 January 2022], available at https://hbr.org/1970/11/how-to-negotiate-in-japan.

Anyone engaged in business negotiations may also need to be aware of regional differences in Kyoto and Osaka's ways of verbal articulation. While in Kyoto (the pre-modern capital of Imperial Japan) indirectness in conversational Japanese (much like the way people speak in the current capital of Tokyo) is common, in the historical merchant city Osaka widely known directness is either a cultural trait or an anomaly in Japanese communication styles.[52] A common joke is when Kyoto-ites say something like "How about having *ochazuke* rice soup?", their guests would take leave by making excuses that they needed to get back while on the other hand, Tokyoites rarely invite others to their homes.[53]

If the non-Japanese team of negotiators is unfamiliar with contextual cultural reading or interpretation of non-verbal communications, then an intermediary who can interpret such signals would be helpful. Resonating with such emotional sensitivity is helpful for the negotiations. Interpreters who can read body language and contextual communications would be very helpful to the negotiation process. When negotiations break down, sometimes it is useful to engage an intermediary familiar with both parties to remove the roadblock and offer solutions to resume the negotiation process. The intermediary can be from the same *sakuru* (university clubs or circles), alumni club or the same high school as the Japanese negotiators. In Japan, the old boys/girls' alumni club is very important as they may have grown up and forged their friendships amidst the same cohort of students throughout their academic careers.

8. Time, Timelines, Timeliness

Based on all that has been discussed, we can expect that negotiating with Yamamoto and his team is going to take much time and patience. Some experts recommend not to prematurely jump to conclusions when things are done differently from the West.[54] There are several angles we can take

[52] Richie, S. "East and West: Differences between the Kanto and Kansai regions" dated 15 June 2019 in WorkInJapan.today [downloaded on 15 June 2019], available at https://workinjapan.today/culture/east-and-west-differences-between-the-kanto-and-kansai-regions/.
[53] *Ibid.*
[54] Van Zandt, Howard F. "How to Negotiate in Japan" dated November 1970 in Magazine/ *Harvard Business Review* (HBR) [downloaded on 1 January 2022], available at https://hbr.org/1970/11/how-to-negotiate-in-japan.

when it comes to being patient about timelines. Given the Japanese work ethics — maybe it makes them look less hardworking if the turnaround is quick. Everyone must be seen to be putting in more time. According to pre-pandemic figures from the government, Japanese workers only consumed 52.4% of their paid leave entitlement in 2018.[55] In fact, employees typically do not have paid sick leave. Such a gruelling work culture gave birth to the term *karoshi* — "death from overwork". The law-makers had to pass a law to limit over-time work and mandate taking leave.[56] Sometimes, sick leave in Japan is not taken up even when eligible.

Japanese expect a high level of meticulousness in their team members. They typically undertake very detailed research and background work before engaging in a negotiation. Communication between team members would be open and transparent so that they all share the same level of information before negotiating. The *ringisho* system of sharing information where each member puts her/his seal to having read the common memo before the negotiation ensures a strong exchange and sharing of information. Questions or opposition are raised internally within the team very much ahead of negotiations. Thus, a glaring mistake made by a single team member is viewed negatively. However, the same standards may not be expected from the opposing party.

Due to the consensus-seeking culture, it takes time for Japanese negotiators to reach a decision. Negotiation rhythms may have lengthy periods of silence with punctuations of light conversations (which may also contain subject matter that are of secondary relevance to the primary subject matter) and eventually, after much *nemawashi* (tying up the roots to bind the plant, a bonsai term), a consensus is reached.[57] Every single member (including the lower-ranking team members) is consulted before a decision

[55] Ministry of Health, Labour and Welfare (MHLW), "Kekka no Gaiyou (The Summary of the Outcome)" undated in Ministry of Health, Labour and Welfare (MHLW) [downloaded on 1 January 2022], available at https://www.mhlw.go.jp/toukei/itiran/roudou/jikan/syurou/19/dl/gaiyou01.pdf (document is in Japanese).
[56] Work Style Reform Legislation was passed in 2018 to place limits on overtime work to 45 hours per month with a maximum of 360 hours in a year. However, high skilled professional workers (those who jobs require specialised skills and earn at least an annual salary of USD95,000, are exempt from such limitation).
[57] Van Zandt, Howard F. "How to Negotiate in Japan" dated November 1970 in Magazine/ *Harvard Business Review* (HBR) [downloaded on 1 January 2022], available at https://hbr.org/1970/11/how-to-negotiate-in-japan.

is reached. Thus, the non-Japanese negotiating team must be patient and not overly interpret delays in decision-making as a form of rejection. They should contextualize delays as part of an effortful consensus-seeking procedure. Japanese are also very procedure-minded and follow operational manuals closely. This may also result in bureaucracy that delays the decision-making process. The longer time taken to achieve consensus is also related to the desire for predictability rather than springing surprises in the negotiations or the post-negotiation implementation period.

Exhaustive and time-consuming explanations of terms and conditions are useful in this aspect to eliminate any possibility of surprises and ambiguities in the terms. Thorough explanation of every point in the negotiation is greatly appreciated by Japanese negotiators. Presentation summaries, briefs and/or reports/manuals are often helpful for this process. Japanese negotiators have a strong preference for written/printed/published materials and this applies to the use of name cards (*meishi*) and annual post-mailing of new year greeting cards as well. Therefore, try not to jump to conclusion if the Japanese party to the negotiations requires more time for consideration.

During this period, non-Japanese negotiating parties are advised to keep all channels of communication open and unobstructed for ad-hoc communications about the deal. Sometimes, these additional nuggets of information are needed by the Japanese negotiators to convince any resistance or opposition at their end. Sometimes, detailed sets of data are sought by the Japanese for this purpose as well. During the negotiation meetings, disagreements can be expressed, but once consensus is attained, it becomes awkward and uneasy to block the collectively agreed upon decision because a unilateral disapproval can disrupt Japanese groupism and the Japanese leader's authority may be negatively impacted (given that business terms and proposals emanate or were already discussed extensively with her/his juniors).[58]

Bibliography

Bazerman, Curhan, J. R., Moore, D. A., & Valley, K. L. (2000). Negotiation. *Annual Review of Psychology*, 51(1), 279–314. https://doi.org/10.1146/annurev.psych.51.1.279.

---

[58] *Ibid.*

Graham, John, L. & Mark Lam, N. "The Chinese Negotiation" dated 1 October 2003 in *Harvard Business Review* [downloaded on 1 January 2022], available at https://hbr.org/2003/10/the-chinese-negotiation.

Hall, E.T. (1976). *Beyond Culture*, Anchor, Garden City, N.Y.

International Labour Office, "Women in managerial and leadership positions in the G20", (2021) available at: https://www.ilo.org/wcmsp5/groups/public/---dgreports/---ddg_p/documents/publication/wcms_762098.pdf.

Janosik, R. J. (1987). Rethinking the culture-negotiation link. *Negotiation Journal*, 3, 385–395.

Katz, L. "Negotiating International Business — Japan" dated 2017 in Negotiating International Business — The Negotiator's Reference Guide to 50 Countries Around the World [downloaded on 1 January 2022], available at http://www.leadershipcrossroads.com/mat/cou/Japan.pdf.

Lau, V. "Kansai vs. Kanto: Japan's most bitter regional feud" dated 29 April 2015 in CNN [downloaded on 1 January 2022], available at https://edition.cnn.com/travel/article/discover-japan-kansai-vs-kanto/index.html.

Lee, Brett, J. & Park, J. H. (2012). East Asians' social heterogeneity: Differences in norms among Chinese, Japanese, and Korean Negotiators. *Negotiation Journal*, 28(4), 429–452. https://doi.org/10.1111/j.1571-9979.2012.00350.x.

Lewicki, R. J., Saunders, D. M., & Barry, B. (2021). *Essentials of Negotiation* (7th ed.). McGraw-Hill International Edition, pp. 48–55.

Miles, E. W. & Clenney, E. F. (2010). Gender differences in negotiation: A status characteristics theory view. *Negotiation and Conflict Management Research*, 3(2), 130–144.

Ministry of Health, Labour and Welfare (MHLW). "Kekka no Gaiyou (The Summary of the Outcome)" undated in Ministry of Health, Labour and Welfare (MHLW) [downloaded on 1 January 2022], available at https://www.mhlw.go.jp/toukei/itiran/roudou/jikan/syurou/19/dl/gaiyou01.pdf.

Paddock, E. L. & Kray, L. J. (2011). The role of gender in negotiation. Negotiation Excellence: Successful Deal Making, 229–245. Research Collection Lee Kong Chian School of Business. Available at: https://ink.library.smu.edu.sg/lkcsb_research/3176.

Richie, S. "East and West: Differences between the Kanto and Kansai regions" dated 15 June 2019 in WorkInJapan.today [downloaded on 15 June 2019], available at https://workinjapan.today/culture/east-and-west-differences-between-the-kanto-and-kansai-regions/.

Talhelm, T. "'Rice Theory' Explains North-South China Cultural Differences, Study Shows" dated 8 May 2014 in UVA Today (University of Virgina News) [downloaded on 1 January 2022], available at https://news.virginia.edu/content/rice-theory-explains-north-south-china-cultural-differences-study-shows.

Van Zandt, Howard F. "How to Negotiate in Japan" dated November 1970 in Magazine/*Harvard Business Review* (HBR) [downloaded on 1 January 2022], available at https://hbr.org/1970/11/how-to-negotiate-in-japan.

Walton, R. E. & McKersie, R. B. (1965). *A Behavioral Theory of Labor Negotiations: An Analysis of a Social Interaction System.* New York: McGraw-Hill.

World Economic Forum (WEF). "Global Gender Gap Report 2022 INSIGHT REPORT JULY 2022" dated 13 July 2022 in World Economic Forum website [downloaded on 13 July 2022], available at https://www.weforum.org/reports/global-gender-gap-report-2022/.

Japan Quiz

1. The Japanese word for negotiation is '_____'. It is written in Kanji and derived from Chinese characters.
   A. Bousho
   B. Housho
   C. Sansho
   D. Kōshō

2. Traditionally, the top elite stratum which are occupied by the _____class instead of scholar gentry officials. Fill in the blank.
   A. artisanal
   B. warrior
   C. brahmin
   D. merchant

3. Consensus building is extremely important in Japan's group-oriented business culture. True or false?
   A. True
   B. False

4. Japan usually prioritizes employment opportunities as a goal for its companies/country rather than (or in addition to) profit-making. That is why the Japanese name for 'companies' is 'kaisha', flipping the characters for 'shakai' which means society. Is this general characterization true or false?
   A. True
   B. False

5. Japanese name for 'companies' is '_____', flipping the char-
   acters for '_____' which means society. Fill in the two blanks
   accordingly.
   A. gongxi, shehui
   B. taisha, shakou
   C. kaisha, shakai
   D. kaiseki, shakai

6. The Japanese civilization and society defined themselves as the
   '_____' people. Fill in the blank.
   A. Han
   B. Aztec
   C. wa
   D. Sun

7. Japanese proverb *deru kugi wa utareru*, meaning "the nail that sticks
   out must be hammered down" has become an American proverb, too.
   True or false?
   A. True
   B. False

8. Japanese view of outsiders is clearly defined as the 'in' (_____)
   and 'out' (_____-) groups. Fill in the two blanks.
   A. uni, soto
   B. mi, soto
   C. uchi, soto
   D. uchi, sato

9. *Senpai–kohai* traditions can be translated as?
   A. samurai–artisan traditions
   B. father–daughter traditions
   C. mother–son traditions
   D. senior–junior traditions

10. Personal feelings are not revealed during any social events, including
    negotiations. Therefore, the non-Japanese team of negotiators may
    also have to restrain their tendencies to inject feelings and intentions
    into the negotiations unless they are crucial for the process itself. Is
    this general characterization true or false?
    A. True
    B. False

Answer Bank

1. D
2. B
3. B
4. A
5. C
6. C
7. A
8. C
9. D
10. A

Chapter 4

The Korean Negotiator

The Korean word for negotiation is *hyeobsang*. It is written in Hangul 협상.

1. The Environment (South Korea)

South Korea was one of the dynamic four tiger (sometimes known as the four dragon) economies that studied and indigenized Japan's state-led economic development from the 1960s to the 1990s and emerged as a major economic power (and even became a geopolitical Middle Power). At the point of South Korean membership into the OECD (Organization of Economic Cooperation and Development) in the mid-1990s, the economy was already part of the international supply chain, producing products like semi-conductor chips, ships, petrochemicals, electronics, and automobiles, and with OECD guidance, Korean per capita GDP went up from 6% of the OECD average in 1970 to 97% in 2019.[1] OECD is effectively the wealthy nation's club that coordinates global economic policy while dispensing aid, assistance and support to other developing economies. This shows that the Korean economy has indeed come of age.

---

[1] With accelerated industrialization and birth-control campaigns, the fertility rate of the Korean population declined from 4.5 in 1970 to 1.6 in 1989 with nuclear families bearing one or two kids, increasing the gender-blind education opportunities for them, closing the education gender gap and propelling some educated women into white collar executive/ professional jobs.

In order to build up South Korea's economy, the state-centered Park Chung-hee administration decided to nurture large Korean conglomerates, known as chaebols, characterized by their sizable capital and technological prowess in heavy industries that immediately differentiated them from the Small and Medium-Sized Enterprises (SMEs). The chaebols came into being in the 1970s and underpinned Korea's postwar economic development. An iron triangle of cooperation between the state, private sector and chaebols was formed. The chaebols received preferential treatment, low-interest loans, government guarantees and subsidies from the state to ensure their success. The government then disciplined and rationalized the private sector to maximize economic outputs, and pacified the militant labor forces. The chaebols may have enjoyed state support in the 1960s and 1970s, but they also fostered entrepreneurship, business acumen and successful risk-taking that resulted in economic growth, even when state support was weak at certain historical periods.[2] In other words, when negotiators are engaged in talks with chaebols, the bargaining power of these conglomerates is immense indeed.

From the 1960s to 2020s, the South Korean economy expanded by approximately 800 times from USD$2 billion in 1961 to USD$1.6 trillion in 2019.[3] SMEs manufactured 45.7% of the country's products, with their numbers increasing to more than 3.35 million SMEs (99.9%) [compared to 2916 big-scale enterprises (0.1%)] employing 87.7% of the labor force with rapid export growth in the 2000s].[4]

[2] Kim, E. M. (April 2017). Korea's evolving business — Government relationship. In J. Page & F. Tarp (Eds.), *The Practice of Industrial Policy: Government-Business Coordination in Africa and East Asia* (Chapter 6). (UK: Oxford University Press), [downloaded on 1 January 2022], available at https://academic.oup.com/book/26495/chapter/194950127 (un-paginated electronic copy).

[3] Yang, H. (25 October 2021). "Gender Equality: Korea has Come a Long Way, but There is More Work to Do." Organization of Economic Cooperation and Development (OECD) website [downloaded on 25 October 2021], available at https://www.oecd.org/country/korea/thematic-focus/gender-equality-korea-has-come-a-long-way-but-there-is-more-work-to-do-8bb81613/.

[4] Kim, E. M. (April 2017). Korea's evolving business — Government relationship. In J. Page & F. Tarp (Eds.), *The Practice of Industrial Policy: Government-Business Coordination in Africa and East Asia* (Chapter 6). (UK: Oxford University Press), 2017, [downloaded on 1 January 2022], available at https://academic.oup.com/book/26495/chapter/194950127 (un-paginated electronic copy).

2. Culture

There are practitioners who opine that the presence of cohesive groupism in Korean society emerges from a strong foundation in Confucianism. Confucianism as a system of governance and social order quickly spread to Korea. It appears to have exerted its soft power cultural influence on Korean society since at least the founding of the Lee Dynasty in 1392.[5] In fact, Confucianism even became a religion in Korea and Vietnam (the only Southeast Asian state to have been influenced by Confucianism, arising from 1,000 years of Chinese rule). Together with Japan, scholars have argued that this was the Confucian sphere of influence in Northeast Asia.

Other than Confucianism, various other forms of influences have exerted their hold on Korean culture. Additionally, Korean culture as a whole has been influenced by shamanism, Buddhism and Daoism hybridized with continual foreign influences particularly from China, and the Koreans have indigenized these influences to build their own Korean identity, language and traditional customs.[6] While democratic South Korea retained such traditional influences, its Stalinist totalitarian Northern counterpart was imbued with a new form of ideology. North Korean traditionalism was systematically eliminated by the Soviet Union when they began the occupation of North Korea after WWII. They de-recognized the Korean traditional family system and Confucian philosophy in North Korea, thus getting rid of historical lineage archival records by incineration and ended the kinship system.[7] Therefore, in the case of North Korea, many traditional features of business negotiations were eliminated from state practice.

Aside from traditional culture, it may be interesting to note that both North and South Korea view K-pop (or contemporary Korean Popular Culture) differently. For South Koreans, there is both social continuity and discontinuity in the products. For example, the military-like training

---

[5] Sun, M. (December 2009). A comparison of business negotiation behavior between Korea and China. *International Journal of Business and Management*, 4(12), 212 [downloaded on 1 January 2022], available at https://pdfs.semanticscholar.org/ccfc/201493ae2e5ced61467 653696c4ecb34571d.pdf.

[6] Lee, Chan & Yu, Woo-ik (undated). "Cultural life." Britannica.com [downloaded on 1 January 2022], available at https://www.britannica.com/place/North-Korea/Cultural-life.

[7] *Ibid.*

camps for pop idols reek of social hierarchy with seniors and coaches disciplining the young idols-in-training to drill dance moves with great precision. Idols are also strictly prohibited from romantic relationships and immoral behavior. All these strict impositions of cultural norms preserve strong continuity of the ancient Confucian morality standards. However, the same K-pop products also de-construct Confucian values like gender identity with the boy idols' gender fluidity in terms of fashion aesthetics and sometimes constructed non-binary identities.

On the other hand, K-pop is banned in both North Korea and China for the same reason. Both communist states consider K-pop a dissonance against traditional Confucian values of gender relations. From the state perspective, the disruption of traditional gender relations may affect birth rates that in turn have a negative impact on strategic dimensions like military security (e.g. decrease in childbirths due to abandonment of gendered heterosexual norms) and economic security (ageing population results in economic decline). Therefore, contemporary Korean popular culture has a different impact on North and South Korea, unlike traditional value systems. The implication is that negotiations or business socials with North Koreans need to be more sensitive when it comes to praising contemporary Korean popular culture and its impact on the traditional family value systems.

Other than geographical proximity, it is highly possible that culture plays a role in accelerating the bilateral business relationships between South Korea and China, especially ever since they reached rapprochement after the collapse of the Soviet Union in 1992. That was the year that they re-engaged with each other officially and carried out state diplomacy as well as private sector exchanges. The two countries progressed very quickly from being ideological and Cold War enemies to intimate economic and business partners within a matter of 10 years,[8] mediated through the same Confucian roots in their traditions. [By 2000, China was the third largest trading partner with South Korea and between 2003–2007 China was the biggest trading partner with South Korea (and has remained in that

[8] Sun, M. (December 2009). A comparison of business negotiation behavior between Korea and China. *International Journal of Business and Management*, 4(12), 212 [downloaded on 1 January 2022], available at https://pdfs.semanticscholar.org/ccfc/201493ae2e5ced61467653696c4ecb34571d.pdf.

position ever since) while South Korea became the sixth largest trading partner with China in 2008.[9]] Like other Northeast Asian cultures, South Korea is communitarian in nature and de-emphasizes individualism in favor of groupism. Like Japan, South Korean society emphasizes harmonious relationships within society. The Chinese have an ideological counterpart to social harmony that is hybridized with socialism from the Hu Jintao era, manifested through the ideological campaign of *hexie shehui* (harmonious society).

Hofstede's Cultural Dimensions (South Korea)

- **Power distance**

South Korea's score of 60 is the second lowest among the countries covered in this book, after Japan's (54). A challenge that foreign businesspersons experience in South Korea is the seemingly authority-less structure of the South Korean negotiating style, which many foreigners (particularly Westerners) find puzzling and frustrating.[10] Analysts say this is especially the case with South Korean family-owned or family-dominated firms as the patriarch or matriarch does not typically join in the negotiations and so targeting negotiations at the appropriate authority may be difficult, leading to negotiation delays.[11] South Koreans are very conscious of power structures and may feel slighted if a foreign firm dispatches negotiators who have lower appointments than their Korean counterparts, making them more emotional compared to other Northeast Asians.[12]

North Korean Stalinist totalitarianism does not allow private enterprises to flourish or become too powerful to challenge the Party or the state. Therefore, the situation in the North is different, but the attitudes remain the same. American negotiators and observers who work with North Korean negotiating teams in disarmament talks noted that they felt insulted

---

[9] *Ibid.*

[10] Coyner, T. (4 October 2007). "Korean Concepts of Negotiating." *Korea Times* [downloaded on 4 October 2007], available at http://www.koreatimes.co.kr/www/news/special/2007/10/175_11313.html.

[11] *Ibid.*

[12] Wang, Hui-ya Anny. (August 2016). A study of negotiating strategies in South Korea. *Journal of Literature and Art Studies*, 6(8), 953 [downloaded on 1 January 2022], available at https://pdfs.semanticscholar.org/4b55/963c764aaa41e907835c90ba597ec81acc23.pdf.

when their negotiators are met with American counterparts perceived to be lower ranking than the North Korean delegation members (especially the leader of the delegation).

- **Individualism–Collectivism**

South Korea's individualism score at 18 is the second lowest in this book, beating only Indonesia (14). Collectivism within in-groups has a long history in Korea. Dubbed the Hermit Kingdom, Korea has traditionally been defending itself against nomadic tribes and foreigners for most of its history, and thus, it has been othering non-Koreans as literally formless non-humans or 'barbarians'. This is also similar to the Chinese and Japanese, who label foreigners as *dongyi* (Chinese hanyu pinyin) and *nanban* (Japanese for 'southern barbarians'). Confucianism does not take kindly to what it considers to be 'non-civilized barbarians' (a politically incorrect view by today's standards). However, when a foreigner is accepted into a business or collegial relationship, they will be accorded the treatment relevant to their position and role.

One reason why some practitioners argue that South Korean negotiators are comparatively more individualistic than their Japanese counterparts is that individual rewards of a successfully concluded negotiation sometimes motivates some Korean negotiators to work towards sealing the business deal.[13] Because of the belief that business relationships are still relevant at the individual or group level rather than totally delegating it to company-level institutional relationships, showing modesty in individual-to-individual interactions remains important.[14] Personal commitments are needed to sustain the implementation of the contract stipulations and, for foreign partners interested to strike a deal (and maintain the deal) with the South Koreans, it is important (just like dealing with any other Northeast Asians) that they must not make their Korean counterparts feel patronized or lose face.[15]

---

[13] *Ibid.*

[14] Katz, L. (2008). "Negotiating International Business — South Korea." "Negotiating International Business — The Negotiator's Reference Guide to 50 Countries Around the World" hosted on Leadershipcrossroads.com [downloaded on 1 January 2022], available at http://www.leadershipcrossroads.com/mat/cou/southkorea.pdf.

[15] Coyner, T. (October 4, 2007). "Korean Concepts of Negotiating." *Korea Times* [downloaded on 4 October 2007], available at http://www.koreatimes.co.kr/www/news/special/2007/10/175_11313.html.

South Korean people are on friendly terms with friends and respect them as well as show them generosity and kindness, but such outreach would be withdrawn if there is no pre-existing relationship.[16] The South Korean groupist and collectivist society is such that, like Japan and China, all members of a unit take collective responsibility for other in-group members, and South Koreans (to a certain extent, the Japanese, too) differentiate clearly between in-group comrades (kind and courteous) and external parties (may even be abrasive).[17] Due to the social structure of groupism and an emphasis placed on teamwork, non-Korean negotiating teams are advised to stay engaged with the entire team and pay especial attention to the senior managers who are considered influential deciders and to avoid conflicts with them.[18]

- **Uncertainty Avoidance**

South Korea's score for this index is 85, which is the second highest in this book, coming after only Japan (85).

3. Communication

The Korean culture, like many (East) Asian cultures, is a high-context culture. Inferential skills are necessary to understanding meanings in high-context communication, but such skills are not required in low-context communication. Nonverbal communication therefore plays a larger and more significant role in high-context communication. Simple physical gestures are also important. Greeting with a bow, a handshake and eye contact are well-regarded (similar to the contemporary Chinese practice, whereas the Japanese practice a much more elaborate ritual of bowing only), along with business card exchanges (which is to be received with a respectful head-nodding acknowledgement).[19] [This contrasts with the

---

[16] Wang, Hui-ya Anny. (August 2016). A study of negotiating strategies in South Korea. *Journal of Literature and Art Studies*, 6(8), 952 [downloaded on 1 January 2022], available at https://pdfs.semanticscholar.org/4b55/963c764aaa41e907835c90ba597ec81acc23.pdf.

[17] *Ibid.*, p. 953.

[18] *Ibid.*

[19] Wang, Hui-ya Anny. (August 2016). A study of negotiating strategies in South Korea. *Journal of Literature and Art Studies*, 6(8), 953 [downloaded on 1 January 2022], available at https://pdfs.semanticscholar.org/4b55/963c764aaa41e907835c90ba597ec81acc23.pdf.

more ritualistic Japanese way of receiving the cards with both hands while bowing and then ritually reading the card's contents.] South Korean greeting is then followed by ritualistic first-meeting greetings with almost no formal business discussion in favor of harmless pleasantries, trivial housekeeping and travel anecdotes and, therefore, the first meeting is considered benign but essential for the foundation of a good business relationship.[20]

There is also a fair bit of nonverbal communication, too. South Korea negotiators often try to keep a consistent *kibun* (feeling or a stable state of mind, which has the same meaning in Japanese language, too, and is equivalent to the Chinese *qifen* or atmospherics) in their work–life routine and often avoid negativity in their conversations to maintain harmony in business relationships.[21] *Inhwa* harmony is a core element of Korea's groupist society that highlights consensus and loyalty to one's seniors who are then concerned with their juniors' well-being.[22] *Nunchi* visual sighting of nonverbal communication and understanding body language are important in Korean communication patterns, e.g. a senior colleague asking her/his junior if she/he is hungry may actually be signaling to the junior that he/she wants to eat now, therefore, if the junior replies in the negative, it would hurt the senior's *kibun*.[23] In general, East Asian conversations tend to deploy metaphoric phrases, implicit references/meanings and body language (unlike North American straight-talking).[24] Some argue that, because some Westerners (like Americans) are more individualistic and assertive than others, they run into more obstacles during negotiations.[25]

However, in one respect the Korean negotiator (both North and South) is different from their East Asian counterpart. When it comes to saying

---

[20] *Ibid.*

[21] *Ibid.*, p. 952.

[22] *Ibid.*

[23] *Ibid.*

[24] Kim, M.-J., Wang, L., & Park, M.-S. (September 21, 2015). Different levels of trust in global business negotiation: A comparative study about Canadians and Korean perspective on doing business negotiation with Chinese. *International Commerce and Information Review,* 17(3), 160 [downloaded on 1 January 2022], available at https://koreascience.kr/article/JAKO201534164960105.pdf.

[25] Graham, J. L. & Lam, N. M. (October 1, 2003). "The Chinese Negotiation." *Harvard Business Review* [downloaded on 1 January 2022], available at https://hbr.org/2003/10/the-chinese-negotiation.

"no" and rejecting your proposals or offers — they are rather direct. In this respect, it may be said that they are more individualistic or Westernized when compared with the other Northeast Asian countries.

4. Negotiation Strategies: Distributive or Integrative

4.1 *South Korea*

Like all other Northeast Asian cultures, South Korea is not a litigative society and prefers to shun legal court battles involving contract law in resolving business disagreements. Korean negotiations are conceptualized as a component part of a relationship, rather than a textualized agreement, and, in any case, a textual contract may not be considered as binding in the same way as it is in the Western societies as contracts are subjected to human relations and personal contacts.[26] Having said this, younger South Koreans who are more Westernized and educated in Western business law may exhibit different thinking.

There may also be generational differences between Korean negotiators, given that elderly South Korean negotiators tend to be more traditional and conservative while younger generations of individuals, particularly cosmopolitan Seoul residents, tend to be more adept and knowledgeable in Western business negotiation styles.[27] Westernization is not a new phenomenon, but was gradually indigenized over more than a century of contact with the West by a previously insular kingdom (widely nicknamed historically as the 'Hermit Kingdom'). Westernization started in the late 19th century, grafted onto Korean traditions and combined harmoniously until the 1940s,[28] alongside ongoing Japanese modernization of the Peninsula.

[26] Coyner, T. (October 4, 2007). "Korean Concepts of Negotiating." *Korea Times* [downloaded on 4 October 2007], available at http://www.koreatimes.co.kr/www/news/special/2007/10/175_11313.html.

[27] Katz, L. (2008). "Negotiating International Business — South Korea." *Negotiating International Business — The Negotiator's Reference Guide to 50 Countries Around the World* hosted on Leadershipcrossroads.com [downloaded on 1 January 2022], available at http://www.leadershipcrossroads.com/mat/cou/southkorea.pdf.

[28] Lee, C. and Yu, Woo-ik. (undated). "Cultural life." Britannica.com [downloaded on 1 January 2022], available at https://www.britannica.com/place/North-Korea/Cultural-life.

After the end of WWII in 1945, Westernization and modernization continued under American tutelage and support.

Like all other Northeast Asian economies, human relations based on trust and win–win scenarios (mutual benefits) are absolutely essential for the negotiation process. The element of trust is defined in the following way. It is the positive projection of the other party's intentionality which can mitigate linguistic, legal and cultural risks/complications in cross-cultural negotiations.[29] Human relations are essential for making the connections and introductions that link foreign parties with South Korean businesses to put the latter at ease in working with foreigners. Here, South Korea is pretty much in lock step with the other CJK members (China and Japan) whose business cultures are also oriented towards utilizing human relationships to resolve disagreements.

The *inhwa* harmony in South Korean culture[30] focuses on the emotional aspect of the relationship. If you build a positive emotional relationship with the South Korean negotiator and consider their *kibun* (feelings) — you will have taken the important first step towards an integrative negotiation. As a gesture of reciprocity, the South Korean negotiator is less likely to engage in distributive tactics because this will hurt your *kibun*. During negotiation, you should be prepared, and make room, for them being emotional or outspoken (you should have seen enough K dramas to appreciate such scenes). This is a form of self-expression and an opportunity for you to also lower your own inhibitions. Reinforcing your intuition or *nunchi* skills will help you greatly during such moments. That they are emotionally expressive makes the South Korean negotiators more direct and forthcoming than their other Northeast Asian counterparts. Ultimately, it is your ability to connect with the South Korean negotiator with the way you handle their and your emotions that trumps the many rounds of dining and drinking.

[29] Kim, M.-J., Wang, L., & Park, M.-S. (September 21, 2015). Different levels of trust in global business negotiation: A comparative study about Canadians and Korean perspective on doing business negotiation with Chinese. *International Commerce and Information Review*, 17(3), 158 [downloaded on 1 January 2022], available at https://koreascience.kr/article/JAKO201534164960105.pdf.

[30] Lee, B. J. & Park, J. H. (2012). East Asians' social heterogeneity: Differences in norms among Chinese, Japanese, and Korean Negotiators. *Negotiation Journal*, 28(4), 429–452. https://doi.org/10.1111/j.1571-9979.2012.00350.x.

However, negotiations which seem integrative may suddenly turn distributive, due to poor *kibun*. Because of their high Uncertainty Avoidance score (85), if the South Korean negotiator senses that their position or interest is being threatened — they will change tack. When this happens, you need to manage any seemingly unreasonable or even aggressive behavior to stay the integrative course.

Sustained continuous contact with South Korean companies is essential for maintaining the relationship even after strong foundations have been built up, so negotiators have to make time and maintain patience for such efforts and always keep in mind the idea of a long-term business relationship.[31] Therefore, non-Korean firms often designate specific South Korean employees to develop long-term relationships with other firms to build up human relations and bridge their companies with such personal connections (*ingan gwangye*, similar to Japanese *ningen kankei* or Chinese *guanxi* — in fact, the root words for all three are based on the same characters) and work with "inside sales people" in the partner's firm.[32] These bridging folks are typically junior managers facilitating the main negotiation process by lending their views on the priority points for their respective firms and second-guessing the personalities of the individuals involved (application of psychoanalysis) in the negotiations process while assessing strategically competitive offers.[33]

4.2 North Korea

Given that North and South Koreas have been separated ideologically for almost seven decades, it may be interesting to study the differences between the negotiating styles of the two Koreas. Because North Korea had been under punishing UN (United Nations) sanctions imposed on them for their nuclear weapons programs, it is effectively marginalized from the international business community and, thus, knowledge about its

---

[31] Wang, Hui-ya Anny. (August 2016). A study of negotiating strategies in South Korea. *Journal of Literature and Art Studies*, 6(8), 952 [downloaded on 1 January 2022], available at https://pdfs.semanticscholar.org/4b55/963c764aaa41e907835c90ba597ec81acc23.pdf.

[32] Coyner, T. (October 4, 2007). "Korean concepts of negotiating." *Korea Times* [downloaded on 4 October 2007], available at http://www.koreatimes.co.kr/www/news/special/2007/10/175_11313.html.

[33] *Ibid.*

business negotiations style is scant. Foreigners who have real-life negotiation experience with the North Koreans have noted that they have a predictable pattern of behavior.

On June 4, 1993, Vice Foreign Minister Kang Sok Ju from North Korea and his delegation flew to New York to participate in negotiations concerning North Korea's withdrawal from the Nuclear Non-Proliferation Treaty (NPT). At the US mission to the United Nations, the foreign minister was met by the State Department's Ken Quinones before coming into contact with Robert L. Gallucci (Assistant Secretary of State for political–military affairs).[34] Some scholars opined that Kang may have felt disrespected by the low rank of the US party meeting him, but it was simply not possible for the US to greet Kang with the equivalent protocol, given that Pyongyang had openly flouted the rules of the UN in their nuclear testing.[35] This situation was somewhat analogous to the South Koreans feeling slighted at negotiations if their non-Korean counterparts arranged parties of unequivalent ranks to sit at the negotiation table.

In hindsight, some analysts felt that negotiating with North Koreans had been over-informed by negotiating experiences with Cold War-era Communist China at Panmunjom during 1951–1953 and literature like *How Communists Negotiate* by Admiral C. Turner Joy (the head negotiator in the armistice talks).[36] Turner Joy's first-hand experience in North Korean negotiating styles may have overemphasized the strong features of the North Korean negotiation style while demonizing their intents.[37] It highlighted North Korean tendencies for force-feeding the agenda with space for only minimal one-sided concessions, ramping up psych warfare away from the negotiations, constant delays for fatiguing the opposing party, reneging on promises, raising distractions from the main items of discussion, practising truth denial or avoidance and carrying out deliberate re-interpretation of agreed items.[38]

---

[34] Snyder, S. (January 8, 2003). "Understanding North Korean Negotiating Behavior." USIP website [downloaded on 1 January 2022], available at https://www.usip.org/press/2003/01/understanding-north-korean-negotiating-behavior.

[35] *Ibid.*

[36] *Ibid.*

[37] *Ibid.*

[38] *Ibid.*

Because of hardened and fossilized positions over time, North Koreans began to favor a zero-sum game approach to negotiations, often with an attitude analogous to a battle for legitimacy (short of fighting a war). Kim Do Tae's (Korea Institute of National Unification) research, a study covering more than 20 years of inter-Korean dialogue, indicated North Korean negotiating objectives are not present at the table but are incidental and primed towards shoring up their global status or putting down South Koreans.[39] Turner Joy indicated that Chinese and Korean cultures appeared to have a stronger influence on negotiating styles than the ideology of communism, although it is difficult to delineate between Chinese and North Korean influences, given the Chinese led much of the armistice talks.[40]

The US–Democratic People's Republic of Korea (DPRK) Summits in Hanoi in 2019 and the earlier one in Singapore indicated that the North Koreans negotiated with high stakes. After the US did not accede to Pyongyang's position to remove substantial economic sanctions levied on Pyongyang since 2017, North Korean Foreign Minister (FM) Ri Yong Ho argued:

> … as we take steps toward denuclearization, the most important issue is security, but we thought it would be more burdensome for the US to take military-related measures, which is why we saw partial lifting of sanctions as corresponding action.[41]

This rationale illuminates Pyongyang's previous calculation: that partial sanctions relief for partial denuclearization would be an acceptable outcome.[42]

The failure of the summits suggests that North Korean negotiating behavior has been insisting on getting concessions on the economic sanctions while justifying its provocative actions towards what it considers as the cessation of US hostilities, resumption of nuclear program and

---

[39] *Ibid.*

[40] *Ibid.*

[41] Sangsoo, L. & Villa, R. (December 21, 2021). "North Korea's Signaling on Nuclear Weapons and Negotiations." 38 North [downloaded on 21 December 2021], available at https://www.38north.org/2021/12/north-koreas-signaling-on-nuclear-weapons-and-negotiations/.

[42] *Ibid.*

cutting off talks known as a "power-for-power" policy.[43] This is a useful lesson picked up when it comes to any state-to-state or state-to-business negotiations in terms of increasing leverage and pursuing equilibrium against opponents with stronger positions.

However, experts observed that it was more sophisticated than just the "power-for-power" principle and includes a "goodwill-for-goodwill" policy as well, opening the door just enough for resuming dialogue with the US under conditions favorable to the regime, prompting the US to offer a concrete package.[44] While this wait for the perceived right conditions is ongoing, North Korea appears to keep up a position of strength. Ri Pyong Chol, vice chairperson of the Central Committee of the Workers' Party of Korea (WPK), reiterated the sustained nuclear program tests were scheduled North Korean "self-defense" exercises, in effect normalizing the military capabilities of the country[45] to keep up pressure on the other negotiating party.[46]

Sustained pressure meant, some experts opined, that the Biden administration's talk offers "anywhere, anytime" were interestingly perceived by North Korea's Choe Son Hui, first Vice Foreign Minister, as a "delaying-time trick." All these bear fruitful lessons for any potential economic or business negotiations with North Koreans.[47] They are likely to sustain a position of strength throughout the negotiations for maximum pressure while demanding nothing less than a favorable tangible offer from the other party.

Any negotiator with North Koreans thus needs to be able to analyze and understand the leveraging and balancing of the power-for-power and goodwill-for-goodwill strategies. In fact, the North Korean openly declare such strategies up front, as Choe Son Hui articulated to North Korean state-owned media: "We already clarified that we will counter the US on the principle of power for power and goodwill for goodwill."[48] This indicates that North Korean negotiations require cajoling with parallel,

---

[43] *Ibid.*

[44] *Ibid.*

[45] *Ibid.*

[46] *Ibid.*

[47] *Ibid.*

[48] *Ibid.*

pragmatic concessions for confidence-building signaling to open the gateway to initiate a negotiation based on trust building, and one has to bear in mind such parallel secondary concessions are only valid for starting talks and not sustaining them. Negotiators call this "a baseline of trust and mutual confidence necessary for further negotiations."[49]

5. Concession-making & Hardball Tactics

Experiential precedents have a persuasive impact on ongoing negotiations, while constant reminders of long-term benefits and commitments to the relationship remind South Korean negotiators that one is willing to maintain that relationship based on familiarity, mutual respect and trust.[50] Like the Chinese culture, "saving face" (*chemyeon* in Korean, *mianzi* in Chinese and *mentsu* in Japanese) is important and therefore, maintaining relationships with a friendly disposition and practicing self-restraint in emotional discharge without embarrassing the other parties is crucial. Introducing abrasive topics must be done with great care in the private realm while maintaining respect, humility, patience and courtesy for the other party and avoiding critical comments about one's rivals.[51]

On the other hand, South Korean business negotiations place more premium on the trust factor. For some scholars, the element of trust reveals the formerly dormant inclination for cooperation hidden by security covers of defensive-aggressive behavior and thus trust is a crucial element for developing relationships in negotiations (including cross-cultural ones).[52] In South Korea, establishing trust over time in negotiations is extremely important as discussed throughout this chapter.

---

[49] *Ibid.*

[50] Katz, L. (2008). "Negotiating International Business — South Korea." *Negotiating International Business — The Negotiator's Reference Guide to 50 Countries around the World* hosted on Leadershipcrossroads.com [downloaded on 1 January 2022], available at http://www.leadershipcrossroads.com/mat/cou/southkorea.pdf.

[51] *Ibid.*

[52] Kim, M.-J., Wang, L., & Park, M.-S. (September 21, 2015). Different levels of trust in global business negotiation: A comparative study about Canadians and Korean perspective on doing business negotiation with Chinese. *International Commerce and Information Review,* 17(3), 158 [downloaded on 1 January 2022], available at https://koreascience.kr/article/JAKO201534164960105.pdf.

The South Korean negotiators are tenacious (and their Northern counterparts, more so) and will usually not make much concessions in a distributive setting. They may delay or prolong the negotiation to extract concessions from you. In fact, using brinksmanship in order to ascertain your bottom-line is not uncommon.[53] In sum, among the countries discussed in this book, the concession-making behavior of this Asian negotiator is likely the most oppressive of all.

When it comes to hardball tactics, there may not be much differentiation between the North and South Korean negotiators as they share fundamental cultural characteristics; differing mainly in political ideologies. Thus, you may encounter the use of aggression, intimidation and deception.

North Korean negotiation tactics are designed for negotiating against much stronger entities. Despite being weaker, North Korea has shown that they can have a more favorable outcome than anticipated by manipulating the pace and speed of negotiations.[54] They even took care to score diplomatic victories by making demands in exchange for concessions in the pace of negotiations, e.g. expelling Japan from the negotiations process while threatening on–off relations with South Korea as a chip in extracting concessions.[55] Thus, hardball manipulation is a core concept in negotiations with North Koreans.

The divergence of North Korean culture away from traditional Korean culture as a whole is found in the influx of communist ideology that reinforces class consciousness and spreads the superiority and independence of Korean culture.[56] In the case of North Korea, ideological factors have influenced the way North Koreans behave, especially in

---

[53] Snyder, S. (1999). Patterns of negotiation in a South Korean cultural context. *Asian Survey, 39*(3), 394–417. https://doi.org/10.2307/3021205.

[54] Zhou, I. F. & van Wyk, J.-A. (August 10, 2021). North Korea's entrapment and time delay tactics during nuclear negotiations. *Asian Journal of Peacebuilding, 9*(2), 417 [downloaded on 10 August 2021], available at https://ipus.snu.ac.kr/eng/wp-content/uploads/sites/2/2021/11/09_Ian-Fleming-Zhou-and-van-Wyk.pdf.

[55] *Ibid.*

[56] Lee, Chan & Yu, Woo-ik. (undated). "Cultural life." Britannica.com [downloaded on 1 January 2022], available at https://www.britannica.com/place/North-Korea/Cultural-life.

international political negotiations. Due to the authoritarian nature of the North Korean state, even private sector negotiations are not entirely non-governmental, given the one-party system that extends its tentacles into all aspects of reality and life in North Korea. The North Korean state is self-aware of its weaker position in international negotiations. The state has thus developed negotiation techniques to deal with strong adversaries.

The North Koreans use "smokescreen" techniques quite easily. This was often applied in the denuclearization negotiations. And some experts argue that Pyongyang manipulated South Korean appeasement to blunt the directness and strength of US negotiation approaches. Some US experts consider this as an entrapment that South Korean negotiators fell for when the North Koreans manipulated their South Korean counterparts to constrain US actions whenever discussions centered on imposing trade sanctions. The US has consistently stuck to a position of CVID (Complete Verifiable Irreversible Denuclearization), but Pyongyang simply refuses to give up its nuclear weapons program as it sees that program as an ultimate guarantee of the existence of its statehood. This effectively substituted the sticks of nukes for the carrots of lifting of economic sanctions. Smokescreen techniques involve using time delays to mask North Koreans' true intentions by making false statements amounting to a willingness to change to greater cooperation if certain conditionalities are fulfilled (when there are no intentions to do so).[57]

6. Role of Women

Korea is a male-dominated society. The number of women in its business leadership positions remains one of the lowest among the developed economies. This applies even to North Korea where socialism was supposedly able to level the playing field for women.

---

[57] Zhou, I. F. & van Wyk, J.-A. (August 10, 2021). North Korea's entrapment and time delay tactics during nuclear negotiations. *Asian Journal of Peacebuilding, 9*(2), 415 [downloaded on 10 August 2021], available at https://ipus.snu.ac.kr/eng/wp-content/uploads/sites/2/2021/11/09_Ian-Fleming-Zhou-and-van-Wyk.pdf.

Global Gender Gap Report 2022 INSIGHT REPORT JULY 2022			
EAST ASIA & the PACIFIC	**Rank**		
Country	**Regional (19)**	**Global (146)**	**Score**
Philippines	2	19	0.783
Singapore	4	49	0.734
Thailand	8	79	0.709
Vietnam	9	83	0.705
Indonesia	10	92	0.697
Korea (South)	**12**	**99**	**0.689**
China	13	102	0.682
Malaysia	14	103	0.681
Japan	19	116	0.650

Source: "Global Gender Gap Report 2022." World Economic Forum. July 13, 2022. https://www.weforum.org/reports/global-gender-gap-report-2022/digest.

While South Korea falls behind Southeast Asian countries (with the exception of Malaysia) in both regional and global ranking, it is ahead of the other Northeast Asian countries. The reasons attributed to South Korea's leading ranking in Northeast Asia is generally attributed to its successful economic globalization that resulted in higher women participation in the economy, gender-neutral education policies, changing societal mindsets, amongst other reasons.

In terms of gender equality, some researchers argue that the separation of gender roles in the workforce is still entrenched in people's mindsets and is resistant to progress from the traditional perception of the female role in housework. Some elderly Korean husbands call their other halves Djip-saram (translated as the 'home person' doing voluntary household chores like looking after kids) while the men are termed *Bakat-Yangban* (the male outside the house).[58] The word *Yangban* generally means noble or aristocratic in Korean language. The Japanese similarly have

---

[58]Yang, H. (October 25, 2021). "Gender equality: Korea has Come a Long Way, but There is More Work to Do." Organization of Economic Cooperation and Development (OECD) website [downloaded on 25 October 2021] , available at https://www.oecd.org/country/korea/thematic-focus/gender-equality-korea-has-come-a-long-way-but-there-is-more-work-to-do-8bb81613/

almost stopped using *kannai* or domestic person in their spoken language, preferring to use *tsuma* or wife instead. Like in other Northeast Asian Confucian states, the status of women in South Korea is changing fast. With accelerated industrialization and birth-control campaigns, the fertility rate of the South Korean population declined from 4.5 in 1970 to 1.6 in 1989 with nuclear families bearing one or two kids becoming the norm, increasing the gender-blind education opportunities for them, closing the education gender gap and propelling some educated women into white collar executive/professional jobs.[59]

North Korean demographics have fared even worse due to mass starvation, international economic sanctions, lack of market forces in the agricultural sector and dogmatic adherence to *juche,* self-reliance. Its population today is only half the size of its southern counterpart. North Korean women's social status is less influenced by demographics. It has more to do with ideological moulding of minds. North Korean state's education trajectory went in a different direction. Soviet-style re-education programmed individuals to follow party lines, restricting the private sphere of everyday life and individual rights while communist self-reliance or *juche* created austere conditions for livelihoods.[60] Socialism also meant that North Korean women had their status elevated, given that totalitarianism is also gender-blind and party policies applied equally to all theoretically.

South Korea, on the other hand, was fully vested into the international system. As the South Korean economy internationalized, South Korean women's participation rate in the workforce expanded from 49% in 1990 to 60% in 2019 (majority in service jobs), leading to greater gender equity in the society and changing mindsets, too.[61] South Korean women's participation rate in higher education expanded faster than their male counterparts' since 2013 and, in 2020, women's enrolment rate was 71.3% (5% higher than male enrolment), becoming a crucial factor in bringing about

[59] *Ibid.*
[60] Lee, Chan & Yu, Woo-ik. (undated), "Cultural life." Britannica.com [downloaded on 1 January 2022], available at https://www.britannica.com/place/North-Korea/Cultural-life.
[61] Yang, H. (October 25, 2021). "Gender Equality: Korea has Come a Long Way, but There is More Work to Do." Organization of Economic Cooperation and Development (OECD) website [downloaded on 25 October 2021], available at https://www.oecd.org/country/korea/thematic-focus/gender-equality-korea-has-come-a-long-way-but-there-is-more-work-to-do-8bb81613/.

gender equality in contemporary South Korea.[62] While there is a gender difference in high school educational participation among individuals aged 55 and above, it does not exist among South Korean youths, though the next gender parity challenge is in salaries in employment.[63]

In terms of salaries, South Korean women receive 33.3% lower than their male colleagues on average, but for South Koreans in their twenties with similar educational qualifications and years of working experience, there is insignificant or even negative gender pay gap.[64] In addition, above 60% of South Korean teachers (including varsity academics) are females, while females in government committees more than doubled from 2010 to 2020, going beyond 40%.[65] The number of women ministers also went beyond 33% in 2020 and the number of women business leaders hit 1.4 million (making up approximately 40% in 2017).[66] In contrast, austere living conditions meant that North Korean women have fewer corporate opportunities as their South Korean counterparts. Given that all North Koreans (other than the Pyongyang elites) regardless of gender are equally affected by the harsh economic conditions in their country, any business negotiations with the North Korean state is likely to prioritize economic benefits for the country.

Despite the gender achievements and emancipation in South Korea, some argue that the older generations of Koreans (including those in senior management) tend to be more gender-conscious. In the past, South Korean women were allocated the role of managing large, extended family units, therefore, senior management in some companies have been cautious in sending women for negotiations. This is especially in the case of negotiating with more conservative elderly senior partners, although, in overcoming corporate resistance to their advancement, more South Korean women have become successful entrepreneurs, leading to changes in gender rela-

---

[62] *Ibid.*

[63] *Ibid.*

[64] *Ibid.*

[65] Yang, H. (October 25, 2021). "Gender Equality: Korea has Come a Long Way, but There is More Work to Do." Organization of Economic Cooperation and Development (OECD) website [downloaded on 25 October 2021], available at https://www.oecd.org/country/korea/thematicfocus/gender-equality-korea-has-come-a-long-way-but-there-is-more-work-to-do-8bb81613/.

[66] *Ibid.*

tions in South Korea.[67] In comparative terms, the South Korean society is less masculine than Japan as it appears to score higher in the area of feminine values like 'working in order to live', managerial consensus, valuing equality, solidarity, quality work lives and conflict resolution through compromise/negotiation, supportive approach towards information provision to stakeholders, public relations, investor relations/marketing.[68]

It may also be interesting to note that, at the time when this chapter was written in 2022, a significant number of young Korean men were revolting against what they deemed to be an unfair playing field for them in the context of what they perceived as the excesses of feminism. They felt demasculinized as jobs were perceived to have been taken away from them due to political-correctness and wokeness pressures exerted by feminists advocating gender equality at the workplace. And, in their view, all this was happening at a time when they felt oppressed by high taxation and costs of living. The consequence of this revolt was voting in a conservative South Korean president who campaigned on promises to listen to their voices and address the social concerns of young men. Given that this is a new development, it remains to be seen how this will impact gender aspects of business negotiation and other business practices.

7. Intermediary/Interpreter

Negotiations are generally classifiable into three parts: antecedent phase (pre-negotiation stage and preparations), the concurrent phase (ongoing process), and the consequent phase (post-negotiation stage) and negotiation behavior throughout all three phases can affect their outcome.[69] Entertainment activities are seen as very important rituals in

---

[67] Wang, Hui-ya Anny. (August 2016). A study of negotiating strategies in South Korea. *Journal of Literature and Art Studies*, 6(8), 952 [downloaded on 1 January 2022], available at https://pdfs.semanticscholar.org/4b55/963c764aaa41e907835c90ba597ec81acc23.pdf.

[68] Lee, K.-H. & Herold, D. M. (2006). Cultural relevance in corporate sustainability management: A comparison between Korea and Japan. *Asian Journal of Sustainability and Social Responsibility*, 1, 14 [downloaded on 1 January 2022], available at https://ajssr.springeropen.com/track/pdf/10.1186/s41180-016-0003-2.pdf.

[69] Sun, M. (December 2009). A comparison of business negotiation behavior between Korea and China. *International Journal of Business and Management*, 4(12), 212 [downloaded on 1 January 2022], available at https://pdfs.semanticscholar.org/ccfc/201493ae2e5ced61467653696c4ecb34571d.pdf.

the pre-negotiation antecedent phase. Instead of profit-making to the exclusion of all other factors, South Koreans prefer to have sustainable growth and good personal relationships and one way to break the ice with them is through entertainment activities (such as drinking parties and enjoying the moment).[70] Given that South Korean negotiators tend to articulate vague terms, foreign negotiating teams may wish to reinforce their understanding of their Korean counterparts' articulations by framing those utterances in their own terms and exchanging written notes for verification.[71]

Using interpretors and constantly clarifying terms that are vague are very useful tools for a successful negotiation while not rushing to settle the negotiations within a short time (even when one is on a short business travel schedule as impatience is seen as a weakness) and mitigating any expectations of fast conclusions to negotiations.[72] The element of time consciousness differs between East Asians and North Americans. North Americans tend to conceptualize time as a finite resource and a highly valuable commodity, much more than South Korea or China, and this would then impact on whether communication styles are straightforward, patiently tolerant of time expended or contextually based on atmospherics and negotiation conditions.[73] Having patience in going through a long-drawn decision-making culture (especially in negotiations with *chaebol* or conglomerates) and ensuring that no vital points are given up easily, the foreign negotiator can inform the South Korean partner of the flight schedule in advance for greater potential success.[74]

---

[70] Coyner, T. (October 4, 2007). "Korean Concepts of Negotiating." *Korea Times* [downloaded on 4 October 2007], available at http://www.koreatimes.co.kr/www/news/special/2007/10/175_11313.html.

[71] *Ibid.*

[72] *Ibid.*

[73] Kim, M.-J., Wang, L., & Park, M.-S. (September 21, 2015). Different levels of trust in global business negotiation: A comparative study about Canadians and Korean perspective on doing business negotiation with Chinese. *International Commerce and Information Review,* 17(3), 160 [downloaded on 1 January 2022], available at https://koreascience.kr/article/JAKO201534164960105.pdf.

[74] Coyner, T. (October 4, 2007). "Korean Concepts of Negotiating." *Korea Times* [downloaded on 4 October 2007], available at http://www.koreatimes.co.kr/www/news/special/2007/10/175_11313.html.

Sometimes, even an external third-party facilitator, a paid translator or a consultant can step in to help out with the negotiations.[75] In the case of a breakdown in negotiations, non-Korean negotiators are encouraged not to feel despair but to create a positive atmosphere for future possibilities. In fact, this is the general advice given to all negotiators dealing with Northeast Asians. Given that the South Korean business landscape is not a vast community and business groups are tightly-knit, the preservation of one's standing in such a market is important for future ventures plus the creation of future enemies needs to be avoided at all costs.[76]

8. Time, Timelines, Timeliness

Based on all that has been discussed, we can expect that negotiating with Korean negotiators is going to take much time and patience. Within South Korean conceptualization of business negotiations, there is future-orientation to a contract. However, one differentiation with Japan is that while Japanese negotiation cultures may develop long-term relationships over time, South Koreans prefer that the bonds be forged before initiating business interactions as both sides need to be at ease with the relationship.[77] Even after gaining the trust of the South Korean business partner, a caveat is that they may not automatically trust others from the same company and so, because of this, the same representatives to the negotiations have to be maintained, otherwise any changes in personnel may mean restarting the whole negotiation process altogether.[78]

Trust appears to take a backseat to maximum manipulation for optimal advantage in the North Korean case. Observers of North Korean negotiation tactics noted that weaker parties in a negotiation can be influenced by any pre-conceived notions of the structural outcome of negotiations by utilizing strategies such as time delay tactics alongside entrapment. Components of such tactics can include: retarding negotiations to the

---

[75] Ibid.
[76] Ibid.
[77] Katz, L. (2008). "Negotiating International Business — South Korea." "Negotiating International Business — The Negotiator's Reference Guide to 50 Countries Around the World" hosted on Leadershipcrossroads.com [downloaded on 1 January 2022], available at http://www.leadershipcrossroads.com/mat/cou/southkorea.pdf.
[78] Ibid.

maximum, preventing a final agreement, delaying negotiations by diversion, lengthening negotiations until an unrelated environmental or domestic change happens and tiring out negotiators until they give concessions (entrapping).[79] Time delays can only make an impact if the other side's negotiators do not possess any viable alternative and North Korea's decision to delay stages of the nuclear disarmament negotiations is a good example of the strategic use of this principle.[80] North Korean state negotiators utilized the delay to cause frictions in the US alliance pretending to be seeking a better alternative to the one currently proposed while laying the fault with the United States as being unwilling to cooperate.[81] Therefore, using time delay tactics, North Korea managed to keep their nuclear weaponry agenda intact.

Bibliography

Coyner, T. (October 4, 2007). "Korean Concepts of Negotiating." *Korea Times* [downloaded on 4 October 2007], available at http://www.koreatimes.co.kr/www/news/special/2007/10/175_11313.html.

Graham, J. L. & Lam, N. M. (October 1, 2003). "The Chinese Negotiation." *Harvard Business Review* [downloaded on 1 January 2022], available at https://hbr.org/2003/10/the-chinese-negotiation.

Hofstede Insights. (2022). "Compare Countries." Hofstede Insights [downloaded on 1 January 2022], available at https://www.hofstede-insights.com/product/compare-countries/.

Katz, L. (2008). "Negotiating International Business — South Korea." "Negotiating International Business — The Negotiator's Reference Guide to 50 Countries around the World" hosted on Leadershipcrossroads.com [downloaded on 1 January 2022], available at http://www.leadershipcrossroads.com/mat/cou/southkorea.pdf.

Kim, E. M. (April 2017). Korea's evolving business — Government relationship. In J. Page & F. Tarp (Eds.), *The Practice of Industrial Policy: Government-Business Coordination in Africa and East Asia* (Chapter 6). (UK: Oxford

---

[79] Zhou, I. F. & van Wyk, J.-A. (August 10, 2021). North Korea's entrapment and time delay tactics during nuclear negotiations. *Asian Journal of Peacebuilding*, 9(2), 411 [downloaded on 10 August 2021], available at https://ipus.snu.ac.kr/eng/wp-content/uploads/sites/2/2021/11/09_Ian-Fleming-Zhou-and-van-Wyk.pdf.

[80] *Ibid.*, p. 416.

[81] *Ibid.*

University Press), 2017, [downloaded on 1 January 2022], available at https://academic.oup.com/book/26495/chapter/194950127 (un-paginated electronic copy).

Kim, M.-J., Wang, L., & Park, M.-S. (September 21, 2015). "Different levels of trust in global business negotiation: A comparative study about Canadians and Korean perspective on doing business negotiation with Chinese. *International Commerce and Information Review*, 17(3), 155–176 [downloaded on 1 January 2022], available at https://koreascience.kr/article/JAKO201534164960105.pdf.

Lee, Chan & Yu, Woo-ik. (undated). "Cultural life." Britannica.com [downloaded on 1 January 2022], available at https://www.britannica.com/place/North-Korea/Cultural-life.

Lee, K.-H. & Herold, D. M. (2006). Cultural relevance in corporate sustainability management: A comparison between Korea and Japan. *Journal of Sustainability and Social Responsibility*, 1, 1–21 [downloaded on 1 January 2022], available at https://ajssr.springeropen.com/track/pdf/10.1186/s41180-016-0003-2.pdf.

Snyder, S. (January 8, 2003). "Understanding North Korean negotiating behavior. USIP website [downloaded on 1 January 2022], available at https://www.usip.org/press/2003/01/understanding-north-korean-negotiating-behavior.

Sun, M. (December 2009). A comparison of business negotiation behavior between Korea and China. *International Journal of Business and Management*, 4(12), 212–218 [downloaded on 1 January 2022], available at https://pdfs.semanticscholar.org/ccfc/201493ae2e5ced61467653696c4ecb34571d.pdf.

Wang, Hui-ya Anny. (August 2016). A study of negotiating strategies in South Korea. *Journal of Literature and Art Studies*, 6(8), 951–957 [downloaded on 1 January 2022], available at https://pdfs.semanticscholar.org/4b55/963c764aaa41e907835c90ba597ec81acc23.pdf.

Yang, H. (October 25, 2021). "Gender Equality: Korea has Come a Long Way, but There is More Work to Do." Organization of Economic Cooperation and Development (OECD) website [downloaded on 25 October 2021], available at https://www.oecd.org/country/korea/thematic-focus/gender-equality-korea-has-come-a-long-way-but-there-is-more-work-to-do-8bb81613/.

Zhou, I. F. & van Wyk, J.-A. (August 10, 2021). North Korea's entrapment and time delay tactics during nuclear negotiations. *Asian Journal of Peacebuilding*, 9(2), 411–426 [downloaded on 10 August 2021], available at https://ipus.snu.ac.kr/eng/wp-content/uploads/sites/2/2021/11/09_Ian-Fleming-Zhou-and-van-Wyk.pdf.

Korea Quiz

1. South Korea was one of the dynamic four _____ (sometimes known as the four dragon) economies that studied and indigenized Japan's state-led economic development from the 1960s to the 1990s and emerged as a major economic power. Fill in the blank.
   A. porcupine
   B. leopard
   C. tiger
   D. snake

2. The Korean word for negotiation is '_____'. Fill in the blank.
   A. saram-ei
   B. hyeobsang
   C. hyundai
   D. arirang

3. In order to build up South Korea's economy, the state-centered Park Chung-hee administration decided to nurture large Korean conglomerates known as _____characterized by their sizable capital and technological prowess in heavy industries that immediately differentiated them from the Small and Medium-Sized Enterprises (SMEs). Fill in the blank.
   A. zaibatsu
   B. jituan
   C. keiretsu
   D. chaebols

4. Other than Confucianism, various other forms of influences have exerted their hold on Korean culture. Additionally, Korean culture as a whole has been influenced by shamanism, Buddhism and Daoism hybridized with continual foreign influences particularly from China, and the Koreans have indigenized these influences to build their own Korean identity, language and traditional customs. Is this general characterization true or false?
   A. True
   B. False

5. _____is the abbreviation of contemporary Korean Popular Culture. Fill in the blank.
   A. Bubblegumpop
   B. Mandopop
   C. K-pop
   D. J-pop

6. North Korean Stalinist totalitarianism does not allow private enterprises to flourish or become too powerful to challenge the Party or the state. Is this true or false?
   A. True
   B. False

7. Korea was traditionally dubbed the _____Kingdom. Fill in the blank.
   A. Middle
   B. Hermit
   C. Sunshine
   D. Middle Earth

8. The South Korean groupist and collectivist society means that, like Japan and China, all members of a unit take collective responsibility for other in-group members. Is this general characterization true or false?
   A. True
   B. False

9. _____ harmony is a core element of Korea's groupist society that highlights consensus and loyalty to one's seniors who are then concerned with their juniors' well-being. Fill in the blank.
   A. Inyoung
   B. Innin
   C. Inhwa
   D. Hwasong

10. If you build a positive emotional relationship with the South Korean negotiator and consider their _____(feelings) — you will have taken the important first step towards an integrative negotiation. Fill in the blank.
    A. kiki
    B. kinmen
    C. keemun
    D. kibun

Answer Bank

1. C
2. B
3. D
4. A
5. C
6. A
7. B
8. A
9. C
10. D

Chapter 5

The Malaysian Negotiator

The Bahasa Melayu word for negotiation is *Berunding*.

1. The Environment

Malaysia is an important and outstanding stakeholder in economic regionalism. Within the Association of Southeast Asian Nations (ASEAN), in the ASEAN Free Trade Area (AFTA) made up of Thailand, Malaysia, Brunei, Indonesia, Vietnam, Cambodia, Laos and Myanmar, the rapid economic development of Malaysia stands out along with that of Thailand and Singapore (the leading economies in that region). AFTA has become part of a wider regional initiative with the inclusion of three Northeast Asian regional powers (CJK or China, Japan, Korea) that has evolved into the more macro architecture of Regional Comprehensive Economic Partnership (RCEP). It is currently the largest free trade pact in the world.

Malaysia is involved in the regional initiatives of the US-centered IPEF (Indo-Pacific Economic Framework), Japan (and Australia)-facilitated CPTPP (Comprehensive and Progressive Agreement for Trans Pacific Partnership) and many other pro-trade agreements, which makes the country an important economic player in the region. Malaysia is also part of the fast-growing ASEAN Economic Community (AEC), the second most developed economic regional organization after the European Union (EU) consisting of the 10 member states of ASEAN (Indonesia, Malaysia, the Philippines, Singapore, Thailand, Brunei that joined in 1985 and

CLMV or Cambodia–Laos–Myanmar and Vietnam that joined in the 1990s). At the point of this writing, East Timor or Timor Leste which obtained observer status in late 2022 may potentially become the 11th member. This is a fast-growing region with net population growth and likelihood of becoming a dynamic consumer market with more than 600 million consumers.

As Malaysia is on the verge of becoming a developed economy (the stated target formulated by the veteran politician Mahathir Mohammad's former administration was Wawasan 2020, but this goal was slightly detracted by the COVID-19 pandemic), changes are happening to the Malaysian economic structure. Along with moving up the value-added chain in the global economy, Malaysia is slowly transitioning to the service industry, therefore sales and other industrial sectoral negotiations will become increasingly important, along with the boom in consulting and tourism services in the 21st century.[1] This also means that understanding the cultural aspects of business negotiations with Malaysian businesses will increase in importance.

2. Culture

Malaysia is a multicultural society with Malays in the majority (58% of the populace), followed by the Chinese (24%) and Indians (8%),[2] out of a population of approximately 24 million,[3] and their worldviews and

---

[1] Chang, L.-C. C. (2020). "A Comparison of Taiwan and Malaysia in Negotiation Styles." Universiti Utara Malaysia Course Franchise Business Management (FBPME3023) studoc website [downloaded on 1 January 2023], available at https://www.studocu.com/my/document/universiti-utara-malaysia/franchise-business-management/a-comparison-of-taiwan-and-malaysia-in-negotiation-styles/21649420.

[2] Katz, L. (March 2008). "Negotiating International Business — Malaysia." *Negotiating International Business — The Negotiator's Reference Guide to 50 Countries around the World and Mount San Antonio College* [downloaded on 1 January 2023], available at https://instruction2.mtsac.edu/rjagodka/BUSM_51_Project/Negotiating/Malaysia.pdf, p. 1.

[3] Chang, L.-C. C. (2020). "A Comparison of Taiwan and Malaysia in Negotiation Styles." Universiti Utara Malaysia Course Franchise Business Management (FBPME3023) studoc website [downloaded on 1 January 2023], available at https://www.studocu.com/my/document/universiti-utara-malaysia/franchise-business-management/a-comparison-of-taiwan-and-malaysia-in-negotiation-styles/21649420.

outlooks are civilizationally distinct from each other. Historically, Malaysia received cultural influences from the Islamic, Chinese and Indian civilizations, which accounts for Malaysia's strong strain of cultural diversity.[4] The indigenous Malays (*bumiputeras or bumiputras* translated literally into "sons of the soil") hold majority political power and they practice the state religion of Islam, thus imposing Syriah or Sharia Islamic laws and lifestyle choices (like halal cuisines) on the Muslim community (which also includes Arabic and Indian Muslims in addition to the Malays).

Religion plays a significant role among many groups within the Malaysian society. Personal space and sometimes Islamic decorum lead to an avoidance of physical touch (other than shaking hands), especially touching the head (including cute kids if you meet them) as both Muslims and Hindus consider the left hand ritually unclean and to be avoided.[5] In addition to physical contact taboos, there are some cultural values which bind Malays together. Some studies on Malaysian value systems indicated that Malays emphasize respect for others, Islam, humility, indirectness and courtesy; and ethnic Chinese valued diligence, perseverance, academic pursuits, financial gains and family; while Malaysian Indians held a fear of divinity and prioritized their sense of belonging, kinship, family and loyalty.[6]

According to the World Economic Forum (2016), Malaysia has the third largest Chinese population in the world residing outside of China.[7]

---

[4] *Ibid.*

[5] Katz, L. (March 2008). "Negotiating International Business — Malaysia." Negotiating International Business — The Negotiator's Reference Guide to 50 Countries around the World and Mount San Antonio College [downloaded on 1 January 2023], available at https://instruction2.mtsac.edu/rjagodka/BUSM_51_Project/Negotiating/Malaysia.pdf, p. 2.

[6] Awang, S., Maros, M., & Ibrahim, N. (May 2012). Malay values in intercultural communication. *International Journal of Social Science and Humanity*, 2(3), 201 [downloaded on 1 January 2023], available at http://www.ijssh.org/papers/96-CH219.

[7] *"Where Are the Largest Chinese Populations Outside of China? | Thailand or Indonesia: Which Country Has the Largest Chinese Population? | By World Economic Forum | Facebook."* https://www.facebook.com/worldeconomicforum/videos/where-are-the-largest-chinese-populations-outside-of-china/10153549858561479/. (Accessed November 8, 2022).

Hofstede's Cultural Dimensions

• **Power Distance**

In terms of "Power Distance" or the "acceptance of unequal power distribution in an organization within a society,"[8] social hierarchy is important in Malaysian negotiations' culture and it reflects one's social status, rank in life and seniority. Therefore, most leaders in negotiation teams are typically seniors and Malaysian culture tends to treat seniors with respect (and that also means avoiding smoking and wearing sunglasses in front of them as a mark of respect).[9]

Some studies have indicated that Malaysia has the highest ranking Power Distance Index and cultures with high power distance based on gender, race, seniority, academic performance, birth, achievements, family status, etc.[10] Nonverbal communication in Malaysia is sensitized to social hierarchy and rank. Some body language expressions can denote certain nuances that can affect perceptions of social rank and seniority. Sucking in air through the gaps in the teeth indicates negativity while maintaining constant eye contact is offensive and should be avoided as far as possible, one should therefore look downwards when interacting with elderly or/and senior-ranking Malaysians.[11] Higher power distance index ranking translates to greater acceptance that superiors or seniors have more power than

[8] Chang, L.-C. C. (2020). "A Comparison of Taiwan and Malaysia in Negotiation Styles." Universiti Utara Malaysia Course Franchise Business Management (FBPME3023) studoc website [downloaded on 1 January 2023], available at https://www.studocu.com/my/document/universiti-utara-malaysia/franchise-business-management/a-comparison-of-taiwan-and-malaysia-in-negotiation-styles/21649420.

[9] Katz, L. (March 2008). "Negotiating International Business — Malaysia." Negotiating International Business — The Negotiator's Reference Guide to 50 Countries around the World and Mount San Antonio College, p. 1 [downloaded on 1 January 2023], available at https://instruction2.mtsac.edu/rjagodka/BUSM_51_Project/Negotiating/Malaysia.pdf.

[10] Hashim, H. M. (2010). "International Negotiation Styles: A Perspective of Malaysian Diplomats." CORE (Connecting Repositories) Research Service, p. 50 [downloaded on 1 January 2023], available at https://core.ac.uk/download/pdf/56361749.pdf.

[11] Katz, L. (March 2008). "Negotiating International Business — Malaysia." Negotiating International Business — The Negotiator's Reference Guide to 50 Countries Around the World and Mount San Antonio College, p. 2 [downloaded on 1 January 2023], available at https://instruction2.mtsac.edu/rjagodka/BUSM_51_Project/Negotiating/Malaysia.pdf.

their subordinates lower down in the social hierarchy[12] and body language plays a part in conveying this acceptance.

Ultimately, like in the rest of East Asia, the "face" factor is important here, therefore avoid causing undue embarrassment to the other party, damage to their reputation and social status by remaining poker-faced, self-restraining, tactful and diplomatic throughout the negotiations.[13]

- **Individualism–Collectivism**

A groupist culture or an individual representing that culture is concerned about their own interests as well as that of others and they are likely to focus on cooperative strategies for problem/conflict resolution, while a society that prioritizes their interests more than that of others tends to be more individualistic and selects collaboration strategies.[14] Like most East Asian societies, Malaysia is a groupist, communitarian and harmony-oriented country, so individualistic demands are subjugated to that of the team or community one belongs to, with the individual showing compliance to the team objectives in order to maintain harmonious relationships with other team members.[15]

Self-consciousness/awareness represented by individualism is typically robust in a comparatively loose (and open) social structure, but, in a collective society/community like Malaysia, individuals are socialized into a group identity from a young age in a tightly organized societal structure,

---

[12] Hashim, H. M. (2010). "International Negotiation Styles: A Perspective of Malaysian Diplomats." CORE (Connecting Repositories) Research Service, p. 50 [downloaded on 1 January 2023], available at https://core.ac.uk/download/pdf/56361749.pdf.

[13] Katz, L. (March 2008). "Negotiating International Business — Malaysia." Negotiating International Business — The Negotiator's Reference Guide to 50 Countries around the World and Mount San Antonio College, p. 1 [downloaded on 1 January 2023], available at https://instruction2.mtsac.edu/rjagodka/BUSM_51_Project/Negotiating/Malaysia.pdf.

[14] Chang, L.-C. C. (2020). "A Comparison of Taiwan and Malaysia in Negotiation Styles." Universiti Utara Malaysia Course Franchise Business Management (FBPME3023) studoc website [downloaded on 1 January 2023], available at https://www.studocu.com/my/document/universiti-utara-malaysia/franchise-business-management/a-comparison-of-taiwan-and-malaysia-in-negotiation-styles/21649420.

[15] Katz, L. (March 2008). "Negotiating International Business — Malaysia." Negotiating International Business — The Negotiator's Reference Guide to 50 Countries Around the World and Mount San Antonio College, p. 1 [downloaded on 1 January 2023], available at https://instruction2.mtsac.edu/rjagodka/BUSM_51_Project/Negotiating/Malaysia.pdf.

although some studies have shown that it is not as groupist as their Northeast Asian counterparts like Taiwan.[16] Therefore, many experts consider Malaysia to be comparatively mildly collectivist.[17] Malaysians tend to have a strong community spirit (*gotong royong*) and an East Asian cultural inclination to help each other within the community while paying attention to others' feelings and opinions (sometimes even anticipating how others would judge and evaluate them, especially within their networks) to preserve social harmony.[18] Because of these social rituals and norms, the dominant Malay majority lives in social harmony with the other races and this scenario even poses as an ideal model for other societies to emulate.[19]

- **Uncertainty Avoidance**

Overall, Malaysia is considered a weak uncertainty avoidance society.[20] Uncertainty avoidance is the limit "to which a society feels threatened by uncertain or unknown situations."[21] Compared to Western negotiators, Malaysians appear to be less inclined towards selecting the withdrawal

[16] Chang, L.-C. C. (2020). "A Comparison of Taiwan and Malaysia in Negotiation Styles." Universiti Utara Malaysia Course Franchise Business Management (FBPME3023) studoc website [downloaded on 1 January 2023], available at https://www.studocu.com/my/document/universiti-utara-malaysia/franchise-business-management/a-comparison-of-taiwan-and-malaysia-in-negotiation-styles/21649420.

[17] Hashim, H. M. (2010). "International Negotiation Styles: A Perspective of Malaysian Diplomats." CORE (Connecting Repositories) Research Service, p. 51 [downloaded on 1 January 2023], available at https://core.ac.uk/download/pdf/56361749.pdf.

[18] Chang, L.-C. C. (2020). "A Comparison of Taiwan and Malaysia in Negotiation Styles." Universiti Utara Malaysia Course Franchise Business Management (FBPME3023) studoc website [downloaded on 1 January 2023], available at https://www.studocu.com/my/document/universiti-utara-malaysia/franchise-business-management/a-comparison-of-taiwan-and-malaysia-in-negotiation-styles/21649420.

[19] Awang, S., Maros, M., & Ibrahim, N. (May 2012). Malay values in intercultural communication. *International Journal of Social Science and Humanity*, 2(3), 202 [downloaded on 1 January 2023], available at http://www.ijssh.org/papers/96-CH219.pdf.

[20] Hashim, H. M. (2010). "International Negotiation Styles: A Perspective of Malaysian Diplomats." CORE (Connecting Repositories) Research Service, p. 51 [downloaded on 1 January 2023], available at https://core.ac.uk/download/pdf/56361749.pdf.

[21] Chang, L.-C. C. (2020). "A comparison of Taiwan and Malaysia in Negotiation Styles." Universiti Utara Malaysia Course Franchise Business Management (FBPME3023) studoc website [downloaded on 1 January 2023], available at https://www.studocu.com/my/document/universiti-utara-malaysia/franchise-business-management/a-comparison-of-taiwan-and-malaysia-in-negotiation-styles/21649420.

strategy than their Northeast Asian counterparts by accepting risks.[22] They do not feel intimidated in going back to the business arena market after giving up on a current deal in favor of locating another entity that they feel they can work with in the longer term.[23] Western negotiators by comparison are tolerant of ambiguity and do not feel intimidated by ambiguous situations, with greater adaptability to change.[24]

However, compared to Northeast Asian negotiators like the Taiwanese, Malaysians have a greater comparative tendency to focus on a competitive rather than withdrawal strategy, negotiation disagreements may face uncertainties and so non-Malaysian negotiators who are used to high uncertainty avoidance may have less interest in dealing with Malaysians and select other partners that are more collaborative or consultative.[25] Among the Malaysians, the overseas diasporic ethnic Chinese in Malaysia may show a higher degree of uncertainty avoidance and place greater trust in family networks or friendship-based connections (both of which are features of their diasporic *guanxi* networks).[26] Since Malaysians have longer-term orientation and are more comfortable with uncertainty, some studies have shown that Malaysian individuals chose the accommodation strategy in service industry negotiations.[27] This may be an important point to note, given that Malaysia is transitioning into a

[22] *Ibid.*

[23] *Ibid.*

[24] Hashim, H. M. (2010). "International Negotiation Styles: A Perspective of Malaysian Diplomats." CORE (Connecting Repositories) Research Service, p. 51 [downloaded on 1 January 2023], available at https://core.ac.uk/download/pdf/56361749.pdf.

[25] Chang, L.-C. C. (2020). "A Comparison of Taiwan and Malaysia in Negotiation Styles." Universiti Utara Malaysia Course Franchise Business Management (FBPME3023) studoc website [downloaded on 1 January 2023], available at https://www.studocu.com/my/document/universiti-utara-malaysia/franchise-business-management/a-comparison-of-taiwan-and-malaysia-in-negotiation-styles/21649420.

[26] Hashim, H. M. (2010). "International Negotiation Styles: A Perspective of Malaysian Diplomats." CORE (Connecting Repositories) Research Service, p. 51 [downloaded on 1 January 2023], available at https://core.ac.uk/download/pdf/56361749.pdf.

[27] Chang, L.-C. C. (2020). "A comparison of Taiwan and Malaysia in Negotiation Styles." Universiti Utara Malaysia Course Franchise Business Management (FBPME3023) studoc website [downloaded on 1 January 2023], available at https://www.studocu.com/my/document/universiti-utara-malaysia/franchise-business-management/a-comparison-of-taiwan-and-malaysia-in-negotiation-styles/21649420.

service-oriented economy with its economic upgrade in the regional economic architecture.

3. Communication

In building long-term and trustworthy relations with the Malaysian team, showing respect for them is of utmost importance as Malaysian negotiators generally prefer to create strong personal connections first before business dealings and all Malaysians (regardless of race) prefer to work with familiar and likeable individuals.[28] This is especially visible in the case of Malaysian ethnic Chinese[29] who tend to place more emphasis on *guanxi* ties with friends, sworn brothers, family members, relatives or trusted subordinates. Sensitive and unpleasant conversations with the Malaysian negotiators must be held privately (without public outbursts and indications of being upset), carefully and with great care in order not to disrespect the Malaysians.[30] In certain limited contexts, Malaysians may use humor as a tool to reduce tensions and conflicts while downplaying hierarchical gaps and differences.[31]

Malaysians, especially perhaps the Malays, prefer indirect communication (which may be perceived as beating around the bush by Westerners) to convey their true feelings and intentions.[32] Malaysians therefore veer towards a neutral culture which tends to suppress their true feelings while

---

[28] Katz, L. (March 2008). "Negotiating International Business — Malaysia." Negotiating International Business — The Negotiator's Reference Guide to 50 Countries around the World and Mount San Antonio College, p. 1 [downloaded on 1 January 2023], available at https://instruction2.mtsac.edu/rjagodka/BUSM_51_Project/Negotiating/Malaysia.pdf.

[29] Hashim, H. M. (2010). "International Negotiation Styles: A Perspective of Malaysian Diplomats." CORE (Connecting Repositories) Research Service, p. 51 [downloaded on 1 January 2023], available at https://core.ac.uk/download/pdf/56361749.pdf.

[30] Katz, L. (March 2008). "Negotiating International Business — Malaysia." Negotiating International Business — The Negotiator's Reference Guide to 50 Countries Around the World and Mount San Antonio College, p. 1 [downloaded on 1 January 2023], available at https://instruction2.mtsac.edu/rjagodka/BUSM_51_Project/Negotiating/Malaysia.pdf.

[31] Awang, S., Maros, M., & Ibrahim, N. (May 2012). Malay values in intercultural communication. *International Journal of Social Science and Humanity*, 2(3), 202 [downloaded on 1 January 2023], available at http://www.ijssh.org/papers/96-CH219.pdf.

[32] *Ibid.*

those from affective cultures directly exhibit their emotions.[33] Noisy and excitable mannerisms may be conceived as a form of lack of self-restraint, while uncontrolled displays of emotions are to be avoided, and communications should be carried out with awareness of personal space of about a distance of two to three feet.[34]

With generational changes and economic development, more young Malaysians have travelled overseas for foreign education (particularly to the West) and brought back Western ideas like having less hierarchical conformity and also English language proficiency.[35] For the majority, however, most still speak mainly Bahasa Melayu. The official language Bahasa Melayu is spoken by bureaucrats and civil servants although some may speak English with varying proficiencies (pidgin or localized English language have their own special character, charms, diction, lexicon and context which can potentially result in language barriers), thus translators should be present in the negotiating teams on both sides in cross-cultural negotiations.[36] Thus, it may be advisable to hire a local interpreter who not only speaks the language but also understands the cultural nuances of Bahasa Melayu speakers or Malay-accented English. Bahasa Melayu is considered one of the constantly evolving features of the indigenous Malay civilization which is said to be a millennium old, starting from the time when Malays started occupying the Malay archipelago.[37] Besides the

---

[33] Hashim, H. M. (2010). "International Negotiation Styles: A Perspective of Malaysian Diplomats." CORE (Connecting Repositories) Research Service, p. 55 [downloaded on 1 January 2023], available at https://core.ac.uk/download/pdf/56361749.pdf.

[34] Katz, L. (March 2008). "Negotiating International Business — Malaysia." Negotiating International Business — The Negotiator's Reference Guide to 50 Countries Around the World and Mount San Antonio College, p. 2 [downloaded on 1 January 2023], available at https://instruction2.mtsac.edu/rjagodka/BUSM_51_Project/Negotiating/Malaysia.pdf.

[35] Hashim, H. M. (2010). "International Negotiation Styles: A Perspective of Malaysian Diplomats." CORE (Connecting Repositories) Research Service, p. 62 [downloaded on 1 January 2023], available at https://core.ac.uk/download/pdf/56361749.pdf.

[36] Katz, L. (March 2008). "Negotiating International Business — Malaysia." Negotiating International Business — The Negotiator's Reference Guide to 50 Countries Around the World and Mount San Antonio College, p. 2 [downloaded on 1 January 2023], available at https://instruction2.mtsac.edu/rjagodka/BUSM_51_Project/Negotiating/Malaysia.pdf.

[37] Hashim, H. M. (2010). "International Negotiation Styles: A Perspective of Malaysian Diplomats." CORE (Connecting Repositories) Research Service, p. 11 [downloaded on 1 January 2023], available at https://core.ac.uk/download/pdf/56361749.pdf.

historical significance, the Federal Constitution of Malaysia, which is the ultimate, supreme piece of legislation in the country, defined a Malay as someone who is a Muslim, speaks Malay and implements Malay culture in his/her life.[38] Thus, Bahasa Melayu lies at the heart of being a native bumiputera Malay in both cultural and legal aspects.

Other than the dominant Malay national language, minority ethnic groups also exhibit their idiosyncratic communication patterns, norms and rituals. Sometimes, specific ethnic groups in Malaysia have certain cultural nuances in their communication. For example, Malaysian ethnic Chinese consider it courteous to pattern their speech in both positive and negative expressions when couching decisions, e.g. "Do you want to eat this or not?"[39] Across racial lines, Malaysians are likely to practice elaborate displays of courtesy in standardized social rituals that are attuned towards seniority and situational contexts.[40] For example, pointing at individuals or things is done by utilizing an open palm or with the right thumb and not the index finger and some groups like the Chinese Malaysians place their right index finger on their nose when referring to themselves rather than pointing to the chest (a Western custom).[41]

4. Negotiation Strategies: Distributive or Integrative

The Malaysian negotiation style tends to be more integrative. This is due to the long-term orientation of Malaysian-style business relationships,

---

[38] Awang, S., Maros, M., & Ibrahim, N. (May 2012). Malay values in intercultural communication. *International Journal of Social Science and Humanity*, 2(3), p. 201 [downloaded on 1 January 2023], available at http://www.ijssh.org/papers/96-CH219.pdf.

[39] Katz, L. (March 2008). "Negotiating International Business — Malaysia." Negotiating International Business — The Negotiator's Reference Guide to 50 Countries Around the World and Mount San Antonio College, p. 2 [downloaded on 1 January 2023], available at https://instruction2.mtsac.edu/rjagodka/BUSM_51_Project/Negotiating/Malaysia.pdf.

[40] Hashim, H. M. (2010). "International Negotiation Styles: A Perspective of Malaysian Diplomats." CORE (Connecting Repositories) Research Service, p. 63 [downloaded on 1 January 2023], available at https://core.ac.uk/download/pdf/56361749.pdf.

[41] Katz, L. (March 2008). "Negotiating International Business — Malaysia." Negotiating International Business — The Negotiator's Reference Guide to 50 Countries Around the World and Mount San Antonio College, p. 2 [downloaded on 1 January 2023], available at https://instruction2.mtsac.edu/rjagodka/BUSM_51_Project/Negotiating/Malaysia.pdf.

with a tendency to avoid conflicts/tensions in any relationships. Providing negative feedback can be clumsy in interactions, often treated with seriousness by Malaysians and can result in the loss of "face."[42] Comfort in working with others, building friendships and good human relations are extremely important in Malaysia. Once you have accumulated private social capital and friendships (the longer, the better), the greater the success in negotiations. Related to this point, Malaysian business relationships and negotiation styles tend to occur between individuals rather than institutions so when a negotiator has obtained the trust and comfort of the Malaysian partners, the whole process has to be redone again if the individuals in the negotiating team are changed as trust is not immediately transferable between negotiators.[43] Therefore, it is advisable not to change the membership of the negotiating team once rapport is built up with the Malaysian negotiators.

When negotiating and/or doing business, showing tolerance and understanding may be more acceptable than legalistic and rational attitudes when interacting with Malaysians.[44] Courtesy and being humble are considered positive qualities and they are not necessarily contrary to negotiation success as Malaysians may be patient but they are also persistent in trying to reach their negotiation targets, thus some negotiators recommend mirroring such practices when interacting with them.[45] Humility in Malay communication may mean self-deprecation, avoidance of self-praise, avoidance of overstatement in

---

[42] Hashim, H. M. (2010). "International Negotiation Styles: A Perspective of Malaysian Diplomats." CORE (Connecting Repositories) Research Service, p. 63 [downloaded on 1 January 2023], available at https://core.ac.uk/download/pdf/56361749.pdf.

[43] Katz, L. (March 2008). "Negotiating International Business — Malaysia." Negotiating International Business — The Negotiator's Reference Guide to 50 Countries Around the World and Mount San Antonio College, p. 1 [downloaded on 1 January 2023], available at https://instruction2.mtsac.edu/rjagodka/BUSM_51_Project/Negotiating/Malaysia.pdf.

[44] Hashim, H. M. (2010). "International Negotiation Styles: A Perspective of Malaysian Diplomats." CORE (Connecting Repositories) Research Service, p. 63 [downloaded on 1 January 2023], available at https://core.ac.uk/download/pdf/56361749.pdf.

[45] Katz, L. (March 2008). "Negotiating International Business — Malaysia." Negotiating International Business — The Negotiator's Reference Guide to 50 Countries around the World and Mount San Antonio College, p. 1 [downloaded on 1 January 2023], available at https://instruction2.mtsac.edu/rjagodka/BUSM_51_Project/Negotiating/Malaysia.pdf.

favor of understatement, being cautious of appearing arrogant and the use of apologetic behavior and words.[46]

5. Concession-making and Hardball Tactics

High-context cultures tend to be more implicit in their ways of communication with internalized messages, codifications of meaning, exhibiting more nonverbal communications, hiding reactions and having clear boundaries between in and out groups.[47] Therefore, successful negotiators would need to mirror Malaysian nonverbal communications or verbal nuances as any robust direct, upfront and straightforward form of communication may be perceived as abrasive, discourteous or aggressive; and the only exception to this rule is the interactions between two strangers who can then outright reject each other (which would invariably end any potential future negotiations).[48]

The Malaysian business stakeholders tend to be less direct in articulating ideas and may show discomfort in critiquing their peers and juniors.[49] To prevent any accidental loss of face, indirect high-context communication is preferred. Malaysians expressing "yes" may not actually imply positive responses and usually mean they heard and understood the message but not necessarily agree with it; moreover conversations are bereft of a jarring "no" in favor of ambiguity. Ambiguity may be couched in the form of "I am not sure," "we will think about it," "this will require further

---

[46] Awang, S., Maros, M., & Ibrahim, N. (May 2012). Malay values in intercultural communication. *International Journal of Social Science and Humanity*, 2(3), 202 [downloaded on 1 January 2023], available at http://www.ijssh.org/papers/96-CH219.pdf.

[47] Hashim, H. M. (2010). "International Negotiation Styles: A Perspective of Malaysian Diplomats." CORE (Connecting Repositories) Research Service, p. 49 [downloaded on 1 January 2023], available at https://core.ac.uk/download/pdf/56361749.pdf.

[48] Katz, L. (March 2008). "Negotiating International Business — Malaysia." Negotiating International Business — The Negotiator's Reference Guide to 50 Countries Around the World and Mount San Antonio College, p. 2 [downloaded on 1 January 2023], available at https://instruction2.mtsac.edu/rjagodka/BUSM_51_Project/Negotiating/Malaysia.pdf.

[49] Hashim, H. M. (2010). "International Negotiation Styles: A Perspective of Malaysian Diplomats." CORE (Connecting Repositories) Research Service, p. 63 [downloaded on 1 January 2023], available at https://core.ac.uk/download/pdf/56361749.pdf.

investigation," "yes, but …," a half enthusiastic/unconvincing "yes" and/or simply no response, all of which can actually signal a rejection.[50]

Third parties are particularly useful for managing ambiguities and uncertainties, especially in articulating negative news.[51] Occasionally, a negative rejection of a proposal may be conveyed through a third party as a way to save face and avoid the abrasiveness of rejection.[52] Use of third parties in negotiations is sometimes advantageous as Malaysian business executives and negotiators have a power distance preference so they may like a structural framework of negotiations drawn up by a neutral authority rather than a competing/negotiating peer.[53]

Negotiators may also have to take into consideration the differential levels of tolerance and patience among different ethnic groups in Malaysia. Most groups, however, have a long-term orientation and are comparatively patient with timelines and schedules. Individuals with short-term orientation conceptualize time as a limited resource and exhibit impatience about it while long-term-oriented individuals conceptualize time as limitless and an infinite resource and therefore show more patience. Within multicultural and multi-ethnic societies, different racial and ethnic groups may have differential attitudes towards scheduling and timelines. In the case of Malaysia, as it is a multi-ethnic society, some studies indicated the ethnic Chinese are more long-term oriented than their Malay counterparts.

[50] Katz, L. (March 2008). "Negotiating International Business — Malaysia." Negotiating International Business — The Negotiator's Reference Guide to 50 Countries Around the World and Mount San Antonio College, p. 2 [downloaded on 1 January 2023], available at https://instruction2.mtsac.edu/rjagodka/BUSM_51_Project/Negotiating/Malaysia.pdf.

[51] Hashim, H. M. (2010). "International Negotiation Styles: A Perspective of Malaysian Diplomats." CORE (Connecting Repositories) Research Service, p. 64 [downloaded on 1 January 2023], available at https://core.ac.uk/download/pdf/56361749.pdf.

[52] Katz, L. (March 2008). "Negotiating International Business — Malaysia." Negotiating International Business — The Negotiator's Reference Guide to 50 Countries Around the World and Mount San Antonio College, p. 2 [downloaded on 1 January 2023], available at https://instruction2.mtsac.edu/rjagodka/BUSM_51_Project/Negotiating/Malaysia.pdf.

[53] Chang, L.-C. C. (2020). "A comparison of Taiwan and Malaysia in Negotiation Styles." Universiti Utara Malaysia Course Franchise Business Management (FBPME3023) studoc website [downloaded on 1 January 2023], available at https://www.studocu.com/my/document/universiti-utara-malaysia/franchise-business-management/a-comparison-of-taiwan-and-malaysia-in-negotiation-styles/21649420.

6. Role of Women

Based on the 2022 Global Gender Gap Report by the World Economic Forum,[54] Malaysia is ranked second last out of 19 countries in the East Asia and the Pacific region — the following table shows all of the other countries covered in this book. For some Malaysians, gender perceptions may also be related to religious beliefs. In terms of the work environment, Malaysian (in particularly Muslim Malaysian) managers show a tendency towards identifying with the group, displaying sensitivity to social issues, believing in cultural hospitality and paying especial attention in maintaining the dignity of men.[55] Non-Malaysian female negotiators in the teams negotiating with their Malaysian counterparts may sensitize themselves to the last point during the negotiation process.

Global Gender Gap Report 2022 INSIGHT REPORT JULY 2022

EAST ASIA & the PACIFIC	Rank		
Country	Regional (19)	Global (146)	Score
Philippines	2	19	0.783
Singapore	4	49	0.734
Thailand	8	79	0.709
Vietnam	9	83	0.705
Indonesia	10	92	0.697
Korea (South)	12	99	0.689
China	13	102	0.682
Malaysia	**14**	**103**	**0.681**
Japan	19	116	0.650

[54] "Global Gender Gap Report 2022." (July 13, 2022). World Economic Forum, available at https://www.weforum.org/reports/global-gender-gap-report-2022/digest. The Global Gender Gap Index benchmarks the current state and evolution of gender parity across four key dimensions (Economic Participation and Opportunity, Educational Attainment, Health and Survival, and Political Empowerment). It is the longest-standing index which tracks progress towards closing these gaps over time since its inception in 2006.

[55] Chang, L.-C. C. (2020). "A comparison of Taiwan and Malaysia in Negotiation Styles." Universiti Utara Malaysia Course Franchise Business Management (FBPME3023) studoc website [downloaded on 1 January 2023], available at https://www.studocu.com/my/document/universiti-utara-malaysia/franchise-business-management/a-comparison-of-taiwan-and-malaysia-in-negotiation-styles/21649420.

Other studies argue that Malaysia is relatively gender-neutral at the workplace, attaining the mid-point between feminine (consensus building, equity, compromise) and masculine (assertiveness, decisiveness, competitiveness, aggression) cultural values.[56] In terms of cultural "Masculinity/Femininity" behaviors, going for tangible achievements, seeking monetary benefits and autonomy are highlighted as examples of masculine qualities.[57] Malaysian males may show tendencies towards (or clamor for) such qualities. All in all, some studies show that Malaysian propensity for consensus-seeking and resolving conflicts through compromise and negotiation appear to be counterbalanced by the tendency to fight and become assertive while competing.[58]

Given this net neutral result, one may need to conceptualize cultural masculinity in comparative rather than absolute terms. For example, they may be more masculine compared to Northeast Asian negotiating styles. Culturally, some studies also indicated Malaysian business executives and negotiators were less risk-adverse, comparatively more individualistic and self-centric (compared to Northeast Asian societies like Taiwan), and at ease with more competition, all of which were considered "masculine" qualities.[59]

7. Intermediary/Interpreter

If a negotiating team is unable to locate or afford simultaneous translation, it may be useful to articulate slowly in brief, basic English sentences with

---

[56] Hashim, H. M. (2010). "International Negotiation Styles: A Perspective of Malaysian Diplomats." CORE (Connecting Repositories) Research Service, p. 53 [downloaded on 1 January 2023], available at https://core.ac.uk/download/pdf/56361749.pdf.

[57] Chang, L.-C. C. (2020). "A Comparison of Taiwan and Malaysia in Negotiation Styles." Universiti Utara Malaysia Course Franchise Business Management (FBPME3023) studoc website [downloaded on 1 January 2023], available at https://www.studocu.com/my/document/universiti-utara-malaysia/franchise-business-management/a-comparison-of-taiwan-and-malaysia-in-negotiation-styles/21649420.

[58] Hashim, H. M. (2010). "International Negotiation Styles: A Perspective of Malaysian Diplomats." CORE (Connecting Repositories) Research Service, pp. 52 and 53 [downloaded on 1 January 2023], available at https://core.ac.uk/download/pdf/56361749.pdf.

[59] Chang, L.-C. C. (2020). "A Comparison of Taiwan and Malaysia in Negotiation Styles." Universiti Utara Malaysia Course Franchise Business Management (FBPME3023) studoc website [downloaded on 1 January 2023], available at https://www.studocu.com/my/document/universiti-utara-malaysia/franchise-business-management/a-comparison-of-taiwan-and-malaysia-in-negotiation-styles/21649420

pauses in between, free from complicated slang and/or jargon and with constant summarization of main points.[60] However, this does not apply to official communication as the civil servants and bureaucrats expect all communications to be done mostly in the Malay language. Therefore, non-Malaysian negotiating teams armed with translators and interpreters may be able to perform better in the negotiations. In addition to the language itself, it would be useful to have interpreters or intermediaries who can understand cultural nuances and nonverbal communications, not just a command of the language itself. Some studies indicate that, in order to fully understand a Malay speaker, his/her verbal articulations may not fully express the true intentions or views, so it is important to understand the body language as well.[61]

Malaysian physical motions and body language are low-key but important in high-context cultural communication and so, all parties to the negotiations should keep an eye on body language for unspoken messages.[62] Some studies pointed out that nonverbal communication is especially prevalent among Malays.[63] There are many examples of this aspect, including those that cut across ethnic lines. In terms of high-context behavior, for example, the Malaysian smile may not represent agreement or being amused as in the West and can be body language for concealing embarrassment, coyness/shyness, disagreement, distress/discomfort, resulting in

[60] Katz, L. (March 2008). "Negotiating International Business — Malaysia." Negotiating International Business — The Negotiator's Reference Guide to 50 Countries Around the World and Mount San Antonio College, p. 2 [downloaded on 1 January 2023], available at https://instruction2.mtsac.edu/rjagodka/BUSM_51_Project/Negotiating/Malaysia.pdf.

[61] Hashim, H. M. (2010). "International Negotiation Styles: A Perspective of Malaysian Diplomats." CORE (Connecting Repositories) Research Service, p. 69 [downloaded on 1 January 2023], available at https://core.ac.uk/download/pdf/56361749.pdf.

[62] Katz, L. (March 2008). "Negotiating International Business — Malaysia." Negotiating International Business — The Negotiator's Reference Guide to 50 Countries Around the World and Mount San Antonio College, p. 2 [downloaded on 1 January 2023], available at https://instruction2.mtsac.edu/rjagodka/BUSM_51_Project/Negotiating/Malaysia.pdf.

[63] Hashim, H. M. (2010). "International Negotiation Styles: A Perspective of Malaysian Diplomats." CORE (Connecting Repositories) Research Service, p. 69 [downloaded on 1 January 2023], available at https://core.ac.uk/download/pdf/56361749.pdf.

Westerners spotting the Malaysian smile or laughter at intervals that in Western negotiation culture may be considered unconventional or even inappropriate.[64]

A major Malay value is the *budi* complex system, which consists of (among other features) Malay politeness expressed through both verbal and nonverbal communications to avoid appearing as uncouth and uncultured.[65] Malaysians articulate their ideas in a subdued and gentle manner punctuated by silence and any responses to a question are predicted by a collected pause (up till 10 seconds and above) to gather the thoughts and the pause does not symbolize any real meaning.[66] Such communication norms appear to be socialized into Malaysians from young. Some scholars opine that Malay youngsters inculcate the values of being "seen and not heard" and avoid directness in speech, thus communicating in an indirect manner to prevent insulting others.[67]

8. Time, Timelines, Timeliness

Some negotiation experts opine that business executives and the bureaucracy tend to have less exposure to other negotiating or corporate cultures other than those in ASEAN, and therefore, this may lead to the conventional thinking that negotiations should be done in the same way and in the

[64] Katz, L. (March 2008). "Negotiating International Business — Malaysia." Negotiating International Business — The Negotiator's Reference Guide to 50 Countries Around the World and Mount San Antonio College, p. 2 [downloaded on 1 January 2023], available at https://instruction2.mtsac.edu/rjagodka/BUSM_51_Project/Negotiating/Malaysia.pdf.

[65] Hashim, H. M. (2010). "International Negotiation Styles: A Perspective of Malaysian Diplomats." CORE (Connecting Repositories) Research Service, p. 67 [downloaded on 1 January 2023], available at https://core.ac.uk/download/pdf/56361749.pdf.

[66] Katz, L. (March 2008). "Negotiating International Business — Malaysia." Negotiating International Business — The Negotiator's Reference Guide to 50 Countries Around the World and Mount San Antonio College, p. 2 [downloaded on 1 January 2023], available at https://instruction2.mtsac.edu/rjagodka/BUSM_51_Project/Negotiating/Malaysia.pdf.

[67] Awang, S., Maros, M., and Ibrahim, N. (May 2012). Malay values in intercultural communication. *International Journal of Social Science and Humanity*, 2(3), 201 [downloaded on 1 January 2023], available at http://www.ijssh.org/papers/96-CH219.pdf.

same pace as in other ASEAN countries.[68] Some researchers believe that a business partnership can only be considered as a long-term relationship of equal status if they can build common identity, objectives, risks and benefits.[69] Therefore, the advice provided by some negotiators is to let the Malaysian negotiation team to set their pace of doing business until one is able to figure out the optimal pace and speed in taking the negotiations forward for maximum success.[70] On the other hand, other scholars highlighted the negotiating feature that Malaysian business stakeholders tend to be extremely terse, direct to the point, and may feel discomfort in excessively wasting time on negotiations and prefer perhaps to reach a compromise sooner than later.[71] Despite such divergent opinions, in general, building a good relationship with the Malaysians needs long-term efforts, thus negotiators recommend proceeding with substantial negotiations only after both sides have developed a certain comfort level with each other.[72]

---

[68] Katz, L. (March 2008). "Negotiating International Business — Malaysia." Negotiating International Business — The Negotiator's Reference Guide to 50 Countries around the World and Mount San Antonio College [downloaded on 1 January uary 2023], available at https://instruction2.mtsac.edu/rjagodka/BUSM_51_Project/Negotiating/Malaysia.pdf.

[69] Soo, H. P. L. (June 2, 2019). A comparison of China and Malaysia in international business negotiation. *Journal of the Messenger*, 11(1A), 154, Special Issue on the School of Multimedia Technology and Communication Postgraduate Symposium [downloaded on 1 January 2023], available at https://journals.usm.ac.id/index.php/the-messenger/article/view/823/909.

[70] Katz, L. (March 2008). "Negotiating International Business — Malaysia." Negotiating International Business — The Negotiator's Reference Guide to 50 Countries Around the World and Mount San Antonio College, p. 1 [downloaded on 1 January uary 2023], available at https://instruction2.mtsac.edu/rjagodka/BUSM_51_Project/Negotiating/Malaysia.pdf.

[71] Chang, L.-C. C. (2020). "A comparison of Taiwan and Malaysia in negotiation styles." Universiti Utara Malaysia Course Franchise Business Management (FBPME3023) studoc website [downloaded on 1 January 2023], available at https://www.studocu.com/my/document/universiti-utara-malaysia/franchise-business-management/a-comparison-of-taiwan-and-malaysia-in-negotiation-styles/21649420.

[72] Katz, L. (March 2008). "Negotiating International Business — Malaysia." Negotiating International Business — The Negotiator's Reference Guide to 50 Countries Around the World and Mount San Antonio College, p. 1 [downloaded on 1 January 2023], available at https://instruction2.mtsac.edu/rjagodka/BUSM_51_Project/Negotiating/Malaysia.pdf.

Bibliography

Awang, S., Maros, M., & Ibrahim, N. (May 2012). Malay values in intercultural communication. *International Journal of Social Science and Humanity*, 2(3), 201–205 [downloaded on 1 January 2023], available at http://www.ijssh.org/papers/96-CH219.pdf.

Chang, L.-C. C. (2020). "A Comparison of Taiwan and Malaysia in Negotiation Styles." Universiti Utara Malaysia Course Franchise Business Management (FBPME3023) studoc website [downloaded on 1 January 2023], available at https://www.studocu.com/my/document/universiti-utara-malaysia/franchise-business-management/a-comparison-of-taiwan-and-malaysia-in-negotiation-styles/21649420.

Hashim, H. M. (2010). "International Negotiation Styles: A Perspective of Malaysian Diplomats." CORE (Connecting Repositories) Research Service [downloaded on 1 January 2023], available at https://core.ac.uk/download/pdf/56361749.pdf.

Katz, L. (March 2008). "Negotiating International Business — Malaysia." Negotiating International Business — The Negotiator's Reference Guide to 50 Countries around the World and Mount San Antonio College [downloaded on 1 January 2023], available at https://instruction2.mtsac.edu/rjagodka/BUSM_51_Project/Negotiating/Malaysia.pdf.

Soo, H. P. L. (June 2, 2019). A comparison of China and Malaysia in international business negotiation. *Journal of the Messenger*, 11(1A), 148–156, Special Issue on the School of Multimedia Technology and Communication Post-graduate Symposium [downloaded on 1 January 2023], available at https://journals.usm.ac.id/index.php/the-messenger/article/view/823/909.

Malaysia Quiz

1. Malaysia is involved in the regional initiatives of the US-centered IPEF (Indo-Pacific Economic Framework) and the Japan (and Australia)-facilitated CPTPP (Comprehensive and Progressive Agreement for Trans Pacific Partnership). True or false?
   A. True
   B. False

2. The indigenous Malays are known as _____, translated literally into 'sons of the soil'. Fill in the blank.
   A. bumiputeras or bumiputras
   B. datuks
   C. tan sris
   D. laksamana

3. Malays practice the state religion of Islam, thus imposing _____ laws. Fill in the blank.
   A. common
   B. Syriah or Sharia
   C. secular
   D. animistic

4. The '_____' factor refers to avoiding causing undue embarrassment to the other party, or damage to their reputation and social status, by remaining poker-faced, self-restraining, tactful and diplomatic throughout the negotiations.
   A. brain
   B. hand
   C. face
   D. leg

5. Nonverbal communication in Malaysia is sensitized to social hierarchy and rank. Some body language expressions can denote certain nuances that can affect perceptions of social rank and seniority. Is this general characterization true or false?
   A. True
   B. False

6. Malaysians tend to have strong community spirit (_____) and an East Asian cultural inclination to help each other within the community. Fill in the blank.
   A. lontong royong
   B. rasa sayang
   C. sotong royong
   D. gotong royong

7. Among the Malaysians, the overseas diasporic ethnic Chinese in Malaysia may show a higher degree of uncertainty avoidance and place greater trust in family networks or friendship-based connections (both of which are features of their diasporic *guanxi* networks). Is this general characterization true or false?
   A. True
   B. False

8. The official language _____ is spoken by bureaucrats and civil servants in Malaysia. Fill in the blank.
   A. Tagalog
   B. Ceylonese
   C. Bahasa Melayu
   D. Sanskrit

9. Humility in Malay communication may mean self-deprecation, avoidance of self-praise, avoidance of overstatement in favor of understatement, being cautious of appearing arrogant and the use of apologetic behavior and words. Is this general characterization true or false?
   A. True
   B. False

10. A major Malay value is the _____ complex system which consists of (among other features) Malay politeness expressed through both verbal and nonverbal communications to avoid appearing as uncouth and uncultured. Fill in the blank.
    A. budiman
    B. buddy
    C. hudi
    D. budi

Answer Bank

1. A
2. A
3. B
4. C
5. A
6. D
7. A
8. C
9. A
10. D

Chapter 6

The Filipino Negotiator

1. The Environment

When the Philippines joined Indonesia, Malaysia, Singapore and Thailand to form ASEAN[1] in 1967, it was a role model for its partners — it had a strong economy with a well-educated English-speaking workforce as well as a parliamentary democracy.[2] However, it then went through a series of boom and bust cycles and even weathered a 14-year martial law rule which ended in 1986. In the 21st century, the Philippines has just started to achieve economic growth rates comparable to fellow middle-income neighbors such as Indonesia, Thailand and Vietnam. After emerging from the COVID-19 pandemic with a new administration, the Philippines appears poised once again for a spectacular economic recovery. Even a sovereign wealth fund is in the pipeline.

The two key contributors to the country's economic well-being are its BPO (Business Process Outsourcing) sector and the remittance from its OFW (Overseas Filipino Workers). BPOs are more than just "call centers" as the services outsourced to the Philippines also include back-office knowledge processing; data transcription, game development; software

---

[1] Association of Southeast Asian Nations. (2020). "The Founding of ASEAN." Asean.org. Available at https://asean.org/the-founding-of-asean/. Indonesia, Malaysia, Philippines, Singapore and Thailand are the five founding member nations of ASEAN which now includes Brunei, Cambodia, Laos, Myanmar and Vietnam.

[2] Church, P. (2017). *Short History of South-East Asia*. Singapore: John Wiley & Sons Inc.

and engineering development.[3] Doubtless, the Filipinos' English proficiency, its high-skilled workforce, together with their cultural connection
to the United States (where major BPO clients are based) are obvious
reasons for the sector's success. According to the Philippine Statistics
Authority, there were some 1.83 million Filipinos overseas in 2021.[4]
Engaged in construction, domestic work, healthcare services, information
technology, business services and the entertainment industry, the remittance from this significant group contributes some 10% of the country's
GDP.[5]

The Philippines is especially sensitive to the dynamics of the US–China
relationship. Both countries are significant trading partners.[6] As a former
colony for 48 years before World War II, the Philippines shares deep historical and cultural linkages with the US. Due to its geographical location,
like several of its Southeast Asian neighbours, the Philippines also has
competing claims against China to territories in the South China Sea/West
Philippine Sea.[7]

When you first arrive in the densely urbanized Metro Manila, the prevalent use of English in speech and signages may evoke a sense that this is a
Westernized country. Moreover, as Catholicism is the dominant religious
faith, the many chapels and the religious decor in public buses and jeep-
neys may reinforce your initial impression. However, it will not be long
before you realize that Filipino negotiators have their own distinct way of
doing business with you.

---

[3] Cabuay, C. & Hill, H. (2019). 5. The Philippine economy: Renewed dynamism, old challenges. In I. Deinla and B. Dressel (Eds.), *From Aquino II to Duterte (2010–2018): Change,
Continuity — And Rupture* (pp. 145–185). Singapore: ISEAS Publishing, https://doi.
org/10.1355/9789814843294-011.

[4] "Statistical Tables on Overseas Filipino Workers | Philippine Statistics Authority." (n.d.).
Psa.gov.ph. Available at https://psa.gov.ph/statistics/survey/labor-force/sof-index.

[5] Cabuay, C. & Hill, H. (2019). 5. The Philippine economy: Renewed dynamism, old challenges. In I. Deinla and B. Dressel (Eds.), *From Aquino II to Duterte (2010–2018): Change,
Continuity — And Rupture* (pp. 145–185). Singapore: ISEAS Publishing, https://doi.
org/10.1355/9789814843294-011.

[6] "Highlights of the Philippine Export and Import Statistics August 2022 (Preliminary) |
Philippine Statistics Authority." (n.d.). Psa.gov.ph. Available at https://psa.gov.ph/content/
highlights-philippine-export-and-import-statistics-august-2022-preliminary#:~:text=The%20
People. (Accessed January 31, 2023).

[7] West Philippines Sea is the official Philippines designation for the South China Sea.

2. Culture

The Philippines[8] is made up of over 7,000 islands which can be grouped into three main clusters — Luzon in the north, Visayas in the centre and Mindanao in the south. These island clusters are diverse in terms of ethnicity, languages and cuisines. Almost 80% of the country's 114 million-strong population are Roman Catholics.[9] The population in the northern islands generally identify as Christian, while it is much more common to find those who identify as Muslim in the southern parts of the Philippines. The largest ethnic group is the Tagalog (25%).[10] The two official languages are Filipino, which is based on the Tagalog language, and English. The country was a Spanish colony for over 300 years. In 1898, it was ceded to the United States following the Spanish–American War. After World War II, the Philippines gained independence in 1946.

It is a complex task to unpack the Filipino culture given its plurality. However, since Manila is the commercial and political centre, the spotlight in this chapter will be on the Tagalog-speaking culture of the capital city in Luzon.[11]

The twin concepts of *kapwa* and *utang na loob* are the foundational pillars of Filipino culture. These terms were present in the Tagalog language before the Spanish colonial period and were used at a time when the basic social structures were villages of close-knit families held together by mutually beneficial alliances under the rule of a chief.[12] During the Spanish rule, the native language was retained and used to translate Christian doctrines instead of forcing the natives to learn Spanish. Thus, the original Tagalog concepts of *kapwa* and *utang na loob* remain intact.

[8] The information in this paragraph is largely obtained from "Philippines — The World Factbook," January 17, 2023. Available at https://www.cia.gov/the-world-factbook/countries/philippines/.
[9] "Philippines — The World Factbook," January 17, 2023. Available at https://www.cia.gov/the-world-factbook/countries/philippines/.
[10] *Ibid.*
[11] Kaut, C. (1961). Utang Na Loob: A system of contractual obligation among Tagalogs. *Southwestern Journal of Anthropology,* 17(3), 256–272.
[12] Jeremiah, R. (2015). Loób and Kapwa: An introduction to a Filipino virtue ethics. *Asian Philosophy,* 25(2), 148–171. doi: 10.1080/09552367.2015.1043173.

Kapwa[13] conveys a sense of fellowship and shared identity. This Tagalog term translates literally to "other", but the Filipinos use it to address another person with the intention of establishing a connection. It is akin to calling someone a fellow being without notions of self or the other. *Kapwa* embeds a worldview and web of meanings unique to the Filipino culture. It focuses on the commonality and shared-ness instead of seeing the other person as the opposite of oneself and vice versa. Thus, when it comes to interacting with another person, embracing *kapwa* means using people-centred perspectives and building relationships. The most important relationship in the Filipino society is the familial relationship. Filipinos generally feel strong and deep attachment towards their families (or *pamilya*) and will readily share with you information or stories about their families or home towns. Family gatherings are frequent and typically involve many members with impromptu group singing and dancing. Familial kinship includes relatives on the father's and mother's side as well as everyone related through marriage. Key friendships that can be traced to childhood or school or work, known as *barkada,* are also important relationships. In the eyes of others, a person who is skilled in practicing *kapwa* will have a strong network of biological and social relationships.

Utang na loob[14] is the concept of reciprocity needed to maintain and solidify the above-mentioned kinship relations. This old Tagalog term can be explained as being a "debt of gratitude". A child's *utang na loob* to his/her parents is immense so must do his/her utmost to repay the gift of life. Neglecting one's own parents will be branded as being *wala* (without) *utang da loob,* which is one of the greatest insults that can be levied against someone in the Philippines. Beyond the moral debt in the parent–child context, this concept is also used to generate a system of cyclical reciprocal obligations. If a favor or a positive gesture from another person is accepted,

---

[13] Explanation of *kapwa* is largely taken from Jeremiah, R. (2015). Loób and Kapwa: An introduction to a Filipino virtue ethics. *Asian Philosophy*, 25(2), 148–171. doi: 10.1080/09552367.2015.1043173.

[14] Explanation of *utang na loob* is largely taken from Kaut, C. (1961). Utang Na Loob: A system of contractual obligation among Tagalogs. *Southwestern Journal of Anthropology,* 17(3), 256–272. For comparison, see the concept of *bun khun* discussed in the Thai Negotiator Chapter which is the notion of a reciprocal relationship underpinned by an element of gratitude.

a "debt of gratitude" is incurred and every Filipino seeks to repay his/her obligation "with interest". Such "interest" then creates another "debt of gratitude", and the cycle goes on. This dynamic process has been described as a form of "one-upmanship".[15] Having *utang na loob* thus strengthens relationships.

Attracted by economic opportunities in the Spanish colony, Chinese traders and migrants, mainly from the Fujian province, began setting up home in the port city of Manila. During Spanish colonial times, the Chinese dominated the retail and wholesale markets and established monopolies over buying and selling operations and continued to expand their economic influence during the American period.[16] To this day, Chinese family-owned businesses remain highly successful in the Philippines. One prominent example is SM Investments Corporation, which was founded by Henry Sy, Senior, and though listed, is controlled by the Sy family.[17] One of the largest conglomerates in the Philippines, SM Investments also expanded its business to China through a network of connections or *guanxi,* referred to as Bamboo network[18] or Dragon network.[19] Tellingly, the company built its first mall[20] in China in Xiamen, Fujian province — the birthplace of the founder.

During the Spanish colonial period, in order to marry the local Filipinos, Chinese settlers were required to convert to Catholicism, which also came with benefits such as less taxes and restrictions on

[15] Holnsteiner, M. (1973). Reciprocity in the lowland Philippines. In F. Lynch & A. De Guzman II (Eds.), *Four Readings on Philippine Values* (4th edn.). Quezon City: Ateneo de Manila.

[16] Masucol, E., Jap, J., & Liu, A. H. (2022). Islands apart: Explaining the Chinese experience in the Philippines. *Frontiers in Political Science,* 4, 836561. doi: 10.3389/fpos.2022.836561.

[17] SM Investments. "At a Glance." Available at https://www.sminvestments.com/about-us/at-a-glance/. (Accessed January 25, 2023).

[18] Tanzer, A. (1994). The bamboo network. *Forbes,* 154(2), 138–144.

[19] Susanto, A. B. & Susanto, P. (2013). *The Dragon Network: Inside Stories of the Most Successful Chinese Family Businesses.* Singapore: John Wiley & Sons.

[20] SM Investments. (September 7, 2015). "SM Prime Wins Gold Award for China Mall." Available at https://www.sminvestments.com/press_release/sm-prime-wins-gold-award-for-china-mall/.

movement.[21] Such unions led to the formation of a Chinese *mestizo*[22] community. It is estimated that Chinese mestizos make up approximately 22.8 million of the total population.[23] Ethnic or pure Chinese comprise a further 1.15 million, which according to the World Economic Forum (2016) is the ninth largest Chinese population in the world residing outside of China.[24] Currently, the term *Tsinoy* is used when referring to both Chinese mestizos and pure Chinese, but that is a usage that is popular rather than legal.[25]

Like the Mainland Chinese, the *Tsinoys* also embrace values such as showing respect to elders and observing filial piety. However, this is not as a result of embracing Confucianism. These values are integral to Filipino familism, Tagalog concepts of *kapwa* and *utang na loob* as well as Christian values. Therefore, when you deal with the *Tsinoys*, you will observe that they have assimilated well into the Filipino community. In particular, the Chinese mestizos have often been viewed more as Filipino than as Chinese.[26] Even the pure ethnic Chinese hope you will treat them more as Filipinos.[27]

---

[21] Masucol, E., Jap, J., & Liu, A. H. (2022). Islands apart: Explaining the Chinese experience in the Philippines. *Frontiers in Political Science*, 4, 836561. doi: 10.3389/fpos.2022.836561.

[22] A Spanish word used in the Philippines to describe people of Filipino and Chinese ancestry.

[23] "Press Release — PRIB: Senate declares Chinese New Year as special working holiday. (n.d.). Legacy.senate.gov.ph. Available at https://legacy.senate.gov.ph/press_release/2013/0121_prib1.asp. (Accessed January 25, 2023).

[24] "*Where Are the Largest Chinese Populations Outside of China? | Thailand or Indonesia: Which Country Has the Largest Chinese Population? | By World Economic Forum | Facebook.*" Available at https://www.facebook.com/worldeconomicforum/videos/where-are-the-largest-chinese-populations-outside-of-china/10153549858561479/. (Accessed November 8, 2022).

[25] Chu, R. T. (2023). From 'Sangley' to 'Chinaman', 'Chinese Mestizo' to 'Tsinoy': Unpacking 'Chinese' identities in the Philippines at the turn of the twentieth-century. *Asian Ethnicity*, 24(1), 7–37.

[26] Masucol, E., Jap, J. & Liu, A. H. (2022). Islands apart: Explaining the Chinese experience in the Philippines. *Frontiers in Political Science*, 4, 836561. doi: 10.3389/fpos.2022.836561.

[27] Chang, L.-C. (2011). A comparison of Taiwanese and Philippine Chinese business negotiation styles. *Social Behavior and Personality*, 39(6), 765–772.

Hofstede's Cultural Dimensions

• Power Distance

For this index, the Philippines (score: 94) is ranked the second highest in this book, after Malaysia (score: 100) who is in the top spot.[28] The socio-economic as well as political status (if any) of a person's biological and social kinship network will define his/her identity and standing.[29] Among themselves, the Filipinos will instinctively take stock of one another person's familial and social network. This will serve as a marker of a person's place in the social hierarchy. Such standing remains quite entrenched and it is not easy to move up social rungs. Gestures and communication patterns will always reflect and acknowledge hierarchy. Failure to do so is an affront. In some cases, the adherence to such power distance structure is so strong that even when personal injustice is suffered at the hands of someone higher up, instead of reacting a Filipino may endure it and wait for an even higher authority to come to his/her rescue. Adhering to *utang na loob* may contribute to social stratification because of the unequal status between the "creditor" and the "debtor". That it is still a strong cultural trait in the society shows that Filipinos accept and adhere to power distance structures in their hierarchical society.

Like other hierarchical societies, age and seniority matter. Many senior roles are occupied by people who are advanced in years. Their observance and respect for hierarchy is also reflected in the way they speak. When speaking to someone of higher status or who is older, a polite form of speech will be used such as ending their sentences or phrase with the word *po* (the equivalent of "sir") to show respect. Even when speaking to their peers, Filipinos will use terms such as *kuya* (older brother) or *ate* (older sister) in addition to their names.

• Individualism–Collectivism

Given the high importance of family and personal networks, it is no surprise that the Filipino culture is group-oriented. From a very young age,

---

[28] Hofstede Insights. "Country Comparison — Hofstede Insights." Available at https://www.hofstede-insights.com/country-comparison/. (Accessed February 6, 2023).

[29] Rodell, P. A. (2018). Chapter 25: A syncretic culture. In M. R. Thompson & E. V. C. Batalla (Eds.), *Routledge Handbook of the Contemporary Philippines* (pp. 321–329). London & New York: Routledge.

a child is taught that the world is full of dangers and it is best for him/her to remain within the realms of the security provided by family and other kinships. By remaining a member of an in-group, especially a strong one with extensive connections, he/she will be safe and have a high chance of prospering. Cultural underpinnings such as *kapwa* promote solidarity, and *utang na loob* promotes loyalty to kinship.

Though a collectivist society, the Philippines' individualism score (32) is still higher than that of the other countries covered in this book, except Japan (46). This is no doubt contributed by the cultural influences of Spain and the US. The Filipino is thus more individualistic than his/her Southeast Asian neighbors. And this is especially true of the business elites. Towards the later part of the Spanish occupation in the 19th century, the elites in the Philippines were sending their children overseas to be educated in Spanish seminaries and universities. This Spanish-educated class of natives were known as *ilustrados* and they led the movement for nationalism. When the US took over, there were initially open hostilities, but the Americans reached a compromise with the *ilustrados,* which enabled the latter to dominate the political and economic structures of the country.[30] In sum, the business and political elites in the Philippines are more bicultural than their counterparts in the region.

- **Uncertainty Avoidance**

The Philippines score is 44 for this index and is comparable to Indonesia's score of 48.[31] Such moderate scores mean that the Filipino society generally adopts a relaxed attitude towards uncertainty and tolerates deviation from norms. The Philippines sits on the Ring of Fire, which is a belt of active volcanoes and earthquake epicentres, and also on the Pacific typhon belt.[32] Filipinos have suffered numerous destructive typhons. Besides having to face multiple natural disaster threats, their business and social environments are also at the mercy of deep-rooted corruption and failed reforms. If there are major deviations from expectations or norms, your

---

[30] Church, P. (2017). *Short History of South-East Asia.* Singapore: John Wiley & Sons Inc.
[31] Hofstede Insights. "Country Comparison — Hofstede Insights." Available at https://www.hofstede-insights.com/country-comparison/. (Accessed February 6, 2023).
[32] "Philippines — The World Factbook," January 17, 2023. Available at https://www.cia.gov/the-world-factbook/countries/philippines/.

Filipino counterpart is likely to be accommodative. Withdrawal is also an option open to them if the differences in interests and positions convince them that you are not the right *suki* candidate.

3. Communication

The official languages are English and Filipino, and in Manila, English proficiency is common. Though the Filipino negotiators may be fluent in English and come across as being cheerful and enthusiastic in conversation, their communication style is generally indirect. They are so subtle that they would not even point directly at an object. Instead, they may point to something or someone by puckering their lips and moving their mouths or chin in the direction they are pointing to. To them, pointing with the index finger is generally an expression of anger.

The indirect form of communication stems from the Filipino's deep desire to avoid *hiya* (embarrassment or shame).[33] This is their way of showing deference to another person and not doing anything to jeopardize the other party's social standing. You may sometimes find your Filipino counterpart too generous with compliments or hospitality, especially if this is the first time they are dealing with you. This may come across as being insincere or unnecessary, but it is their way of ensuring you do not suffer any embarrassment. Not wanting another person to suffer *hiya* is also an extension of showing *kapwa*. Likewise, you should avoid open disagreement or confrontation and display of negative emotions as this may embarrass them, especially in front of third parties. This means that the Filipino negotiator will avoid saying "no" to you directly and will have difficulty expressing their own interests if these interests conflict with yours. Instead of an outright "no" or rejection, they may instead say *bahal na,* which means something along the lines of it is up to God's will. Silence is very rare, and when it happens, it invariably means something is very wrong and the negotiation is at risk. You should always be mindful of the context and atmosphere and understand what the Filipino negotiator is trying to convey

---

[33] Jeremiah, R. (2015). Loób and Kapwa: An introduction to a Filipino virtue ethics. *Asian Philosophy*, 25(2), 148–171, doi: 10.1080/09552367.2015.1043173.

to you. Pay attention to the context, gestures and nonverbal signals.[34] The Filipino negotiator will be sensitive to your nonverbal cues, such as any change in your tone of voice or subtle gestures. They pride themselves in being able to access your "inner world" and know how you really feel about the negotiation process and any outcome that will follow. When they are able to accurately read your reactions, they take it as a reflection of their emotional intelligence. It assures them that they can deepen their relationship with you. This empathy is known in their culture as *pakikiramdam*.[35] It can at times be frustrating because they may ignore whatever you are saying since they hold on to their (baseless) belief that your body language speaks something else. On your side, you should check and verify a few times, to be sure of the underlying meaning, especially if it concerns important aspects of the negotiation process.

While Filipinos often laugh in conversations, in some situations the laughter is their way of covering or averting embarrassment. They use humor to soften their disagreement or rejection, and for the skilled negotiators, it may be their way of making fun or insulting the propositions you have made. Injecting humor in this manner is their way of attacking your position while preserving the relationship. One possible response from you may be to exchange playful banter with them or laugh it off to sidestep the tension. Of course, you do not have to play along if this makes you uncomfortable. There is a strong cultural norm for the Filipino negotiator to use humor to avoid head-on confrontation.[36]

4. Negotiation Strategies: Distributive or Integrative

When they go to the marketplace, Filipinos will typically buy only from their regular suppliers who in turn offer lower prices, better quality or other

---

[34] Katz, L. (2017). *Negotiation International Business — Philippines*. Negotiating International Business — The Negotiator's Reference Guide to 50 Countries Around the World [downloaded on 5 January 2023], available at http://www.leadershipcrossroads.com/mat/cou/Philippines.pdf.

[35] Jeremiah, R. (2015). Loób and Kapwa: An introduction to a Filipino virtue ethics. *Asian Philosophy*, 25(2), 148–171. doi: 10.1080/09552367.2015.1043173.

[36] Teng, C., Mendiola, M. J. B., & Montiel, C. J. (2015). From 'Good Day' to 'Sign Here': Norms shaping negotiations within a face culture. *Negotiation & Conflict Management Research*, 8(4), 228–42. https://doi.org/10.1111/ncmr.12060.

more favorable terms. This forms a *suki* relationship or bond between the buyer and seller. The term *suki* is used to describe anyone who is in a stable, trusted commercial relationship.[37] This *suki* system is also infused by *utang na loob*. The seller reciprocates the patronage by offering a better price to the buyer, who may reciprocate by recommending the seller to his/her friends and so on. When preparing for the negotiation or during the pre-negotiation stage,[38] you should find out whether your Filipino counterpart already has a *suki* relationship with any of your competitors. If there are existing *suki* bonds, you will have an uphill task convincing them to switch over and forge a new relationship with you. Essentially, their *suki* is their go-to partner and they will stick to this relationship unless there are compelling reasons to replace it. So, if you have an opportunity to establish such a bond with the Filipino negotiator, you should maximize the benefits that can come with having a *suki*.

Filipinos have a strong preference for integrative negotiation. Guided by *kapwa* (seeing you as a fellow being) and *pakikiramdam* (showing empathy), the Filipino negotiators will make explicit efforts to seek common ground and maintain a fruitful relationship with you. Especially after negotiations have progressed for some time, they tend to frame the desired negotiation outcomes in cooperative and collective terms — what is good for "us" and "we" or in their language, *kami* or *tayo*, respectively. Information will be shared by the Filipino negotiators, but they are usually tentative and subject to change because everything ultimately depends on whether or not rapport can be built. Nevertheless, there is genuine intention on their part to obtain a win–win outcome for both of you. Aside from seeking mutually beneficial outcomes for both sides, it is also vital to the Filipino negotiators that social interaction is smooth and emotions are properly managed. If they feel that there is no personal rapport between the two parties to the negotiation, or for whatever reasons you are not on the same wavelength or page as them, they would hesitate to do business with

---

[37] Dannhaeuser, N. (1980). The role of the neighborhood store in developing economies: The case of Dagupan City, Philippines. *The Journal of Developing Areas,* 14(2), 157–74. Available at http://www.jstor.org/stable/4190748.

[38] Negotiations are generally classifiable into three parts: Antecedent phase (pre-negotiation stage and preparations), the concurrent phase (ongoing process), and the consequent phase (post-negotiation stage) — See Theoretical Chapter under Negotiation Strategies: Distributive or Integrative.

you. It is for this reason that there will also be a number of social events to punctuate the negotiation process. They will appreciate your willingness to spend time with them, having meals or drinks together and even accepting invitations to go to their family gatherings. On such occasions, you will certainly be asked to sing.

If disagreements and emotions are not properly managed or if there are other obstacles to the rapport-building, the Filipino negotiators may choose to engage in distributive bargaining and maximize gains for themselves. The negotiation dynamics will be different. In the older context, *kapwa* is reserved for someone from the same *barangay* (village) or someone on the same side; outsiders or people on the opposite side do not deserve *kapwa*.[39] In the distributive mode, there is low level of trust and information will be withheld or even replaced with misinformation or misrepresentation. The Filipino negotiators will forsake the need to use humor to mask their disagreement or mitigate any affront. They can be sarcastic and may even use deceptive techniques to distract or block you or bring the negotiation to a swift end if you are not prepared to compromise.[40] Nevertheless, even in the distributive phase, the Filipino is still open to pursuing integrative outcomes and undertaking joint-problem-solving, provided you open up the necessary channels or find the right mediator. One way to switch from the distributive to the integrative mode is to leverage on relationships — have a mutual party known to both sides to help build bridges. The Filipino negotiator will have a huge kinship network (both real and ritualistic) of personal alliances because business in the Philippines relies heavily on personal ties and relationships. Finding the right mediator to whom your Filipino counterpart owes *utang na loob* will go a long way.

The Filipino negotiator's ability to both assert and assuage is reflected in their various responses to the maritime tensions and territorial disputes in the South China Sea/West Philippine Sea.[41] The administration under

[39] Jeremiah, R. (2015). Loób and Kapwa: An introduction to a Filipino virtue ethics. *Asian Philosophy*, 25(2), 148–171. doi: 10.1080/09552367.2015.1043173.

[40] Katz, L. (2017). "Negotiation International Business — Philippines." Negotiating International Business — The Negotiator's Reference Guide to 50 Countries Around the World [downloaded on 5 January 2023], available at http://www.leadershipcrossroads.com/mat/cou/Philippines.pdf.

[41] The information in this paragraph is largely obtained from Masucol, E., Jap, J., & Liu, A. H. (2022). Islands Apart: Explaining the Chinese Experience in the Philippines. *Frontiers in Political Science*, 4, 836561. doi: 10.3389/fpos.2022.836561.

Benigno Aquino III (2010–2016) adopted a distributive approach and filed an arbitration case against China. This resulted in a ruling by the Permanent Court of Arbitration at The Hague that upheld elements of the Philippines' case, but China did not participate in the proceedings. In contrast, the subsequent Duterte administration (2016–2022) prioritized cooperation and adopted policies which focused on win–win aspects of the two countries' relations. In an interview, President Marcos Jr. framed the South China Sea/West Philippine Sea in characteristic relationship-centered terms when he described it as being an "important and unavoidable part of our relationship".[42]

5. Concession-making and Hardball Tactics

The Filipino concession-making pattern is slow and at times seems never-ending. They employ what is called *dagdag,* which literally means adding-on. Just when you thought that you have closed the deal with the final sweetener, the Filipino negotiator will press for one more concession from you. At the same time, they will intimate that they are also prepared to grant you, one (hopefully last) concession in exchange. The Filipino negotiator enjoys such reciprocity, especially near the end of the concurrent phase, because it reflects mutual commitment towards the negotiated outcome. This is also in sync with the circuitry of *utang na loob* and is taken to be a positive sign that both parties will be in a long-term relationship. If you hope to build a *suki* bond, you have to be sensitive to such requests for concessions because a positive reaction will lay the foundation and build trust between the two parties. Show patience, make space for delays and maintain your composure.

You can opt to stand firm and not accede to any further requests for last-minute concessions, especially if doing so will breach your resistance. Because the Filipino negotiators are relationship-oriented, they will be open to "postponing" concession-making to when parties negotiate the next deal or *sa susunod na* (next time).[43] This will be taken to mean that both sides

---

[42] Kawase, K. (2023). "South China Sea Keeps Philippines' Marcos up 'Night and Day.'" *Nikkei Asia,* January 19. Available at https://asia.nikkei.com/Spotlight/Davos-2023/South-China-Sea-keeps-Philippines-Marcos-up-night-and-day.

[43] Teng, C., Mendiola, M. J. B., & Montiel, C. J. (2015). From 'Good Day' to 'Sign Here': Norms shaping negotiations within a face culture. *Negotiation & Conflict Management Research,* 8(4), 228–242. https://doi.org/10.1111/ncmr.12060.

can look forward to better concessions or more generous gestures in the future as the relationship deepens. You can also defer such concession-making to the post-negotiation stage, during which you can expect more bargaining. However, if you commit to granting any concessions in the future, you must remember your "obligation" to keep up the reciprocity, and likewise you can remind your Filipino negotiators if they "owe" you any future concessions. Such exchanges enhance the trust and rapport.

The Filipino negotiators are skilled at using emotional appeals either to oppose your offers or to substantiate theirs.[44] They may try to make you feel guilty in order to appreciate their predicament or difficulty. When this happens, they are hoping to trigger your *kapwa* for you to share their perspectives. Though indirect, their communication style is expressive and colourful. Appeals are commonly accompanied with humility — "please consider", "please understand this is insufficient", "please, we can make this happen". Their facial expressions and body language will reinforce their plea. This will rarely escalate into any form of intimidation or aggression because they do not want to risk losing any face or causing you to suffer *hiya*. However, in this high power-distance society, if the Filipino negotiators occupy very senior positions, they may resort to using threats or even insults. At this point, there will be a change in the pronouns used by them, from the collaborative *tayo* (we, us) to the *kayo* (you). This is where the negotiation may shift from cooperation to competition. This is a crucial inflection point in the negotiation which requires cautious approach. One approach is to seek a break in the negotiation process to de-escalate tensions. The experienced Filipino negotiator will know how to inject humor at the appropriate juncture to enable both sides to save face.[45]

Generally, the Filipino negotiators prefer not to use hardball tactics, which require some display of aggression or hostility, because they place a premium on maintaining smooth interpersonal relationships. However, the younger generation, especially those who have studied overseas or are

---

[44] Katz, L. (2017). "Negotiation International Business — Philippines." *Negotiating International Business — The Negotiator's Reference Guide to 50 Countries Around the World* [downloaded on 5 January 2023], available at http://www.leadershipcrossroads.com/mat/cou/Philippines.pdf.

[45] Teng, C., Mendiola, M. J. B., & C. J. Montiel. (2015). From 'Good Day' to 'Sign Here': Norms shaping negotiations within a face culture. *Negotiation & Conflict Management Research,* 8(4), 228–242. https://doi.org/10.1111/ncmr.12060.

very fluent in the English language, may take a different stance. They are generally more comfortable making demands and rejecting your proposals. When it comes to tangibles such as price, they may simply tell you to "take it or leave it". In a sense, some younger Filipino negotiators have a more straightforward negotiation style. By extension, this may also mean it will be more challenging to build longer-term relationships with them.

6. Role of Women

Among all the countries covered in this book, the Philippines registers the highest level of gender parity. Based on the 2022 Global Gender Gap Report by the World Economic Forum (see the following table), the Philippines is second in the East Asia and Pacific region (after New Zealand and ahead of Australia) and 19th globally, out of 146 countries.[46]

Global Gender Gap Report 2022 INSIGHT REPORT JULY 2022			
EAST ASIA & the PACIFIC	Rank		
Country	Regional (19)	Global (146)	Score
Philippines	**2**	**19**	**0.783**
Singapore	4	49	0.734
Thailand	8	79	0.709
Vietnam	9	83	0.705
Indonesia	10	92	0.697
Korea (South)	12	99	0.689
China	13	102	0.682
Malaysia	14	103	0.681
Japan	19	116	0.650

Source: "Global Gender Gap Report 2022." World Economic Forum. July 13, 2022. https://www.weforum.org/reports/global-gender-gap-report-2022/digest.

---

[46] "Global Gender Gap Report 2022." (July 13, 2022). World Economic Forum. Available at https://www.weforum.org/reports/global-gender-gap-report-2022/digest. The Global Gender Gap Index benchmarks the current state and evolution of gender parity across four key dimensions (Economic Participation and Opportunity, Educational Attainment, Health and Survival, and Political Empowerment). It is the longest-standing index which has been tracking progress towards closing these gaps over time since its inception in 2006.

The Filipino family is based on a bilateral kinship system where neither the male nor the female side has privilege over the other in terms of descent or superiority.[47] Due to this, in traditional society, the women held prominent social roles in the community and remained their husbands' equal partners. Even the highest political offices in the country — its Presidency and Vice-Presidency — have been held by women several times. Among the country's prominent family-owned conglomerates, there are also women in leadership positions. For SM Investment Corporation, the late founder's eldest daughter Teresita T. Sy holds many key positions and is seen to be the de-facto successor.[48] Another well-known example is Robina Gokongwei, the eldest daughter of late tycoon John Gokongwei Jr., who helms the family business empire.[49] For women in corporate leadership positions, the phenomenon known as "glass walls" — i.e., being over-represented in support management functions such as human resources, finance and administration and under-represented in strategic decision-making — is nevertheless still present.[50]

It is possible that you may still face some gender stereotypes when negotiating in the Philippines as a woman. However, being confident and articulate will win you some quick admiration. The Filipino will not put obstacles in your trust building merely on account of your being a female negotiator. In fact, they may even be prepared to accept a more aggressive or masculine behaviour from you. Once rapport is built, you will no doubt receive many social invitations from your Filipino counterpart and they will respect your social comfort zone. Throughout the negotiation process, you must always be careful not to embarrass them or cause them to suffer

---

[47] Rodell, P. A. (2018). Chapter 25: A syncretic culture. In M. R. Thompson & E. V. C. Batalla (Eds.), *Routledge Handbook of the Contemporary Philippines* (pp. 321–329) London & New York: Routledge.

[48] Ylagan, H. C. A. (February 10, 2019). "Primogeniture in Family Business — BusinessWorld Online." BusinessWorld Online. Available at https://www.bworldonline.com/editors-picks/2019/02/10/213590/primogeniture-in-family-business/.

[49] Gonzales, I. (October 27, 2021). "4 Philippine Companies among World's Top 10 Women-Led Firms." Philstar.com. Available at https://www.philstar.com/business/2021/10/27/2136886/4-philippine-companies-among-worlds-top-10-women-led-firms.

[50] "Leading to Success: The Business Case for Women in Business and Management in the Philippines," September 18, 2020. Available at http://www.ilo.org/manila/publications/WCMS_755607/lang--en/index.htm.

hiya — as they expect their boundaries to be respected and will not cut you any slack even if you are a woman.

7. Intermediary/Interpreter

As English is one of two official languages in the country, many Filipinos in Manila are fluent in English. The 2022 English Proficiency Index ranked the Philippines 22nd out of 111 countries.[51] This is higher than other ASEAN countries covered in this book such as Malaysia (24th), Vietnam (60th), Indonesia (81st) and Thailand (97th).[52] You should be mindful of your counterpart's English proficiency and not talk to them in a way that comes across or may be interpreted as being patronizing.

If you intend to engage an intermediary to facilitate relationship building, this should be someone who has a positive *utang na loob* relationship with your Filipino counterpart. With this, the Filipino negotiator may feel more inclined or even obligated to achieve a mutually beneficial outcome. Besides business associates, *barkada* or old friends or someone part of a longtime social network are also an important branch of a Filipino's kinship network. Because these are built over time, the importance of the *barkada* can even rival family ties and should therefore not be underestimated.[53] These long associations will also of course have their system of *utang na loob* vis-à-vis your Filipino counterpart.

However, as discussed, *utang na loob* is a complicated social mechanism of reciprocity. Favors are expected to be repaid and the recipient is generally not in a position to refuse.[54] The Philippines is ranked 116th out of 180 countries by the Transparency International's Corruption Perception Index 2022.[55] This is the lowest ranking among the countries covered in

[51] "EF EPI 2022 — EF English Proficiency Index." Available at https://www.ef.com/wwen/epi/. (Accessed February 8, 2023).
[52] Ibid
[53] Rodell, P. A. (2018). Chapter 25: A syncretic culture. In M. R. Thompson and E. V. C. Batalla (Eds.), *Routledge Handbook of the Contemporary Philippines* (pp. 321–329). London & New York: Routledge.
[54] Kaut, C. (1961). Utang Na Loob: A system of contractual obligation among Tagalogs. *Southwestern Journal of Anthropology,* 17(3), 256–272.
[55] Transparency.org. (January 25, 2022). "Philippines." Available at https://www.transparency.org/en/countries/philippines.

this book.[56] The cultural norm of *utang na loob* no doubt plays an integral part in the corruption in the Philippines because it leads to clientelism. The importance of kinship network is also a contributing factor. Whenever a person occupies an influential political or business position, members of his or her family will enjoy enhanced standing, and with that they are put in a better position to generate and leverage off the system of "indebtedness". Due to these cultural factors, Filipinos seem more tolerant of corruption. Despite having several anti-corruption agencies, there is consistently low probability of detection and punishment for corrupt offences.[57]

The involvement of a third party may thus subject both you and your Filipino counterpart to unintended "obligations" and can complicate matters. Depending on the situation at hand, having a middleman is not always welcome when negotiating in the Philippines.[58] If you decide to enlist the help of an intermediary when negotiating in the Philippines, you should proceed with caution.

8. Time, Timelines and Timeliness

Filipinos are often late when meeting their friends and even for their own social events to which you have been invited. They called this "Filipino Time", which can mean an hour or two after the scheduled time. The atrocious traffic and congestion in the Metro Manila certainly provide legitimate reasons for delay. Also, because senior people may choose to show up late for appointments to reflect their status, the junior members will take the cue and time their appearances. However, for important business meetings, there is a growing trend of timeliness on the part of the Filipino negotiator. You should therefore be punctual for these occasions, especially if the meetings are called by you.

Even if punctual, they will not launch into discussion of formal matters immediately because making small talk will invariably take place first. Negotiations often start slowly because your Filipino counterpart wants to

---

[56] North Korea is also assigned a separate ranking, at 174th place.
[57] Quah, J. S. T. (2018). Chapter 4: Combating corruption. In M. R. Thompson and E. V. C. Batalla (Eds.) *Routledge Handbook of the Contemporary Philippines* (pp. 321–329). London & New York: Routledge.
[58] Chang, L.-C. (2011). A comparison of Taiwanese and Philippine Chinese business negotiation styles. *Social Behavior and Personality,* 39(6), 765–772.

read the room and make sure they tune in correctly as to how you are feeling. Add their indirect style of communication and strong focus to building rapport with you during the negotiation process, the pace of negotiation may be protracted.[59] If there are key deadlines to be met, or if time is of the essence when it comes to some of the tangibles — you should stress the importance of compliance in relationship terms so that your Filipino counterpart knows the importance of keeping to the agreed schedule.

Bibliography

Association of Southeast Asian Nations. (2020). "The Founding of ASEAN." Asean.org. Available at https://asean.org/the-founding-of-asean/.

Cabuay, C., & Hill, H. (2019). 5. The Philippine economy: Renewed dynamism, old challenges. In I. Deinla & B. Dressel (Eds.), *From Aquino II to Duterte (2010–2018): Change, Continuity — And Rupture* (pp. 145–185). Singapore: ISEAS Publishing, available at https://doi.org/10.1355/9789814843294-011.

Chang, L.-C. (2011). A comparison of Taiwanese and Philippine Chinese business negotiation styles. *Social Behavior and Personality,* 39(6), 765–772.

Chu, R. T. (2023). From 'Sangley' to 'Chinaman', 'Chinese Mestizo' to 'Tsinoy': Unpacking 'Chinese' identities in the Philippines at the turn of the Twentieth-Century. *Asian Ethnicity,* 24(1), 7–37.

Church, P. (2017). *Short History of South-East Asia.* Singapore: John Wiley & Sons Inc.

CIA. (January 17, 2023). "Philippines — The World Factbook." Available at https://www.cia.gov/the-world-factbook/countries/philippines/.

Dannhaeuser, N. (1980). The role of the neighborhood store in developing economies: The case of Dagupan City, Philippines. *The Journal of Developing Areas,* 14(2), 157–74. Available at http://www.jstor.org/stable/4190748.

"EF English Proficiency Index 2022." Available at https://www.ef.com/wwen/epi/. (Accessed February 8, 2023).

Gonzales, I. (October 27, 2021). "4 Philippine Companies among World's Top 10 Women-Led Firms." Philstar.com. Available at https://www.philstar.com/business/2021/10/27/2136886/4-philippine-companies-among-worlds-top-10-women-led-firms.

[59] Katz, L. (2017). "Negotiation International Business — Philippines." Negotiating International Business — The Negotiator's Reference Guide to 50 Countries Around the World [downloaded on 5 January 2023], available at http://www.leadershipcrossroads.com/mat/cou/Philippines.pdf.

Government of the Philippines Senate. (n.d.) "Press Release — PRIB: Senate Declares Chinese New Year as Special Working Holiday." Legacy.senate.gov. ph. Available at https://legacy.senate.gov.ph/press_release/2013/0121_prib1. asp. (Accessed January 25, 2023).

Hofstede Insights. "Country Comparison — Hofstede Insights." Available at https://www.hofstede-insights.com/country-comparison/. (Accessed February 6, 2023).

Holnsteiner, M. (1973). Reciprocity in the lowland Philippines. In F. Lynch & A. De Guzman II (Eds.), *Four Readings on Philippine Values* (4th edn.). Quezon City: Ateneo de Manila.

International Labour Organization. (September 18, 2020). "Leading to Success: The Business Case for Women in Business and Management in the Philippines." Available at http://www.ilo.org/manila/publications/WCMS_755607/ lang--en/index.htm.

Jeremiah, R. (2015). Loób and Kapwa: An introduction to a Filipino virtue ethics. *Asian Philosophy*, 25(2), 148–171. doi: 10.1080/09552367.2015.1043173.

Katz, L. (2017). "Negotiation International Business — Philippines." Negotiating International Business — The Negotiator's Reference Guide to 50 Countries Around the World [downloaded on 5 January 2023], available at http://www. leadershipcrossroads.com/mat/cou/Philippines.pdf.

Kaut, C. (1961). Utang Na Loob: A system of contractual obligation among Tagalogs. *Southwestern Journal of Anthropology,* 17(3), 256–272.

Kawase, K. (2023). "South China Sea Keeps Philippines' Marcos up 'Night and Day." *Nikkei Asia*, January 19. Available at https://asia.nikkei.com/Spotlight/ Davos-2023/South-China-Sea-keeps-Philippines-Marcos-up-night-and-day.

Masucol, E., Jap, J., & Liu, A. H. (2022). Islands apart: Explaining the Chinese experience in the Philippines. *Frontiers in Political Science,* 4, 836561. doi: 10.3389/fpos.2022.836561.

Philippine Statistical Authority. (2022). "Highlights of the Philippine Export and Import Statistics August 2022 (Preliminary)." Available at https://psa. gov.ph/content/highlights-philippine-export-and-import-statistics-august-2022-preliminary#:~:text=The%20People. (Accessed January 31, 2023).

Philippine Statistical Authority. "Statistical Tables on Overseas Filipino Workers | Philippine Statistics Authority." (n.d.). Psa.gov.ph. Available at https://psa. gov.ph/statistics/survey/labor-force/sof-index.

Quah, J. S. T. (2018). Chapter 4: Combating corruption. In M. R. Thompson & E. V. C. Batalla (Eds.), *Routledge Handbook of the Contemporary Philippines* (pp. 321–329). London & New York: Routledge.

Rodell, P. A. (2018). Chapter 25: A syncretic culture. In M. R. Thompson & E. V. C. Batalla (Eds.), *Routledge Handbook of the Contemporary Philippines* (pp. 321–329). London & New York: Routledge.

SM Investments. (September 7, 2015). "SM Prime Wins Gold Award for China Mall." Available at https://www.sminvestments.com/press_release/sm-prime-wins-gold-award-for-china-mall/.

SM Investments. "At a Glance," available at https://www.sminvestments.com/about-us/at-a-glance/. (Accessed January 25, 2023).

Susanto, A. B. & Susanto, P. (2013). *The Dragon Network: Inside Stories of the Most Successful Chinese Family Businesses.* Singapore: John Wiley & Sons.

Tanzer, A. (1994). The bamboo network. *Forbes,* 154(2), 138–144.

Teng, C., Mendiola, M. J. B., & Montiel, C. J. (2015). From 'Good Day' to 'Sign Here': Norms shaping negotiations within a face culture. *Negotiation & Conflict Management Research,* 8(4), 228–42. https://doi.org/10.1111/ncmr.12060.

Transparency.org. "Philippines." Available at https://www.transparency.org/en/countries/philippines.

World Economic Forum. (July 13, 2022). "Global Gender Gap Report 2022." Available at https://www.weforum.org/reports/global-gender-gap-report-2022/digest.

World Economic Forum. "Where Are the Largest Chinese Populations Outside of China? | Thailand or Indonesia: Which Country Has the Largest Chinese Population? | By World Economic Forum | Facebook." Available at https://www.facebook.com/worldeconomicforum/videos/where-are-the-largest-chinese-populations-outside-of-china/10153549858561479/. (Accessed November 8, 2022).

Ylagan, H. C. A. (February 10, 2019). "Primogeniture in Family Business — BusinessWorld Online." BusinessWorld Online. https://www.bworldonline.com/editors-picks/2019/02/10/213590/primogeniture-in-family-business/.

Philippines Quiz

1. The two key contributors to the Philippines' economy are Business Process Outsourcing (BPO) and tourism. True or False?
   A. True
   B. False

2. The two official languages are Filipino and English. Filipino is based on the:
   A. Cebuano language
   B. Tagalog language
   C. Malay language
   D. Javanese language

3. *Kapwa* is one of foundational concepts of the Filipino culture. *Kapwa* refers to:
   A. a sense of fellowship and shared identity
   B. the notion of reciprocity
   C. embarrassment or shame
   D. relationship and bond between buyers and sellers

4. *Utang na loob* is the concept of reciprocity that upkeeps and solidifies kinship relations in the Philippines. What does the term mean?
   A. Fellowship
   B. Embarrassment or shame
   C. Giving face
   D. Debt of gratitude

5. Attracted by economic opportunities during Philippines' days as a Spanish colony, Chinese traders and migrants mainly from the _____ province began setting up home in the port city of Manila. Fill in the blank.
   A. Guangdong
   B. Fuzhou
   C. Hainan
   D. Fujian

6. The Filipino's indirect form of communication stems from their deep desire to avoid _____. This is their way of giving face and not jeopardizing the other person's social standing. Fill in the blank.
   A. threatening sense of fellowship between individuals
   B. showing lack of empathy
   C. causing embarrassment
   D. upsetting established commercial dealings

7. Filipinos have a strong preference for _____ negotiation because they are guided by the core cultural concept of *kapwa*. Fill in the blank.
   A. distributive
   B. integrative
   C. mixture of distributive and integrative
   D. contingent

8. The Filipino concession-making involves the use of *dagdag*, which literally means _____. Fill in the blank.
   A. adding-on
   B. changing their last offer
   C. Applying time pressure
   D. ending the negotiation suddenly

9. According to the 2022 Global Gender Gap Report by the World Economic Forum, Philippines' gender parity score is _____ Singapore and is _____ Japan. Fill in the blanks.
   A. lower than; higher than
   B. the same as; higher than
   C. lower than; same as
   D. higher than; higher than

10. When negotiating in the Philippines it is not advisable to involve third parties because this may subject both you and your Filipino counterpart to unintended "obligations" due to their system of *utang na loob,* which is a complicated concept of reciprocity. Is this statement true or false?
    A. True
    B. False

Answer Bank

1. B. False. The two key contributors to the Philippines' economy are the Business Process Outsourcing (BPO) and remittance from its Overseas Filipino Workers (OFW).
2. B
3. A
4. D
5. D
6. C

7. B. Integrative. Filipinos have a strong preference for integrative negotiation because they are guided by the core concept of *kapwa* which makes them see you as a fellow being.
8. A. adding-on. *Dagdag* literally means adding-on i.e. the Filipino negotiator will also press for one more concession even when you believe you have closed the deal with a final sweetener.
9. D. In terms of gender parity, Philippines' score is higher than both Singapore and Japan. Based on the 2022 Global Gender Gap Report, the Philippines is placed second in the East Asia and the Pacific region.
10. A.

Chapter 7

The Singaporean Negotiator

1. The Environment

This small city-state in Southeast Asia is widely regarded as an economic miracle (and one of the original Four Tiger or Dragon Economies mentioned by the World Bank in its report titled "The East Asian Miracle"). With no hinterland and scarce natural resources, Singapore has now a thriving modern economy and one of the highest GDP per capita in the world.[1] When you are in Singapore for your negotiation, you will be impressed by the spotless tree-lined streets and top-class infrastructure in one of the world's most expensive cities.[2]

Against this picture of modernity, it is hard to imagine that the island at the southern tip of the Malay peninsula was just a small enclave of fishing villages populated mainly by a few hundred Malay families at the beginning of the 19th century.[3] In 1819, the British East India Company under Sir Stamford Raffles gained control of the island — known first as *Temasek* (derived from the Malay word *tasek,* which means "lake") and later as

---

[1] International Monetary Fund. (2022). "GDP per Capita, Current Prices." Imf.org, https://www.imf.org/external/datamapper/NGDPDPC@WEO/OEMDC/ADVEC/WEOWORLD.

[2] In 2022, Singapore shared the top spot with New York City. Hannam, P. (2022). "New York and Singapore Top the List of World's Most Expensive Cities in 2022." *The Guardian,* https://www.theguardian.com/business/2022/dec/01/new-york-and-singapore-top-the-list-of-worlds-most-expensive-cities-in-2022.

[3] Church, P. (2017). *Short History of South-East Asia.* Singapore: John Wiley & Sons Inc.

Singapura (which means "lion city" in Sanskrit).[4] The British renamed the island "Singapore" and it became a major entrepot trade port (later a major global transshipment hub) for products from the Southeast Asian region and industrial Europe. Its status as a free port attracted migrants and traders from southern parts of China and the Indian subcontinent, as well as others such as the Javanese and Bugis merchants from Indonesia. Three years of Japanese occupation (1942–1945) during World War II interrupted the British rule. When limited self-government was introduced in 1959, the People's Action Party (PAP) won a landslide victory and a Cambridge-educated lawyer, Lee Kuan Yew, became the country's first prime minister. Lee held that position for three decades and his leadership is largely credited for transforming Singapore from a third-world colonial backwaters to one of the region's economic "Tigers."

After the country gained independence in 1965, the PAP government took a resolutely pragmatist approach and drew up various blueprints for planned development. The overarching national economic strategy was to establish industrial estates (similar to free economic zones) in order to attract foreign investments and to capitalize on the country's strategic geographical location. Low taxes and reliable infrastructure coupled with a legal system modelled on the English common law system and which adopted many British commercial laws made Singapore an attractive hub for finance and trade. Very early on, education was seen as an important tool for nation and economy building. Since 1966, the government pursued a bilingual policy which required students to learn English as well as their respective mother tongues, namely, Chinese, Malay and Tamil (according to the racial background of each individual).[5] A centralized and highly subsidized public education produced a highly skilled and educated workforce to support economic growth and later to help the country transition

---

[4] National Library Board. (2014). "Temasek/Singapura — Singapore History." Singapore, https://eresources.nlb.gov.sg/history/events/d24d6da6-0013-4a12-a6bc-68ad1497148e#:~: text=Temasek%2FSingapura%20%2D%20Singapore%20History&text=The%20name%20% E2%80%9CTemasek%E2%80%9D%20is%20probably,of%20land%20surrounded%20by% 20water. (Accessed February 20, 2023).

[5] Poon, A. (2018). Narrating privilege: Meritocracy and the portrait of the scholar in Singapore Anglophone literature. *Postcolonial Studies,* 21(4), 414–432. (See footnote 29).

from an industrial to a service economy. The strong focus on education also underpinned a merit-based system to reward and promote based on a person's achievement and performance rather than his or her personal connections or race or ethnicity. Meritocracy was championed by Lee Kuan Yew as one of the country's fundamental governing principles and an effective way to root out corruption and rent-seeking. Singapore has consistently occupied top positions in global corruption perception indices and in 2022 it was ranked fifth out of 180 countries by the Transparency International's Corruption Perception Index.[6]

The country's rise from a developing country to a first-world nation in merely five decades is a remarkable story. Today, the country's former humble name "Temasek" is better known as being the name of its sovereign wealth fund, which manages a global portfolio in excess of S$400 billion.[7]

Nevertheless, the Singapore negotiators are keenly aware that their country is a tiny red dot[8] on the world map subject to regional and global economic headwinds and contesting forces. The country's pragmatic government has always imbued its people with a sense of vulnerability and situation awareness and this is reflected in their mindset when they negotiate with you.

2. Culture

Singapore is a multicultural society. Ethnic Chinese make up three-quarters of its almost four-million strong population and the rest are mainly Malays, Indians and Eurasians.[9] The country is thus home to three dominant

---

[6] Transparency.org. (January 25, 2022). "Singapore" https://www.transparency.org/en/countries/singapore.

[7] "Temasek at a Glance." (n.d.). Temasek Corporate Website English. https://www.temasek.com.sg/en/about-us/temasek-at-a-glance.

[8] The description of Singapore as "a little red dot" was made by then Indonesian President Habibie in an interview to *Asian Wall Street Journal* in August 1988. Corsuk, R. & Chua, R. (1998). Singapore strains relations with Indonesia's President. *The Wall Street Journal.* Available at https://www.wsj.com/articles/SB902170180588248000.

[9] CIA. "Singapore — The World Factbook". January 27, 2023. available at https://www.cia.gov/the-world-factbook/countries/singapore/.

cultural groups (the ethnic Chinese, Malays and mixed heritage Eurasians) of East Asia and the Indians from South Asia.[10] Additionally, Singapore hosts close to 1.5 million non-residents from various parts of the world who work or study in the country.[11] The island has been a cultural melting pot since its days as a busy colonial port as part of the British commercial and industrial empire. Then, the living areas of various racial groups were demarcated and this is reflected in present-day Singapore street names and areas such as Bugis Street, Arab Street, Chinatown, Little India and the Malay Village.[12] However, post-independent Singapore introduced a slew of government policies to promote racial and religious harmony and to prevent formation of racial enclaves. Meticulous rules are in place to ensure Singaporeans of different ethnic backgrounds live, study and work together amicably.[13] Singapore has four official languages, namely, English, Malay, Mandarin and Tamil. English is the medium of instruction in schools and Malay, Mandarin and Tamil are taught as second languages. English is thus the first language (the 'working language') and widely used in Singapore. Local speakers also use a brand of colloquial English, known as Singlish in office or work settings, especially when communicating among themselves. Singlish has its own unique sentence structure and grammar and is heavily influenced by Malay, Tamil and Chinese dialects such as Hokkien/Southern Min and Cantonese, as well as the frequent use of non-English fillers such as *hor, lah* and *leh* to add emphasis. Such use engenders a sense of connectedness among Singaporeans of different races. Multiculturalism is also reflected in the food choices available to you when you visit the city state. Your Singaporean counterpart may suggest dining at a hawker center — which is an open-air complex that houses

[10] Osman-Gani, A. M. & Tan, J. S. (2002). Influence of culture on negotiation styles of Asian managers: An empirical study of major cultural/ethnic groups in Singapore. *Thunderbird International Business Review,* 44(6), 819–839.

[11] Department of Statistics Singapore. "Population Trends, 2022." Available at https://www.singstat.gov.sg/-/media/files/publications/population/population2022.ashx#:~:text=Chapter%201%20Population-,Population%20Size%20and%20Growth,June%202022%20(Table%201.1). (Accessed February 14, 2023).

[12] Cordeiro, C. M. (2019). Negotiating with managers from Singapore. In M. A. Khan & N. Ebner (Eds.), *The Palgrave Handbook of Cross-Cultural Business Negotiation.* Cham: Palgrave Macmillan. https://doi.org/10.1007/978-3-030-00277-0_16.

[13] Gov.sg. (April 13, 2020). "HDB's Ethnic Integration Policy: Why It Still Matters." www.gov.sg, available at https://www.gov.sg/article/hdbs-ethnic-integration-policy-why-it-still-matters.

a wide variety of Chinese, Malay or Indian as well as Western dishes adapted to local tastes and context. Hawker centers are typically sited in government-subsidized housing estates known colloquially as "HDB" estates[14] and serve as communal dining spaces. In 2019, Singapore's hawker culture made it to the Unesco (United Nations Educational, Scientific and Cultural Organization) Representative List of Intangible Culture Heritage of Humanity.[15]

The main cultural groups have developed many common values while retaining their respective cultural influences. When you negotiate in Singapore, you may find that there are no dramatic differences in the negotiation styles of the three major ethnic groups.[16] Sometimes, there may be slight subtle differences — the Chinese Singaporean may seek more details and spend more time weighing the pros and cons of your proposals, his or her Indian counterpart may be relatively more people-oriented and you may find the Malay Singaporean generally non-confrontational.[17]

Singapore is the only Association of Southeast Asian Nations (ASEAN)[18] country with an ethnic Chinese-majority population.[19] According to the World Economic Forum (2016), Singapore's Chinese majority is the fifth largest Chinese population in the world residing outside of China.[20] Culturally, there are obvious similarity between the ethnic

[14] "HDB Stands for Housing Development Board and is Singapore's Public Housing Authority." Available at https://www.hdb.gov.sg/cs/infoweb/about-us.
[15] "UNESCO — Hawker Culture in Singapore, Community Dining and Culinary Practices in a Multicultural Urban Context." (n.d). Ich.unesco.org, available at https://ich.unesco.org/en/RL/hawker-culture-in-singapore-community-dining-and-culinary-practices-in-a-multicultural-urban-context-01568.
[16] Osman-Gani, A. M. & Tan, J. S. (2002). Influence of culture on negotiation styles of Asian managers: An empirical study of major cultural/ethnic groups in Singapore. *Thunderbird International Business Review,* 44(6), 819–839.
[17] *Ibid.*
[18] Association of Southeast Asian Nations. (2020). "The Founding of ASEAN." Asean.org, available at https://asean.org/the-founding-of-asean/. Indonesia, Malaysia, Philippines, Singapore and Thailand are the five founding member nations of ASEAN which now includes Brunei, Cambodia, Laos, Myanmar and Vietnam.
[19] Church, P. (2017). *Short History of South-East Asia.* Singapore: John Wiley & Sons Inc.
[20] "Where Are the Largest Chinese Populations Outside of China? | Thailand or Indonesia: Which Country Has the Largest Chinese Population? | By World Economic Forum | Facebook." Available at https://www.facebook.com/worldeconomicforum/videos/where-are-the-largest-chinese-populations-outside-of-china/10153549858561479/. (Accessed November 8, 2022).

Chinese Singaporean negotiator and the Chinese negotiator — such as the embracing of Confucian values and respect for social order and hierarchy. During the country's colonial days, there were already a number of prominent family companies in Singapore owned by second- or third-generation ethnic Chinese, which plugged into the Chinese diaspora in Hong Kong and Southeast Asia.[21] Such networks of *guanxi* (connection) have grown many folds since, especially with the rise of China as an economic powerhouse, and as mentioned earlier are now popularly referred to as Bamboo network[22] or Dragon network.[23] Since 2013, China has been Singapore's (and ASEAN's) largest trading partner and Singapore has been one of the largest (the largest, in fact, at the time of writing) foreign investors in China.[24]

However, in the context of business negotiations, ethnic Chinese Singaporeans are conscious of some noticeable differences between themselves and the Mainland Chinese, even if both speak the same language of Mandarin. The Singaporean negotiators tend to be more focused on details and data; prefer sorting out rules and reasons and largely regard contracts as legal instruments that bring finality. For the Chinese negotiators, the overarching objective is to build relationships and then sort out the working mechanics of business collaborations. They accept that contracts reflect mutual intentions, but these must be recalibrated when circumstances change so that relationships can be maintained.

Hofstede's Cultural Dimensions

- **Power Distance**

Singapore's national score for this index is 74. It is below China's (80) and well below neighboring Malaysia's (100), but is higher than that of Thailand (64) and Japan (54). Though the Singapore negotiator may come across as being more Westernized than their regional counterparts, theirs is still a hierarchical society where respect for elders and reverence for

---

[21] Church, P. (2017). *Short History of South-East Asia*. Singapore: John Wiley & Sons Inc.

[22] Tanzer, A. (1994). The bamboo network. *Forbes,* 154(2), 138–144.

[23] Susanto, A. B. & Susanto, P. (2013). *The Dragon Network: Inside Stories of the Most Successful Chinese Family Businesses.* Singapore: John Wiley & Sons.

[24] "People's Republic of China." (n.d.) www.mfa.gov.sg, available at https://www.mfa.gov.sg/SINGAPORES-FOREIGN-POLICY/Countries-and-Regions/Northeast-Asia/Peoples-Republic-of-China. (Accessed November 28, 2020).

high-ranking office-holders are norms in the society.[25] The ruling party, PAP, is widely accepted as being a paternalistic government and, in the 1990s, Lee Kuan Yew frequently invoked Confucianism to justify building a hierarchical society with strong incorruptible leaders to steer the country. The party's blueprint for Singapore's development and continuing success has always been based on a strong state and state intervention in the economy. As a result, Singaporeans accept that people are not equal (based on meritocracy) and that their place in the social structure depends on their network and, in particular, educational background.

Hierarchy is keenly observed in state-owned enterprise (SOEs) or more commonly called government-linked companies (GLCs) in Singapore. This is especially palpable when the decision-maker is a "scholar" (though not all business or political leaders belong to this category). In Singapore, highly competitive government scholarships are awarded to top academic performers in national examinations, taken when they are 18 years old. These scholarships will fund the recipients' undergraduate education typically at top local or overseas universities and thereafter, in exchange, these graduates will be "bonded" or obligated to work for a number of years in the civil service or public sector. In Singapore parlance, "scholars" refer to these government scholarship holders who are frequently fast-tracked and talent-managed to assume high-level positions in the civil service.[26] When negotiating with an SOE or a government-linked entity, if the decision-maker on the Singapore team appears younger than his or her fellow members, it is frequently the case that you are dealing with an academically outstanding scholar.

- **Individualism–Collectivism**
Despite their exposure and experience interacting with other cultures, Singaporeans are, by and large, group-oriented.[27] For the Individualism index, Singapore's low score of 20 is the same as China's (20), Thailand's

[25] Retna, K. S. & Jones, D. (2013). The 'learning organization' and Singapore culture. *The Learning Organization* 20(4/5), 338–351.

[26] Poon, A. (2018). Narrating privilege: Meritocracy and the portrait of the scholar in Singapore Anglophone literature. *Postcolonial Studies,* 21(4), 414–432.

[27] Katz, L. (2017). "Negotiation International Business — Singapore." Negotiating International Business — The Negotiator's Reference Guide to 50 Countries Around the World [downloaded on 7 February 2023], available at http://www.leadershipcrossroads.com/mat/cou/Singapore.pdf.

(20) and Vietnam's (20).[28] From very early on, racial and religious harmony has been one of the key tenets of government policies. A constant theme in government discourses is that the needs of the community frequently take precedence over individual needs. Though they are competitive and value material success, Singaporeans are collectivist. In-groups in Singapore generally consist of interrelated network of people who share common socio-demographic characteristics, values, beliefs and ways of doing things.[29] If you are negotiating with a team, you may find that the junior members of your Singaporean counterpart generally will not speak up during the meetings or formal discussions. They are usually quiet and reserved and will not want to stand out from the crowd. Acting appropriately in social situations to promote conformity and cooperation is the norm in the society.[30]

- **Uncertainty Avoidance**

Abiding by rules and regulations is the default behavior of the Singaporean negotiator. There is a strong sense of certainty and security as everyone follows well-defined rules. The city-state is well known to some and notorious to others for imposing fines and punishments for antisocial behavior such as littering and vandalism. Even the failure to return food trays at its ubiquitous hawker centers will attract a fine.[31] Within the society, there is high predictability and conformity, so Singaporeans are unaccustomed to thinking about uncertainty. Singapore's low score in this index provides an interesting contrast to Japan's high score (92) even though both peoples are diligent adherents of rules.[32] One possible reason for being on opposite ends of this spectrum may be that whereas the

[28] Hofstede Insights. "Country Comparison — Hofstede Insights." https://www.hofstede-insights.com/country-comparison/. (Accessed February 6, 2023).

[29] Loh, J. (M.I.), Restubog, S. L.D., & Gallois, C. (2009). The nature of workplace boundaries between Australians and Singaporeans in multinational organizations: A qualitative inquiry. *Cross Cultural Management: An International Journal*, 16(4), 367–385. https://doi.org/10.1108/13527600911000348.

[30] *Ibid.*

[31] "News Releases." www.nea.gov.sg, available at https://www.nea.gov.sg/media/news/news/index/mandatory-for-diners-to-return-dirty-trays-crockery-and-clean-table-litter-at-hawker-centres-coffeeshops-and-food-courts.

[32] Hofstede Insights. "Country Comparison — Hofstede Insights." https://www.hofstede-insights.com/country-comparison/. (Accessed February 6, 2023).

Japanese negotiators have a strong dislike for uncertainty (hence high score), their Singapore counterparts are simply not accustomed to dealing with uncertainty (hence low score). Once the agreed negotiated outcomes are committed to writing, if you want to propose any change or variation, the Singapore negotiator will accommodate your request, but this may entail more meetings and discussions, and even starting over again or re-negotiation.

There are of course other perspectives to help appreciate Singapore's low uncertainty avoidance score. One is the cultural plurality in its society. The Singaporean negotiators are constantly exposed to diverse cultures so they can adapt to new ideas and situations, especially if this is congruent with government public discourse. Another is the pragmatic trait in its people, they understand that they have to navigate and cope with ambiguity and complex rules to stay competitive and get things done.

3. Communication

The 2022 English Proficiency Index ranked Singapore at second place, out of 111 countries.[33] For comparison, the ranking of the other ASEAN countries covered in this book are as follows: the Philippines (22nd), Malaysia (24th), Vietnam (60th), Indonesia (81st) and Thailand (97th).[34] Because English is their first language and is the medium of instruction in school, most Singaporeans largely communicate and think in English. This may explain why Singapore is a comparatively lower-context culture when compared with its ASEAN neighbors and other East Asian countries such as China, Japan and South Korea.[35] The Singaporean negotiators rely on written agreements more than nonverbal cues. Unlike their Southeast Asian counterparts, they are less hesitant to say "no" and to reject your proposals or offers. Especially if they are from GLCs (government-linked corporations that may have the state as one of the stakeholders but are run/operated by professional managers) or from the government sector — they will be quick to reject any deviation from templates or precedents that are

[33] EF EPI 2022 — EF English Proficiency Index. https://www.ef.com/wwen/epi/. (Accessed February 8, 2023).
[34] *Ibid.*
[35] Koh, C. B. (2018). *Cross-Cultural Connection in the Suzhou Industrial Park.* HBSP No. NTU163. Boston: Harvard Business Publishing.

in place or have been adopted by their predecessors. Your Singaporean counterpart may politely point out that your suggested approach does not work for them and may even show visible discomfort. However, they may not be able to provide full or proper justification or may be reluctant to supply too much explanation. Open confrontations are extremely rare and harmonious interpersonal interaction is always preferred. In this sense, the Singaporean society is still characterized as being inherently Confucian.[36]

In areas where your interests and positions are at odds with those of the Singaporean negotiator, you will still find that their communication style is less direct and that they prefer a more implicit approach to resolving differences. The Singaporean negotiators are always sensitive to surrounding influencing events or happenings, so you should understand their motivation in order to focus the subject and outcome of your negotiation.[37] They may adopt subtle gestures such as grimacing and shaking of head to convey limitations on their end. As well, laughter may be used to mask embarrassment, disapproval or other feelings of distress. Westerners sometimes observe Singaporeans smiling or laughing at what they might consider inappropriate moments.[38]

As with other East Asian cultures, "saving face" is also important in Singapore. Some Singaporeans may be reluctant to openly admit that they do not understand or disagree with your presentation or proposal, especially if they are with their fellow team members. If you sense any awkwardness or tension on their part, you can encourage questioning or verify with them over less formal settings such as over lunch or coffee breaks. Another way to follow up with the Singaporean negotiator without loss of "face" may be through electronic mails (e-mails). Some of them prefer

---

[36] Loh, J. (M.I.), Restubog, S. L. D., & Gallois, C. (2009). The nature of workplace boundaries between Australians and Singaporeans in multinational organizations: A qualitative inquiry. *Cross Cultural Management: An International Journal*, 16(4) 367–385. https://doi.org/10.1108/13527600911000348.

[37] Cordeiro, C. M. (2019). Negotiating with managers from Singapore. In M. A. Khan & N. Ebner (Eds.), *The Palgrave Handbook of Cross-Cultural Business Negotiation*. Cham: Palgrave Macmillan. https://doi.org/10.1007/978-3-030-00277-0_16.

[38] Katz, L. (2017). "Negotiation International Business — Singapore." Negotiating International Business — The Negotiator's Reference Guide to 50 Countries Around the World [downloaded on 7 February 2023], available at http://www.leadershipcrossroads.com/mat/cou/Singapore.pdf.

expressing their views through e-mails and in particular when the rest of their team members are also doing the same and everyone is copied on the same communication.

4. Negotiation Strategies: Distributive or Integrative

The Singaporean negotiator typically kicks off negotiations with distributive bargaining.

They often prepare well in advance for the negotiation sessions with you. A checklist of items and deliverables will be drawn up to be discussed with you. If negotiating in a team, they will include members equipped with technical expertise with high credentials. During the negotiation, they will be able to articulate their propositions and back them up with facts and figures — and may even send you a soft copy of their multi-paged power-point slides afterwards. You should therefore always be thoroughly familiar about your own product or services and have concrete data and references to support your propositions.

Because of their preparedness and competence — the Singaporean negotiators tend to claim value at the beginning, especially over tangibles such as price and schedules. Also, Singaporeans are competitive and do not like to lose out on good bargains, they will readily describe themselves as being *kiasu* (afraid to lose) in Singlish (originally a Hokkien phrase). The Singapore market is small, so buyers are spoilt for choice and usually expect lowest negotiated prices and prompt delivery. If you are selling to a counterpart from an SOE, you may face a fairly aggressive procurement team that expects a meticulous breakdown of your lump sum quotations. Do not be surprised if they also include penalty clauses for non-compliance with schedules and specifications since this is common practice for them. Moreover, if the team on the Singaporean side has already agreed internally to certain criteria or principles to judge the negotiation outcomes, they will be reluctant to adopt yours. You may find your Singaporean counterparts rigid because they can be quite adamant about following rules or protocol. There will be added frustration for you when they cannot convincingly justify why they are being inflexible or when they refuse to brainstorm new ideas with you. Their low uncertainty avoidance trait sometimes makes the Singaporean negotiators unwilling to explore options outside their own comfort zones.

The Suzhou Industrial Park (SIP) project is a much-publicized inaugural project between the governments of China and Singapore launched in 1994 to jointly develop an industrial township in China's Jiangsu Province.[39] At that time, this was seen as a win–win collaboration between the two countries because it would generate a new income stream for Singapore and help Singapore-based companies expand to China; on the other hand, China could leverage Singapore's township infrastructure and administration building capability. Initially, 65% of the joint venture was owned by a Singapore consortium and 35%, by a Chinese consortium.[40] Even though the Singapore team spoke Mandarin, studied Chinese business practices and understood the role of *guanxi* (connections), various cultural and management differences surfaced which resulted in major changes to the ratio of stakes. In 1999, the two parties reversed their roles — Singapore reduced its stakes to 35% and China increased its ownership to 65%.[41] A Chinese idiom "sharing the same bed but having different dreams" (同床异梦) was even invoked to describe the differences in the two parties' objectives and interests — Singapore's emphasis on transferring "software" (how to develop a township) being contrasted with Chinese's priority on "hardware" (profit-making).[42] At the same time, some cultural differences such as the Singapore side's overt insistence on cost analysis, following technical specifications and signing of a memorandum of understanding (MOU) made the Chinese side feel that there was a lack of trust which hampered relationship building.[43]

The Singaporean negotiator's insistence on following rules and not deviating from specifications is a formidable obstacle to integrative negotiation. Moreover, they are usually constrained by long processes and protocols which underpin deliberation and decision-making. At times, they

---

[39] Sim, C. (2015). *China-Singapore Suzhou Industrial Park. Singapore Infopedia.* Singapore: National Library Board. https://eresources.nlb.gov.sg/infopedia/articles/SIP_2015-02-17_101058.html.

[40] *Ibid.*

[41] Koh, C. B. (2018). *Cross-Cultural Connection in the Suzhou Industrial Park.* HBSP No. NTU163. Boston: Harvard Business Publishing.

[42] *Ibid.*

[43] *Ibid.*

may even come across as being condescending because they believe they have already worked out what is in the best interests of the both of you. Yet, more often than not, your Singaporean counterpart will usually have sound reasons for standing firm in areas that are important to them in the negotiation. If you understand their underlying motivation, you can work on expanding the bargaining mix. For the SIP project, the geotechnical experts on the Singaporean side insisted on the more costly method of filling the low-lying grounds by up to five metres to prepare the site for construction and rejected the Chinese engineers' commonly adopted strategy of draining the site by digging canals and dams.[44] The Singapore team based their design on their study of the last severe flood that struck Suzhou in 1991. This turned out to be prudent because in 1999, the Yangtze River valley was hit by one of the worst floods and the factories in SIP were spared while those in adjacent areas suffered badly.[45]

To create value or pursue more integrative solutions with the Singaporean team, you need to either involve more senior decision-makers from their team or bring in additional relevant technical expertise on your side to get buy-in for your value proposition. The Singaporean negotiators respect hard bargainers if you win them over with facts and figures — and avoid creating direct conflict because "face" is still important for this rational people.[46] Due to their low uncertainty-avoidance score, the Singaporean negotiators can be rather risk-averse and would only be swayed with fact-based persuasion and references to past experiences. Sometimes they stick to 'safe' options because they fear overstepping their authority or making mistakes, both of which will make them lose face. You may need to take the lead to be creative and even draw up a framework or guidelines for brainstorming with your Singaporean counterpart. They welcome your sharing of information and will certainly reciprocate because they are often quite proud of the amount of data they have collected. Like other East Asian cultures, the Singaporean negotiators also

[44] Wong, J. & Lye, L. F. (2020). *Suzhou Industrial Park: Achievements, Challenges and Prospects.* Singapore: World Scientific Publishing Company.
[45] *Ibid.*
[46] Katz, L. (2017) "Negotiation International Business — Singapore." *Negotiating International Business — The Negotiator's Reference Guide to 50 Countries Around the World* [downloaded on 7 February 2023], available at http://www.leadershipcrossroads.com/mat/cou/Singapore.pdf.

value building relationships, but this does not have to be a prerequisite to doing business. They are prepared to negotiate and close a deal with you even while the relationship-building process is on-going.[47] The pragmatic and persistent Singaporean negotiators know the value of win–win outcomes, especially if these bring long-term benefits.

By 2003, SIP recuperated the US$77 million cumulative losses incurred during the first few years of operation and paid its first dividend the following year.[48] In 2006, the two governments signed a further agreement to expand the 70-square-kilometer SIP by another 10 square kilometers to better facilitate flow of goods in and out of the project, which is today widely regarded as a success story and replicated in other Chinese cities.[49] This successful win–win collaboration paved the way for others between the two countries. China and Singapore went on to establish another two Government-to-Government projects, namely, the Tianjin Eco-City in 2007 and the Chongqing Demonstrative Initiative on Strategic Connectivity project (known as Chongqing Connectivity Initiative in abbreviated form) in 2015.[50]

5. Concession-making and Hardball Tactics

It is likely that the Singaporean negotiators have already planned the type and scale of concessions they will offer you. GLCs in particular tend to calibrate their concession-making well in advance and are quite skilled in bargaining trade-offs with you. This bargaining is usually reserved for the more senior members of the team, so you must remember not to cause embarrassment or be dismissive. Generally, the Singaporean negotiators are reluctant to give way on price concessions. In this aspect, the concession-making pattern of the Chinese Singaporean negotiator resembles that of their Mainland Chinese counterpart as both will consider saving money

---

[47] *Ibid.*

[48] Sim, C. (2015). *China-Singapore Suzhou Industrial Park. Singapore Infopedia.* Singapore: National Library Board. Available at https://eresources.nlb.gov.sg/infopedia/articles/SIP_2015-02-17_101058.html.

[49] *Ibid.*

[50] "People's Republic of China." www.mfa.gov.sg, available at https://www.mfa.gov.sg/SINGAPORES-FOREIGN-POLICY/Countries-and-Regions/Northeast-Asia/Peoples-Republic-of-China. (Accessed February 2023).

or *jiejian* (thriftiness) a necessary virtue. They are also time sensitive, so you should be prepared to bargain on timelines and schedules. Though hard bargainers, they are rarely aggressive and will remain polite — even when they use time pressure or exploit your deadlines in the hope that you will close the deal within their desired level. At times, they will pretend to be disappointed or even insulted by your counter-offers and can be quite compelling actors.[51] The concession-making may take place throughout the entire negotiation process, so you should prepare a list of concessions to keep up with your counterpart. You can take the lead in bundling options or concessions to expand the pie. Singaporeans are, above all, pragmatic so they will be willing to make concessions if they can achieve their end goal. Also, they are willing to make trade-offs between short-term and long-term gains.

Remember that because of their rigidity and risk-averse nature, the Singaporean negotiator may at times come across as unreasonable. They do not react well to last minute changes, so you can help by laying these out and giving them time to consult among their team members and seek the approval of key decision-makers. It is common for the Singaporean negotiators, especially those from GLCs or the public sector, to leverage their country's corruption-free reputation and tout the advantages of doing business with them, to lure unilateral concessions from you.

Despite their straightforward no-nonsense negotiation style, you should still be on your guard for deceptive techniques such as misrepresenting values, making false demands or assertions or pretending that they have to follow their bosses' instructions or demands from higher authorities. In sectors which are subject to regulations, the use of a bogey is sometimes practiced. The Singaporean negotiators are familiar with "good cop, bad cop" and other hardball tactics such as "highball/lowball" (using ridiculously high or low starting offers in the hope that the other side will re-evaluate their own openings or position) and "intimidation" (faking anger or fear to force a concession) — since they are exposed to many international business practices. They may adopt and adapt some of these hardball

---

[51] Katz, L. (2017). "Negotiation International Business — Singapore." *Negotiating International Business — The Negotiator's Reference Guide to 50 Countries Around the World* [downloaded on 7 February 2023], available at http://www.leadershipcrossroads. com/mat/cou/Singapore.pdf.

tactics. For instance, they may play the "good cop" with an imaginary "bad cop" — typically some agency or department from the government or in Singlish, *gahmen* — to justify last minute demands or withdrawal of concessions.

6. Role of Women

When you negotiate in Singapore, it is common to find women in top decision-making positions and professional roles. In Singapore, women's educational level is on par with that of their male counterparts.[52] If you are a woman negotiating in Singapore, you will be accorded respect and will not be treated differently.

Women's participation on the boards of the country's 100 largest listed companies is almost 20% at the start of 2022.[53] For GLCs, the picture is even more encouraging, with almost 30% of their boards made up of women as at end of 2021.[54] A ministry body, the Council for Board Diversity, set a target of achieving 25% of women's participation on boards of the 100 largest companies listed on Singapore's Stock Exchange by the end of 2025, and 30% by end-2030.[55] In fact, the country's prominent sovereign wealth fund, Temasek Holdings,[56] was helmed by a female Chief Executive Officer, Ho Ching, for some 17 years, till 2021.[57]

According to the International Labour Office (ILO), Singapore's share of women in senior and middle management roles in 2019 was 37.1% —

---

[52] Department of Statistics. (2022). "Education and Literacy." Singapore, available at https://www.singstat.gov.sg/publications/reference/ebook/population/education-and-literacy.

[53] "More Women on Singapore Company Boards after Pandemic Setback," *The Straits Times*, March 21, 2022. Available at https://www.straitstimes.com/business/companies-markets/more-women-on-singapore-company-boards-after-pandemic-setback.

[54] *Ibid.*

[55] Council for Board Diversity. Available at https://www.councilforboarddiversity.sg/. (Accessed February 23, 2023).

[56] Temasek is a commercial investment company wholly owned by the government of Singapore. However, the government does not direct its investment decisions and assets are owned by the company, which pays taxes and distributes dividends. See: Lim, P. L. (2019). "Temasek Holdings." Singapore Infopedia. Singapore: National Library Board. Available at https://eresources.nlb.gov.sg/infopedia/articles/SIP_2019-07-15_113737.html.

[57] "A look back at outgoing CEO Ho Ching's key contributions at Temasek Holdings." *The Straits Times,* October 1, 2021. https://www.straitstimes.com/business/a-look-back-at-outgoing-ceo-ho-chings-key-contributions-at-temasek-holdings.

comparable to Australia (35.5%) and United States (40.7%) and well ahead of Japan (14.5%).[58] Singapore ranks only below the Philippines, in terms of gender parity among the countries covered in this book, in the 2022 Global Gender Gap Report by the World Economic Forum (see the following table). Its global ranking is 49 out of 146 countries and it is in the fourth position in the East Asia and Pacific region.[59]

Global Gender Gap Report 2022 INSIGHT REPORT JULY 2022			
EAST ASIA & the PACIFIC	Rank		
Country	Regional (19)	Global (146)	Score
Philippines	2	19	0.783
Singapore	**4**	**49**	**0.734**
Thailand	8	79	0.709
Vietnam	9	83	0.705
Indonesia	10	92	0.697
Korea (South)	12	99	0.689
China	13	102	0.682
Malaysia	14	103	0.681
Japan	19	116	0.650

Source: "Global Gender Gap Report 2022." World Economic Forum. July 13, 2022. https://www.weforum.org/reports/global-gender-gap-report-2022/digest.

7. Intermediary/Interpreter

There is generally no need to engage an intermediary when you negotiate in Singapore given their high English language proficiency and exposure

---

[58] International Labour Office. (2021). "Women in Managerial and Leadership Positions in the G20." Available at https://www.ilo.org/wcmsp5/groups/public/---dgreports/---ddg_p/documents/publication/wcms_762098.pdf.

[59] World Economic Forum. (July 13, 2022). "Global Gender Gap Report 2022." Available at https://www.weforum.org/reports/global-gender-gap-report-2022/digest. The Global Gender Gap Index benchmarks the current state and evolution of gender parity across four key dimensions (Economic Participation and Opportunity, Educational Attainment, Health and Survival, and Political Empowerment). It is the longest-standing index which has been tracking progress towards closing these gaps over time since its inception in 2006.

to international business. However, the larger companies and GLCs commonly involve their legal departments during the latter part of the concurrent phase (ongoing process).[60] This is the phase where the differences and conflicts in both sides' positions and interests need to be resolved in order to close the deal. Even in an integrative negotiation, the final stage will require parties to evaluate and settle on the options and alternatives that are acceptable to both sides and this involves value claiming. During such distributive sessions, you will find that the Singaporean negotiators prefer to let their legal counsels or lawyers lead the negotiation. Legal jargon, well-used templates and boilerplate clauses allow your Singapore counterpart to still retain a relatively unemotional negotiating style, which they are more comfortable with. If you have distributive issues which are technical, you can consider the use of third-party neutral experts to boost your case to persuade your Singapore counterpart.

The presence of legal and technical experts helps to maintain the "face" factor for the Singaporean negotiator and provides space for both sides to brainstorm instead of relying on power play to get what each wants. As with other East Asian cultures, building relationships and trust is also important when you negotiate in Singapore. However, relying on relationships alone may not be sufficient to bridge differences and conflicts, effective use of third parties such as lawyers or technical experts can be considered.

8. Time, Timelines and Timeliness

You should be punctual for meetings as well as social events. If you are validly delayed or held up, your Singaporean counterpart will not make a big fuss, but you should nevertheless provide a cogent explanation and a sincere apology. Time is a precious commodity in Singapore and many businesspeople set up back-to-back meetings, so being late can cause inconvenience to others.

---

[60] Negotiations are generally classifiable into three parts: antecedent phase (pre-negotiation stage and preparations), the concurrent phase (ongoing process), and the consequent phase (post-negotiation stage) — see Theoretical Chapter under Negotiation Strategies: Distributive or Integrative.

At the start of meetings, the Singaporean negotiator may make some small talk, but this is usually brief. They may be quite animated if the conversation is about local hawker food or travelling; otherwise, they much prefer to launch straight into discussing matters on the agenda and resume negotiation to tick off their long checklist. However, this does not mean that the pace of negotiation will be fast or inefficient. Since the Singaporean negotiators pay attention to information and details, and are more reliant on written communication, more time will be spent during the concurrent phase (ongoing process), and the consequent phase (post-negotiation stage). For the Singapore team, key decision-makers will want to build consensus and this means that you need to also factor in time for the other side to evaluate and revert to you at various stages of the negotiation. Overall, the Singapore negotiator is time-conscious and generally efficient, but you should be patient if they are detracted or bogged down by details.

Bibliography

Church, P. (2017). *Short History of South-East Asia.* Singapore: John Wiley & Sons Inc.

CIA. (January 27, 2023). "Singapore — The World Factbook." Available at https://www.cia.gov/the-world-factbook/countries/singapore/.

Cordeiro, C. M. (2019). Negotiating with managers from Singapore. In M. A. Khan & N. Ebner (Eds.), *The Palgrave Handbook of Cross-Cultural Business Negotiation.* Cham: Palgrave Macmillan. https://doi.org/10.1007/978-3-030-00277-0_16.

Corsuk, R. & Chua, R. (1998). "Singapore Strains Relations with Indonesia's President." *The Wall Street Journal.* Available at https://www.wsj.com/articles/SB902170180588248000.

Department of Statistics. (2022). "Education and Literacy." Singapore, available at https://www.singstat.gov.sg/publications/reference/ebook/population/education-and-literacy.

Department of Statistics Singapore. "Population Trends, 2022." Available at https://www.singstat.gov.sg/-/media/files/publications/population/population2022.ashx#:~:text=Chapter%201%20Population-,Population%20

Size%20and%20Growth,June%202022%20(Table%201.1). (Accessed February 14, 2023).

EF English Proficiency Index. Available at https://www.ef.com/wwen/epi/. (Accessed February 8, 2023).

Gov.sg. (April 13, 2020). "HDB's Ethnic Integration Policy: Why It Still Matters." Available at https://www.gov.sg/article/hdbs-ethnic-integration-policy-why-it-still-matters.

Hannam, P. (2022). "New York and Singapore Top the List of World's Most Expensive Cities in 2022." *The Guardian*, available at https://www.theguardian.com/business/2022/dec/01/new-york-and-singapore-top-the-list-of-worlds-most-expensive-cities-in-2022.

Hofstede Insights. "Country Comparison — Hofstede Insights." Available at https://www.hofstede-insights.com/country-comparison/. (Accessed February 6, 2023).

International Labour Office. (2021). "Women in Managerial and Leadership Positions in the G20." Available at https://www.ilo.org/wcmsp5/groups/public/---dgreports/---ddg_p/documents/publication/wcms_762098.pdf.

International Monetary Fund. (2022). "GDP per Capita, Current Prices." Imf.org, available at https://www.imf.org/external/datamapper/NGDPDPC@WEO/OEMDC/ADVEC/WEOWORLD.

Katz, L. (2017). "Negotiation International Business — Singapore." Negotiating International Business — The Negotiator's Reference Guide to 50 Countries Around the World [downloaded on 7 February 2023], available at http://www.leadershipcrossroads.com/mat/cou/Singapore.pdf.

Koh, C. B. (2018). *Cross-Cultural Connection in the Suzhou Industrial Park.* HBSP No. NTU163. Boston: Harvard Business Publishing.

Lim, P. L. (2019). "Temasek Holdings". Singapore Infopedia. Singapore: National Library Board. Available at https://eresources.nlb.gov.sg/infopedia/articles/SIP_2019-07-15_113737.html.

Loh, J.(M.I.), Restubog, S. L. D., & Gallois, C. (2009). The nature of workplace boundaries between Australians and Singaporeans in multinational organizations: A qualitative inquiry. *Cross Cultural Management: An International Journal*, 16(4), 367–385. https://doi.org/10.1108/13527600911000348.

"News Releases." www.nea.gov.sg, available at https://www.nea.gov.sg/media/news/news/index/mandatory-for-diners-to-return-dirty-trays-crockery-and-clean-table-litter-at-hawker-centres-coffeeshops-and-food-courts.

National Library Board. (2014). "Temasek/Singapura — Singapore History." Singapore, available at https://eresources.nlb.gov.sg/history/events/d24d6da6-

0013-4a12-a6bc-68ad1497148e#:~:text=Temasek%2FSingapura%20%2D%20Singapore%20History&text=The%20name%20%E2%80%9CTemasek%E2%80%9D%20is%20probably,of%20land%20surrounded%20by%20water. (Accessed February 20, 2023).

Osman-Gani, A. M. & Tan, J. S. (2002). Influence of culture on negotiation styles of Asian managers: An empirical study of major cultural/ethnic groups in Singapore. *Thunderbird International Business Review,* 44(6), 819–839.

"People's Republic of China." (n.d.). www.mfa.gov.sg, available at https://www.mfa.gov.sg/SINGAPORES-FOREIGN-POLICY/Countries-and-Regions/Northeast-Asia/Peoples-Republic-of-China. (Accessed November 28, 2020).

Poon, A. (2018). Narrating privilege: Meritocracy and the portrait of the scholar in Singapore Anglophone literature. *Postcolonial Studies,* 21(4), 414–432.

Retna, K. S. & Jones, D. (2013). The 'learning organisation' and Singapore culture. *The Learning Organization,* 20(4/5), 338–351.

Sim, C. (2015). *China-Singapore Suzhou Industrial Park.* Singapore Infopedia, Singapore: National Library Board. Available at https://eresources.nlb.gov.sg/infopedia/articles/SIP_2015-02-17_101058.html.

Susanto, A. B. & Susanto, P. (2013). *The Dragon Network: Inside Stories of the Most Successful Chinese Family Businesses.* Singapore: John Wiley & Sons.

"Temasek at a Glance." (n.d.). Temasek Corporate Website English, available at https://www.temasek.com.sg/en/about-us/temasek-at-a-glance.

"The Founding of ASEAN." (2020). Asean.org, available at https://asean.org/the-founding-of-asean/.

Tanzer, A. (1994). The bamboo network. *Forbes,* 154(2), 138–144.

The Straits Times. (2021). "A Look Back at Outgoing CEO Ho Ching's Key Contributions at Temasek Holdings." *The Straits Times,* October 1, available at https://www.straitstimes.com/business/a-look-back-at-outgoing-ceo-ho-chings-key-contributions-at-temasek-holdings.

The Straits Times. (2022). "More Women on Singapore Company Boards after Pandemic Setback," March 21, available at https://www.straitstimes.com/business/companies-markets/more-women-on-singapore-company-boards-after-pandemic-setback.

Transparency.org. "Singapore" January 25, 2022. Available at https://www.transparency.org/en/countries/singapore.

"UNESCO — Hawker Culture in Singapore, Community Dining and Culinary Practices in a Multicultural Urban Context." (n.d.). Ich.unesco.org, available at https://ich.unesco.org/en/RL/hawker-culture-in-singapore-community-dining-and-culinary-practices-in-a-multicultural-urban-context-01568.

Wong, J. & Lye, L. F. (2020). *Suzhou Industrial Park: Achievements, Challenges and Prospects.* Singapore: World Scientific Publishing Company.

World Economic Forum. (July 13, 2022). "Global Gender Gap Report 2022." Available at https://www.weforum.org/reports/global-gender-gap-report-2022/digest.

World Economic Forum. "Where Are the Largest Chinese Populations Outside of China? | Thailand or Indonesia: Which Country Has the Largest Chinese Population? | By World Economic Forum | Facebook." Available at https://www.facebook.com/worldeconomicforum/videos/where-are-the-largest-chinese-populations-outside-of-china/10153549858561479/. (Accessed November 8, 2022).

Singapore Quiz

1. Singapore is an attractive hub for finance and trade due to low taxes, reliable infrastructure coupled with a legal system that has adopted many French commercial laws. Is this statement true or false?
   A. True
   B. False

2. The Singaporean negotiators are typically bilingual in English and their mother tongue which may be Chinese, Malay or Tamil according to their racial background. Is this general characterization true or false?
   A. True
   B. False

3. English is the working language, but local speakers also use a brand of colloquial English known as _____ which has its own unique sentence structure and is heavily influenced by Malay, Tamil and Chinese dialects. Fill in the blank.
   A. Taglish
   B. Manglish
   C. Singlish
   D. Tenglish

4. When you negotiate in Singapore, you may find that there are major differences in the negotiation styles of the three major ethnic groups, namely, the Chinese, the Malay and the Indian Singaporeans. Is this general characterization true or false?
   A. True
   B. False

5. In the context of business negotiations, there are some noticeable differences between ethnic Chinese Singaporeans and Mainland Chinese even when the former also speak the same language of Mandarin. Is this general characterization true or false?
   A. True
   B. False

6. Like the Japanese, Singaporeans are also diligent adherents of rules. This explains why both countries score high in Hofstede's Uncertainty Avoidance index. Is this statement true or false?
   A. True
   B. False

7. The Singaporean negotiator typically kicks off negotiations with _____. Fill in the blank.
   A. relationship building
   B. discussion about contract wordings
   C. distributive bargaining
   D. integrative negotiation

8. To create value or pursue integrative solutions with the Singaporean negotiator, you may need to either involve more senior decision-makers from their team or bring in _____. Fill in the blank.
   A. accountants
   B. government officials
   C. intermediaries who are known to them
   D. technical experts in the relevant field

9. In terms of gender parity, Singapore ranks only below the Philippines and ahead of the other ASEAN countries, according to the 2022 Global Gender Gap Report by the World Economic Forum. Is this statement true or false?
   A. True
   B. False

10. Business meetings and social events in Singapore rarely start on time because Singaporeans usually have back-to-back meetings and appointments and will themselves be frequently late. Is this general characterization true or false?
    A. True
    B. False

Answer Bank

1. B
2. A
3. C
4. B
5. A
6. B
7. C
8. D
9. B
10. B

Chapter 8

The Thai Negotiator

1. The Environment

Thailand is the only country in Southeast Asia that has never been colonized by a Western nation. This is why its people are proud to remind *farangs* (foreigners) that "Thailand" means "Land of the Free". "Land of Smiles" is another popular moniker as its people are known for their friendly and pleasant demeanor, making it a top tourist destination for international tourists.

At the same time, this is also a land of multiple contradictions.

The free and friendly country has experienced numerous coup d'etats since 1932.[1] Some were bloodless, such as the first one, led by a group of young army officers which led to the establishment of a constitutional monarchy.[2] Others were violent and are still being commemorated till today.[3] For a country that has not experienced colonization, Thailand has

---

[1] Wongcha-um, P. & Johnson, K. (2020). "Timeline: Thailand's Coups, Kings and Protests." *Reuters*, December 18, available at https://www.reuters.com/article/thailand-protests-youth-history-int-idUSKBN28S1BZ.

[2] Ginsburg, T. (2009). Constitutional afterlife: The continuing impact of Thailand's postpolitical constitution. *International Journal of Constitutional Law,* 7(1), 83–105.

[3] One example being the "October 6 Event" which occurred in 1976. Chia, J. (2021). "Remembering October 6 in Words and Pictures — Thai Enquirer Current Affairs." *Thai Enquirer*, October 6, available at. https://www.thaienquirer.com/19329/remembering-october-6-in-words-and-pictures/.

been run by numerous junta governments. Many of its prominent prime ministers were serving or retired military chiefs. Next, is the heady mix of merit-making and merry-making. When you are in the capital city of Bangkok (called *Krung Thep* by the locals), it is impossible not to be in awe of the numerous ornate, mega-sized *wats* (temples) on both sides of the Chao Phraya river. Every king since the Sukothai period (1239–1438) has been a Buddhist and is also constitutionally required to be one.[4] Buddhism occupies a position of great importance in Thai society.[5] During the many Buddhist holidays, sales of alcohol are banned. Yet, in 2022, Thailand became the first East Asian country to decriminalize use of cannabis nationwide. The government even launched an application called "Plookganja" to help its people grow marijuana and hemp at home.[6] Third, the stark rich and poor divide in the country. Economically, Thailand is one of the success stories in Southeast Asia. Its thriving private enterprises minted many billionaires behind well-known brands such as "Red Bull", "Chang Beer" and "CP Foods." The CP Group (Charoen Pokphand Group) is owned by the prominent Chearavanont family which runs agribusinesses, retail chains (including all 7–11 stores in Thailand) and telecommunications (True Corporation). Its senior chairman, Dhanin Chearavanont has consistently topped the rich list, with an estimated net worth of US$16.9 billion in 2019.[7] Even the country's monarchy sits on huge wealth. King Maha Vajiralongkorn (Rama X) is the richest royal in the world, with an estimated fortune of US$43 billion.[8] Yet, despite such expansive wealth, Thailand has one of the highest income inequalities in

---

[4] "Official Translation CONSTITUTION of the KINGDOM of THAILAND *." (n.d.). Available at https://www.krisdika.go.th/documents/67673/181643/837163_0001. pdf/3d0aab10-e61f-03a4-136a-75003ce4c625. Section 7.

[5] Harding, A. (2007). Buddhism, human rights and constitutional reform in Thailand. *Asian Journal of Comparative Law,* 2(1). https://doi.org/10.2202/1932-0205.1045.

[6] Robinson, G. (2022). "In Thailand, Hold the Drinks and Pass the Cannabis." *Nikkei Asia,* October 26, available at https://asia.nikkei.com/Editor-s-Picks/Tea-Leaves/In-Thailand-hold-the-drinks-and-pass-the-cannabis.

[7] "Thailand's 31 Richest Entrepreneurs Revealed," *South China Morning Post.* November 27, 2019, available at https://www.scmp.com/magazines/style/news-trends/article/3039512/king-maha-vajiralongkorn-may-be-richest-person-thailand.

[8] *Ibid.*

East Asia, with poverty rates rising since 2016.[9] In Bangkok, gated villas and condominiums exist alongside slums with corrugated roofs. When shopping in high-end malls such as ICONSIAM, if you look out of one of its tall glass walls, you see children from a nearby squatter settlement playing in a rubbish heap next to a mucky canal.

Thailand is one of the five founding member countries of ASEAN.[10] Like many other current member countries, the Thai government has been taking steps to recover from the COVID-19 pandemic and to bolster its economy. Similar to Vietnam, it is vying to be a beneficiary of the "China plus one" strategy to attract foreign investment, especially in higher value sectors. "Thailand 4.0" is the government's strategy to move towards a more skilled and technology-oriented economy. To that end, a special economic zone made up of three provinces in eastern Thailand, called the "Eastern Economic Corridor (EEC)" was set up. With the EEC, it is likely to see State-owned Enterprises (SOE) play larger business roles.

2. Culture

Thai culture is informed by the two key institutions in their society, namely Buddhism and the monarchy.

Buddhism is both a source and medium of Thai culture, identity and traditions.[11] Though the country does not have an official state religion, 95% of Thai people are Buddhist.[12] The Buddhist year calendar is used in official documents and daily life.[13] The Thai greeting (*wai*) which consists

---

[9] World Bank. "Thailand Rural Income Diagnostic: Challenges and Opportunities for Rural Farmers," October 20, 2022, available at https://www.worldbank.org/en/country/thailand/publication/thailand-rural-income-diagnostic-challenges-and-opportunities-for-rural-farmers.

[10] Association of Southeast Asian Nations. (2020). "The Founding of ASEAN." Asean.org, available at https://asean.org/the-founding-of-asean/. Indonesia, Malaysia, Philippines, Singapore and Thailand are the 5 founding member nations of ASEAN which now includes Brunei, Cambodia, Laos, Myanmar and Vietnam.

[11] Jackson, P. A. (1990). *Buddhism, Legitimation and Conflict: The Political Functions of Urban Thai Buddhism*. Singapore: Institute of Southeast Asian Studies.

[12] Thai National Census. (2015). Available at https://www.cia.gov/the-world-factbook/countries/thailand/#people-and-society.

[13] The Buddhist Era in Thailand starts in 543 BCE (believed to be the year of Buddha's passing or enlightenment) so the year 2022 CE corresponds to B.E. 2565.

of palms pressed together in a prayer-like fashion accompanied with a slight bow has Buddhist origins. At the coronation of King Vajiralongkorn (Rama X) in 2019, the king proclaimed himself the Royal Patron of Buddhism with the promise that "I will rightfully protect Buddhism forever."[14] When the government communicates social and economic plans to its people to get buy-in, their discourse is couched in terms of Buddhist concepts, and all political groups other than the communist, Christian and Muslim ones, claim to be Buddhist.[15]

The Thai Theravada Buddhist[16] believes deeply in the laws of karma — that a person's verbal, physical and cognitive actions will lead either to merit or demerit depending on whether his/her intention is moral or otherwise.[17] All beings from demons to humans to deities will be ranked in a hierarchy of merit based on karma of past lives and present.[18] Karma accounts for many aspects of life such as gender, social status, talent, wealth and luck. The Thai people fervently believe that their position and success in this life is the result of karma. Those who have better karma — who have accumulated more merit — are superior to others with lesser good karma.[19] All year round, whether at work or at home, the Thais are constantly engaged in rituals and ceremonies that add merit to their present lives and the next. There can be merit-making on one's birthday, when moving to a new home, new company or celebration of any anniversary. In 1991, Professor Suntaree Komin from the National Institute for Development Assistance (NIDA) undertook a landmark research of Thai

---

[14] Reuters. (May 3, 2019). "'I Shall Reign with Righteousness': Thailand Crowns King in Ornate Ceremonies." sec. Emerging Markets, available at https://www.reuters.com/article/us-thailand-king-coronation-idUSKCN1S924H.

[15] Harding, A. (2007). Buddhism, human rights and constitutional reform in Thailand. *Asian Journal of Comparative Law,* 2(1). https://doi.org/10.2202/1932-0205.1045.

[16] Theravada Buddhism is practiced in Thailand, and is prevalent in Sri Lanka, Myanmar, Cambodia and Laos. The Buddhism practiced in China and Vietnam belongs to the Mahayana school. Mahayana Buddhism was also introduced to and contextualized in Japan and South Korea.

[17] Jackson, P. A. (1990). *Buddhism, Legitimation and Conflict: The Political Functions of Urban Thai Buddhism.* Singapore: Institute of Southeast Asian Studies.

[18] Reynolds, C. J. (1976). Buddhist cosmography in Thai history, with special reference to nineteenth-century culture change. *The Journal of Asian Studies,* 35(2), 203–220.

[19] Neil A. E. (2001). *Culture and Power in Traditional Siamese Government.* Southeast Asia Program Series. Ithaca, NY: Southeast Asia Program Publications.

culture by surveying a cross-section of Thai society.[20] Komin explains that while her fellow countrymen are seemingly overwhelmed by the perceived influence of Buddhism on their life, it does not always translate to deep knowledge about the religion. Their attitude is more pragmatic than cosmic — the overarching goal is to accumulate good karma (*bun wassana*) and avoid the bad (usually referred as *kam*). This assures a more comfortable future in the present life and, more importantly, a prosperous life upon rebirth.[21] The Thai people also believe in spirits, astrology, and practice a variety of magical and superstitious behaviors.

After War World II, King Bhumibol Adulyadej became the ninth monarch of Thailand from the Chakri dynasty (Rama IX). One of the longest serving monarchs in the world, his reign lasted for 70 years, from 1946 till 2016. He was much loved by his people. It is very common to see official and other photographs of the ninth king adorn walls of average Thai households. Although a constitutional monarch, the palace's promotion of the image of King Bhumibol's benevolence, virtuosity and centrality to Thai identity positioned him as the pre-eminent and constant figure in their lives — against a backdrop of changing prime ministers, military leaders and countless political parties.[22] King Bhumibol was the grandson of King Chulalongkorn (Rama V) who ruled as an absolute monarch from 1868 to 1910. King Chulalongkorn is credited with modernizing the country in many ways and resisting the tides of colonialism during the turn of the century. The pivotal and long reigns of these two popular rulers helped entrench the position of the monarchy in the hearts of the Thai people. The king is at the pinnacle of the hierarchy in Thai society. He also has the highest amount of karma.[23] To the Thai populace, the king is their strict and caring father who has their interests at heart. In fact, the late King Bhumibol's birthday on 5 December is also Father's Day in Thailand. The position of

---

[20] Komin, S. (1991). *Psychology of the Thai people: Values and behavioral patterns.* Bangkok: Magenta.

[21] Neil A. E. (2001). *Culture and Power in Traditional Siamese Government.* Southeast Asia Program Series. Ithaca, NY: Southeast Asia Program Publications.

[22] "Thailand: Military, Monarchy and the Masses." (n.d.), www.lowyinstitute.org, available at https://www.lowyinstitute.org/the-interpreter/thailand-military-monarchy-masses. (Accessed December 10, 2022).

[23] Wise, J. (2020). *Thailand: History, Politics and the Rule of Law.* Singapore: Marshall Cavendish International (Asia) Private Limited.

the monarch is also enshrined in law. The Thai constitution stipulates that the king "shall be enthroned in a position of revered worship and shall not be violated. No person shall expose the King to any sort of accusation or action."[24] The lèse-majesté law is set out in the country's Penal Code, which says whoever defames, insults or threatens the monarch shall be punished with imprisonment of up to 15 years.[25] In May 2019, King Vajiralongkorn (Rama X) ascended the throne at the age of 64 after the death of his father.

Like its Southeast Asian neighbours, Thailand also experienced waves of Chinese migration when China underwent social and political upheavals. According to the World Economic Forum (2016), Thailand has the second largest Chinese population (7.06 million) in the world residing outside of China, after Indonesia.[26] This means that Chinese Thai make up approximately 14% of its population.[27] As is the case in Indonesia, Malaysia and the Philippines, ethnic Chinese family-owned businesses in Thailand are also hugely successful. These businesses rely on the network of connections or *guanxi* to expand beyond national borders to East Asia and especially to China. As mentioned earlier, such a network is also referred to as Bamboo network[28] or Dragon network.[29] The CP group is one such successful example. The mammoth conglomerate comprises over

[24] "Official Translation Constitution of the Kingdom of Thailand*." (n.d.), available at https://www.krisdika.go.th/documents/67673/181643/837163_0001.pdf/3d0aab10-e61f-03a4-136a-75003ce4c625. Section 6.

[25] "Thailand Criminal Law Text (Translation) | Laws in Thailand." (n.d.) www.thailandlawonline.com, available at https://www.thailandlawonline.com/laws-in-thailand/thailand-criminal-law-text-translation. Section 112. (Accessed December 10, 2022).

[26] "*Where Are the Largest Chinese Populations Outside of China? | Thailand or Indonesia: Which Country Has the Largest Chinese Population? | By World Economic Forum | Facebook.*" available at https://www.facebook.com/worldeconomicforum/videos/where-are-the-largest-chinese-populations-outside-of-china/10153549858561479/. (Accessed November 8, 2022).

[27] Draper, J. & Selway, J. S. (2019). A new dataset on horizontal structural ethnic inequalities in Thailand in order to address sustainable development goal 10. *Social Indicators Research,* 141(1), 275–297. https://doi.org/10.1007/s11205-019-02065-4.

[28] Tanzer, A. (1994). The bamboo network. *Forbes,* 154(2), 138–144.

[29] Susanto, A. B. & Susanto, P. (2013). *The Dragon Network: Inside Stories of the Most Successful Chinese Family Businesses.* Singapore: John Wiley & Sons.

200 companies and invests in 22 countries.[30] It was the first foreign company to register in Shenzhen, China, in 1979 and received the business registration number 0001.[31] The obvious question that follows is whether Confucian values such as loyalty and filial piety influence the culture of this minority group in Thailand, which in turn help build foundations for key *guanxi* (connections).

When you deal with Chinese Thais, you will realize that their business manners are different from that of the mainland Chinese. Few of them speak Mandarin though this may be more common now as a result of China's growing stature. In fact, it is rare to hear them refer to themselves as Sino-Thai. The second and third generation ethnic Chinese identify themselves more as Thai than as part of the Chinese diaspora or overseas Chinese.[32] Values such as respecting elders, observing filial piety are seen as being part of Buddhist precepts and one will certainly incur bad karma if one behaves otherwise. Unlike in Vietnam where Confucian principles abound in Vietnamese vocabulary, many Chinese Thai would be stumped if you ask them to quote any sayings from the sage. They may not have even heard of the great teacher. Among the Chinese ethnic groups in Southeast Asia, the most successful integration into host society has occurred in Thailand.[33] This may explain why Confucianism does not stand out as a single independent influence for the Chinese Thai, whereas it may be embraced by Chinese Indonesians and the Chinese Malaysians to deepen their sense of identity and also as a form of defensive solidarity. In most situations, when you negotiate with a Chinese-Thai negotiator, you would not treat them differently from their fellow countrymen.

[30] Yuda, M. (2019). "Thai Magnate Grooms New Generation for $63bn CP Empire." *Nikkei Asia*, June 14, available at https://asia.nikkei.com/Spotlight/Asian-Family-Conglomerates/Thai-magnate-grooms-new-generation-for-63bn-CP-empire.

[31] "Milestones." (n.d.). www.cpgroupglobal.com, available at https://www.cpgroupglobal.com/en/about-cp/milestones. (Accessed January 1, 2023).

[32] Koning, J. & Verver, M. (2013). Historicizing the 'ethnic' in ethnic entrepreneurship: The case of the ethnic Chinese in Bangkok. *Entrepreneurship and Regional Development*, 25(5–6), 325–348.

[33] Susanto, A. B. & Susanto, P. (2013). *The Dragon Network: Inside Stories of the Most Successful Chinese Family Businesses*. Singapore: John Wiley & Sons.

Hofstede's Cultural Dimensions

• **Power Distance**

Thailand's national score for this index is 64 — the third lowest among the countries covered in this book.[34] Only South Korea (60) and Japan (54) have lower scores.[35] Thailand's score is lowest among the Southeast Asian nations — meaning it is the least tolerant of unequal distribution of power compared to its neighboring countries such as Indonesia, Malaysia, Philippines and Singapore.

In Komin's seminal study, she explained that Thai people are ego oriented and have a deep sense of pride and dignity.[36] Therefore, notwithstanding their calm and gentle demeanor, they can be easily provoked and react with sudden emotions if they feel insulted or belittled. This ego is different from the concept of "face" discussed in many other chapters of this book because the ego is primarily about self-esteem. In East Asia, "face" is more about the individual's social role within his/her community. However, a Thai person's "ego" will also be hurt if someone very close to the "self" is also included, such as his/her parents. When the line is crossed and the ego is violated, it will trigger a sudden volatile reaction. Thus, incidents of sudden breakdown in relationships and ensuing violence are not met with surprise within the Thai community. They understand that someone's ego must have taken a hit.

At the same time, the Thai understand that people are intrinsically unequal. The difference in power, status and social position is explained by the concept of karma.[37] Within traditional Buddhist cosmology, the concept of karma "gives order and regularity to the universe much as Newtonian laws of Western science give order and regularity to the physical universe."[38] To the Thai Buddhists, hierarchical social relations are natural and make rational sense. The king, as the being with the highest

---

[34] See the Theoretical Chapter which compares the scores of the countries covered in this book.

[35] *Ibid.*

[36] Komin, Suntaree. 1991. *Psychology of the Thai people: Values and behavioral patterns.* Bangkok: Magenta.

[37] Neil A. Englehart. 2001. *Culture and Power in Traditional Siamese Government.* Southeast Asia Program Series. Ithaca, N.Y.: Southeast Asia Program Publications.

[38] Reynolds, Craig J. 1976. *Buddhist Cosmography in Thai History, with Special Reference to Nineteenth-Century Culture Change. The Journal of Asian Studies,* 35(2): 203–220.

merit and the chief patron of the religion, sits at the pinnacle of this hierarchy. Even within the monastic community (the *Sangha*), hierarchy is practiced. When monks go out to beg for food, the most senior ranked monk will be first in line. Needless to say, within the military, hierarchy is also of utmost importance.

The Thai negotiators therefore expect their junior subordinates to follow instructions. In addition to rank, respect for elders is also deeply embedded within Thai social and business culture. Your Thai counterpart may even take offence if you are too young or if you send a junior person to negotiate with them. The complaint *dek kern pai* (too young) may be levied. Even though company brochures and publicity materials invariably use images of the young, this is only superficial. Decision-making and power is still vested with the senior members of the team. And do not be surprised if these senior members are also rather elderly. Since the 2014 coup, many SOEs in Thailand have military personnel on their boards or in executive positions, this adds a further layer of hierarchy which you should be mindful of when dealing with them. However, the junior or younger members on the team are also treated pleasantly and with courtesy. The Thai understand that ego is important and so will avoid conflict and clashes. Thus, though unequal distribution of power is generally accepted, smooth interpersonal interaction is still the order of the day.

- **Individualism–Collectivism**

Thailand is a collectivist society. Its individualism score is 20, same as China, Singapore and Vietnam — these countries are all ranked third lowest among the countries in this book.[39]

The Thai people have a shared identity and are proud of their "Thainess" (*khwampen thai*). This identity was shaped during the reign of King Chulalongkorn from the 1890s when the state initiated a series of government policies aimed at assimilating its populations. Such efforts continued even during the successive military governments after the monarchy turned constitutional.[40] Language, religion and social practices were standardized and the name of the country was also changed from

---

[39] Hofstede Insights. "Country Comparison — Hofstede Insights," available at https://www.hofstede-insights.com/country-comparison/. (Accessed February 6, 2023).

[40] Ricks, J. I. (2019). Proud to be Thai: The puzzling absence of ethnicity-based political cleavages in Northeastern Thailand. *Pacific Affairs*, 92(2), 257–285.

Siam to Thailand in 1939 to gird this identity.[41] Further, during the long reign of King Bhumibol, the fusing of royal and Buddhist elements into a meta-narrative for the country also helped to reinforce the "Thai-ness" discourse.[42]

This shared identity may explain why ethnic Chinese are more successfully integrated into Thai society when compared with Indonesia and Malaysia. The main street in Bangkok's Chinatown, called Yaowarat Road, is frequented by all Thais and not just the ethnic Chinese among them. Open gestures of acceptance by the monarchy, in particular, King Bhumibol, as well as the Buddhist character of the society contribute to the high integration of ethnic Chinese.[43] This is the central theme of the display and exhibition at the Yaowarat Chinatown Heritage Centre. The Asian Financial Crisis in 1997 was in fact triggered by the slump in the baht and is nicknamed the 'Tom Yum Kung Crisis'. Although the ethnic Chinese owned a significant portion of the nation's wealth and assets, there was no reported uprising or riots against this minority group, unlike in Indonesia. In fact, when some politicians attempted to blame the Chinese Thai business community for the crisis, there was a public outcry.[44]

Of course, one other major factor that contributes to the collectivist character of the society is its long-standing rice farming culture. In 2019, Thailand was ranked the 12th largest agricultural producer worldwide and the sixth largest rice exporter.[45] As elaborated in the chapter on the Chinese negotiators, rice cultivation requires mutual reliance and interdependence which underpins collectivism. In Thailand, people ask after one another by saying *"gin khao yung"* which translates literally to "have you eaten rice yet" — reflecting the deep influence of the rice culture.

---

[41] *Ibid.*

[42] Fong, J. (2009). Sacred nationalism: The Thai monarchy and primordial nation construction. *Journal of Contemporary Asia,* 39(4), 673–696.

[43] Koning, J. & Verver, M. (2013). "Historicizing the 'ethnic' in ethnic entrepreneurship: The case of the ethnic Chinese in Bangkok." *Entrepreneurship and Regional Development,* 25(5–6), 325–348.

[44] In 1997, the Thai prime minister, Chavalit Yongchaiyudh, blamed the Sino-Thai business community for the economic crisis and faced a public outcry after which Chavalit apologized and claimed he had been misunderstood : Wise, James. 2020. *Thailand: History, politics and the rule of law.* SG: Marshall Cavendish International (Asia) Private Limited.

[45] BOI : The Board of Investment of Thailand. July 1, 2022, available at https://www.boi.go.th/.

Therefore, in the collectivist Thai society, relationships are extremely important and maintaining relationships in every situation is deemed a priority. Every Thai business person's first instinct is to build up his or her business network and reciprocal relationships that will bring gains to both sides. You will sense this very early on when dealing with the Thai negotiators. Their interactions with you are generally sincere and genuine. Even if the negotiation with you does not yield the desired outcome, they will still retain you within their network and look forward to continuing the relationship for another occasion. On your part, you need to be mindful that when interacting with them you exhibit the appropriate attitude whenever conversations and discussions touch on the monarchy, the military and, of course, the main religion in the country. Otherwise, it will make the Thai negotiators feel ill at ease.

- **Uncertainty Avoidance**

Thailand has a national score of 64 and is ranked third highest in this book, after Japan (92) and South Korea (85).[46] At fourth position is Indonesia (48).[47] Like Japan and South Korea, Thailand is a homogenous society. Also, it has never been colonized, unlike the other Southeast Asian countries. These two factors may explain why the Thai have less tolerance for uncertainty as there was no external impetus to force them to adapt. However, this is a people who have lived through many coups. During the 70-year reign of the late King Bhumibol, Thailand saw 10 successful coups which ousted elected governments and had the constitution rewritten 17 times.[48] At the time of writing this chapter, the latest coup occurred in 2014 and saw the junta government in power till 2019 after which it transitioned to a military-dominated semi-elected government. There is preference for predictability, but if the situation requires, the Thai negotiator will readily adapt and rise to the occasion.

---

[46] Hofstede Insights. "Country Comparison — Hofstede Insights." Accessed February 6, 2023, available at https://www.hofstede-insights.com/country-comparison/.
[47] See the Theoretical Chapter which compares the scores of the countries covered in this book.
[48] Wongcha-um, P. & Johnson, K. (2020). "Timeline: Thailand's Coups, Kings and Protests." *Reuters*, December 18, available at https://www.reuters.com/article/thailand-protests-youth-history-int-idUSKBN28S1BZ.

3. Communication

Thai people generally speak in soft-tones and rely heavily on the context
to convey meanings. The language itself reflects differences in gender,
rank, distance and closeness of relationships. Depending on how polite or
familiar they want to be, the Thai communicator can choose among many
types of first person and second person pronouns. In fact, the language is
so complex that many Thai speakers choose not to use any pronouns when
talking among themselves so the listener will have to guess from the context whether the sentence is addressed to them.

However, what makes the Thai negotiators difficult to decipher is their
kreng jai belief system. *Kreng jai* may be translated as consideration for
the other person's feelings and ego. Tremendous emphasis is placed on not
crossing the line to wound another's ego that some Thai people will even
inform you that this is the first rule of all Thai interactions.[49] This exhorts
the individual to do everything within his/her power to not cause any sort
of distress or loss of face to the other person. Invariably, it requires self-
sacrifice in order to keep the other person's ego intact. In Thai companies
or even Thai subsidiaries of foreign companies, *Kreng jai* is a common
explanation for why performance appraisals, whether of peers, subordinates or especially of superiors, are inaccurate or challenging.[50] In business
settings, this indigenous social construct is used by the Thai negotiator to
observe the correct hierarchy with you and maintain a pleasant relationship. In other words, whatever the Thai negotiators feel, they would rather
not say or find difficulty to accurately communicate to you — they will
invoke *kreng jai* to absolve themselves. However, their body language may
give them away. When speaking to your Thai counterpart, you may sense
from their body language that something is not quite right or that some
information is being withheld or masked. Yet, when you press them, they
will explain that they feel *kreng jai* and rather not say. This is frustrating in
particular when honest communication is needed to resolve key pain
points. When you demonstrate consideration for the feelings of your Thai

---

[49] Komin, S. (1991). *Psychology of the Thai People: Values and Behavioral Patterns.*
Bangkok: Magenta.
[50] Andrews, T. G. & Chompusri, N. (2013). Understanding organizational practice adoption
at the Thai subsidiary corporation: Antecedents and consequences of Kreng Jai.
Management International Review, 53(1), 61–82.

counterpart or show that you do not want to impose on them or put them through unnecessary trouble or inconvenience — this will be appreciated as being *kreng jai*. This is "giving face" to the Thai negotiator, which will be deeply appreciated. One practical takeaway on this note is that you should not expect too much from the Thai negotiator when it comes to electronic communications. They generally prefer face-to-face interactions when it comes to negotiation, even if it is not the first time they have done a deal with you.

Of course, like other East Asian countries, some younger Thais may not be as hindered or conditioned by the *kreng jai* culture. Many wealthy Thai families send their children to study in the US and you can effortlessly pick them out from the crowd. Their accent and mannerism and even the way they dress will set them apart.

One trait that may set the Thai negotiator apart from those from other East Asian countries covered in this book may be their sense of fun or what Komin described as their "fun-pleasure" orientation or *sanuk* (having fun or enjoying oneself).[51] This explains why they generally prefer to keep social interactions pleasant and may sometimes come across as being slightly frivolous. Humor and good jokes are always appreciated. Even when meeting for the first time, your Thai host may tease you slightly over non-personal inconsequential things. They do this quite naturally and it is a genuine gesture to make a connection. If you find time to watch some Thai commercials or movies in between your negotiation sessions, you will quickly see that this fun and pleasure strategy is pervasive.[52] During the pre-negotiation stage or antecedent phase of the negotiation, when relationship building is starting — you will be charmed by your Thai negotiator; in particular in informal settings such as over a meal or coffee or just making small talk.

Overall, keeping communication positive, friendly and having some fun along the way to building and maintaining business relationships in Thailand is the right approach.

---

[51] Komin, S. (1991). *Psychology of the Thai People: Values and Behavioral Patterns*. Bangkok: Magenta.

[52] Punyapiroje, C. & Morrison, M. A. (2007). Behind the smile: Reading cultural values in Thai advertising. *Asian Journal of Communication,* 17(3), 318–336.

4. Negotiation Strategies: Distributive or Integrative

The Thai negotiators have both the personality and the propensity to be integrative. They are always smiling, friendly and fun-loving. You will feel at ease very quickly as face-to-face interactions with the Thai are frequently pleasant. You will be disarmed by their ubiquitous *wai* gestures with palms together whenever they see you or thank you. Negotiations are viewed as a joint problem-solving process.[53] To most Thais, their first instinct is to build a smooth relationship with you. You will often be told that without a relationship, you cannot sell a single piece of equipment, whatever the price.[54]

The goal of the Thai negotiator would be to establish a reciprocal relationship with you underpinned by an element of gratitude, commonly translated as *bun khun*.[55] If you have a *bun khun* relationship — it means you acknowledge what the other party has done or will do for you and hope to repay that gesture with an equivalent or greater response. Using Buddhist lens, it can be explained as your accepting a good turn from the other person and wanting to repay so that you will not be indebted, and incur bad karma.[56] So, if you sell something to a Thai buyer, being in a *bun khun* relationship means that you will regard the purchase as a positive act and will reciprocate by giving a favorable price. And this relationship (hopefully) continues and, in return, the Thai buyer will make a repeat purchase or refer other customers to you. One way is to see this as an effort to build deeper and longer-term relationships; beyond mere commercial transactions. A cynical angle will reveal the extractive and obligatory nature of *bun khun* relationships — because one party may be held ransom and is forced to return the favor. In any case, in business

[53] Katz, L. (2017). "Negotiation International Business — Thailand." Negotiating International Business — The Negotiator's Reference Guide to 50 Countries Around the World [downloaded on 5 January 2023], available at http://www.leadershipcrossroads.com/mat/cou/Thailand.pdf.

[54] Punturaumporn, B. & Hale, C. L. (2003). Business negotiations in Thailand: Navigating the challenges of traditions vs. change. Available at SSRN: https://ssrn.com/abstract=400520 or http://dx.doi.org/10.2139/ssrn.400520.

[55] A similar concept is *utang na loob* which is discussed in the Filipino Negotiator Chapter. The notion of a reciprocal relationship underpinned by an element of gratitude.

[56] Komin, S. (1991). *Psychology of the Thai People: Values and Behavioral Patterns.* Bangkok: Magenta.

settings, the Thai negotiator's strong preference is to ensure that they are comfortable dealing with you and that they see potentiality in the relationship.

However, you should not be surprised if the Thai negotiator is not familiar with your culture. Even though the country receives record number of international tourists, its people are generally not informed about foreign cultures. After all, this homogenous society has never been colonized and interaction with tourists is generally transactional and centered around provision of services.

One foreign culture that the Thai people are more familiar with, compared with other nationalities, would be the Japanese culture. For the past decade, Japan has consistently been the number one Foreign Direct Investment (FDI) source country contributing about 30% of accumulated FDI into Thailand.[57] It is estimated that about 6,000 Japanese companies operate in the second largest economy in Southeast Asia.[58] There are numerous joint ventures between Japanese companies and leading corporate players, both in the private and public sectors. For instance, the CP Group formed a joint venture with Meiji Co. Ltd, a major food company, in 1989 to market dairy products to Thai consumers.[59] This vibrant bilateral business relation is a result of cultural diplomacy that has been undertaken by the Japanese government and its business community since the early 1970s.[60] The Japanese government helped establish the Technology Promotion Association (Thailand–Japan) abbreviated as "TPA" and the Japanese Studies Centre at Thammasat University. The Japanese Studies Centre supports learning, scholarship and research about Japan and various Japan-related subjects, largely in the area of social sciences. The TPA essentially replicates the same effort, but in the area of

---

[57] BOI: The Board of Investment of Thailand. 2021. Boi.go.th, available at https://www.boi.go.th/index.php?page=press_releases_detail&topic_id=131040&language=zh.

[58] *Bangkok Post.* (November 18, 2022). "Japan, Thailand Ink New Economic Partnership Plan." Available at https://www.bangkokpost.com, https://www.bangkokpost.com/business/2440742/japan-thailand-ink-new-economic-partnership-plan.

[59] CP-Meiji. "CP-Meiji." available at https://www.cpmeiji.com/sg/about-us. (Accessed January 5, 2023).

[60] The information in this paragraph are taken from Thipakorn, S. (2015). Japan's cultural diplomacy: Influence on Thai society. *Rian Thai: International Journal of Thai Studies*, 8, 209–226.

Japanese technology and engineering. These efforts institutionalized the deep understanding and wide dissemination of knowledge about Japanese people and their culture.

It also helps that these two nationalities have much in common. Both countries have a constitutional monarchy, are collectivist and have a deep appreciation of hierarchy. At the same time, both people are also conscious of the areas where they are different or opposite and seek to learn from each other. For instance, where the Thai are fun-loving and need *sanuk* in their lives, the Japanese frequently come across as being too serious or stern. However, some observers note that once these two nationalities start to interact and work together, they adapt and pick up traits from each other. The Japanese become more confident about their sense of humor and the Thai, more time-conscious and pay greater attention to details.[61] Thus, even if the Thai negotiators always seem at ease with you and are accommodating, do not assume that they are familiar with your culture. This learning process takes time and patience.

Another cautionary note about the Thai negotiator is their flexibility and adaptability to situations. Komin explained that because they place high value on forging personal relationships, they tend to be more situation-oriented rather than principle-oriented.[62] Therefore, although the Thai negotiator works on establishing a relationship with you, they also need to balance a host of other relationships. As they need to constantly navigate through changing positions and interests, they will not hesitate to change tack to go with the new flow. The Thai negotiators always prefer a win–win scenario, but not always with the same party.

In sum, because the Thai negotiators are looking to build a longer-term relationship, they are prepared to share information and trust you. Especially if feelings of *kreng jai* have been established and both sides are aware where the boundaries lie, there are many opportunities to find out what each other's interests and needs are, in order to work towards a win–win outcome.

[61] Swierczek, F. W. & Onishi, J. (2003). Culture and conflict: Japanese managers and Thai subordinates. *Personnel Review*, 32(2), 187–210.
[62] Komin, S. (1991). *Psychology of the Thai People: Values and Behavioral Patterns*. Bangkok: Magenta.

5. Concession-making and Hardball Tactics

The Thai negotiators are extremely skilled at concession-making. This give-and-take exercise is where they build rapport and decide how much they like you. During negotiation, their responses are fluid and flexible; much like the way they would navigate the Bangkok traffic. Besides driving, one can take the sky-train, the underground subway, book a ride on a motorcycle or take a boat ferry to travel down one of the *klongs* (canals*)*. There are many choices and combinations of ways to get from one point to another. Moreover, the Thai people are adept at bargaining as well as haggling[63] and will always inject some *sanuk* to make sure they extract some fun out of you.

It is typical for the Thai negotiator to begin the negotiation process by assuring you that they are always open to concessions because this sets the right tone for relationship building. However, they are invariably reluctant to make the first move or to commit to the concessions which they have been alluding to. It is not always necessary to negotiate in teams, unlike in other parts of East Asia. Although it is a collective and hierarchal society, the decision-makers are usually involved in key parts of the negotiation, and sometimes they may be assisted by a handful of others. However, because business people in Thailand have a complex network of external parties which may include their business associates, government officials and even the military, decision-making must factor in multiple considerations. Therefore, you must give your Thai counterpart time to revert and you may need to go through several rounds before concessions are firmed up. It may sometimes feel as if the goal post never stops moving, but you need to be patient. On your part, you should not put your offers of concessions in writing during the early stages of the negotiation process. Even if you have to commit, you should have the necessary preambles to allow you to make changes or even retract. Make a list of the concessions which you are prepared to give and rely on the *bun khun* relationship with your Thai counterpart to exchange favors.

---

[63] Katz, L. (2017). "Negotiation International Business — Thailand." Negotiating International Business — The Negotiator's Reference Guide to 50 Countries Around the World [downloaded on 5 January 2023], available at http://www.leadershipcrossroads.com/mat/cou/Thailand.pdf.

When negotiating over tangibles such as price and timing of delivery and payment, you may observe that the Thai negotiator is not always price- or time-sensitive. They will be prepared to pay your quoted price or accommodate your timelines provided they are convinced that what you are offering is a value proposition. The price the Thai negotiator is prepared to buy or sell at depends on the level of relationship they can establish with you. Therefore, do not be alarmed if you find that they are selling the same equipment to another buyer at a different price from what they quoted you. Aside from the relationship factor, another challenge you may face is fixing the tangibles in the negotiation. The Thai negotiators frequently package several variables as a single proposition. For instance, you may consider that parties have already agreed on the unit price, but a change in, for example, the choice of law clause or arbitration clause may somehow lead to further bargaining. This is one of the more challenging aspects of Thai concession-making — there may be many moving parts, so you need to be clear what are your boundaries and resistance points. One approach is for you to be firm about what the variables are that you would accept as forming the "package" for negotiation purposes.

You may realize that their flexibility at the negotiation table can be a double-edged sword.[64] The Thai negotiator may come across as being random, disorganized and even insincere.

Deception is more commonly practiced than you would expect.[65] Though the Thai people believe deeply in karma, how to attribute and justify karma is a subjective undertaking. Komin explains that this can readily be a scapegoat concept to help one mitigate one's conscience.[66] Your Thai counterpart may have no choice but to make false concessions, misrepresent, bluff or even tell an outright lie because it is the bad luck of

---

[64] Punturaumporn, B. & Hale, C. L. (2003). "Business Negotiations in Thailand: Navigating the Challenges of Traditions vs. Change." Available at SSRN: https://ssrn.com/abstract=400520 or http://dx.doi.org/10.2139/ssrn.400520.

[65] Katz, L. (2017). "Negotiation International Business — Thailand." Negotiating International Business — The Negotiator's Reference Guide to 50 Countries Around the World [downloaded on 5 January 2023], available at http://www.leadershipcrossroads.com/mat/cou/Thailand.pdf.

[66] Komin, S. (1991). *Psychology of the Thai People: Values and Behavioral Patterns.* Bangkok: Magenta.

the situation or simply your *kam* or bad karma that brought this on. Therefore, even though you may be primarily engaged in an integrative negotiation with a lot of on-going relationship building, you should still look out for the use of a bogey — for instance telling you that they need prior approval of an external party or a waiver from one of their commercial partners.

It is rare for the Thai negotiator to use hardball tactics that require aggression or intimidation because they much prefer pleasant and smooth dealings. You should thus avoid such tactics as well. However, they may abruptly suspend the negotiation or keep away from the negotiating table for a long period of time and keep you guessing what is going on. Unfortunately, this can occur quite frequently. In part, it may be due to their constant changing and unstable political environment. Or, it may be a tactic to distract or upset the momentum of negotiation. You should always initiate some communication and contact, even if they are merely social calls, so that your Thai counterpart knows that you are still invested in the relationship.

6. Role of Women

Global Gender Gap Report 2022 INSIGHT REPORT JULY 2022

EAST ASIA & the PACIFIC	Rank		
Country	Regional (19)	Global (146)	Score
Philippines	2	19	0.783
Singapore	4	49	0.734
Thailand	**8**	**79**	**0.709**
Vietnam	9	83	0.705
Indonesia	10	92	0.697
Korea (South)	12	99	0.689
China	13	102	0.682
Malaysia	14	103	0.681
Japan	19	116	0.650

Source: "Global Gender Gap Report 2022." 2022. World Economic Forum. July 13, 2022. https://www.weforum.org/reports/global-gender-gap-report-2022/digest.

Based on the 2022 Global Gender Gap Report by the World Economic Forum (see the previous table), Thailand is ranked eighth in the East Asia and Pacific region, and 79th globally, out of 146 countries.[67] This means that its gender equality ranking is ahead of all of the other countries discussed in this book, except for Philippines and Singapore.

Nevertheless, given the hierarchical nature of Thai society, there are still stereotypical attitudes about the roles and responsibilities of women. Though the CP Group is a family-owned conglomerate, women within the family are not allowed to be involved.[68] This means that wives, sisters and daughters cannot be shareholders or employees of the business. Senior Chairman, Dhanin Chearavanont, explained that the rule was put in place in accordance with traditional Chinese family values.[69] Thus, when the richest businessman sought audience with King Vajiralongkorn within days after the latter's coronation, he only brought along his two sons as his chosen successors.[70] Indeed, a quick review of the top business families in Thailand would mostly show that the second-generation leaders are mainly the male descendants. This inequality also exists on the religious front. In Thailand, monks are highly respected and receive preferential treatment such as priority entry and seating on public transportation. However, only men can become monks. Thailand's national Buddhist ruling body, the Supreme Sangha Council, refused to recognize female monks or *bhikkhunis*.[71] Thai women who aspire to become *bhikkhunis* have to travel to

---

[67] "Global Gender Gap Report 2022." (July 13, 2022). World Economic Forum, available at https://www.weforum.org/reports/global-gender-gap-report-2022/digest. The Global Gender Gap Index benchmarks the current state and evolution of gender parity across four key dimensions (Economic Participation and Opportunity, Educational Attainment, Health and Survival, and Political Empowerment). It is the longest-standing index which tracks progress towards closing these gaps over time since its inception in 2006.

[68] Kirby, W. C. & Manty, T. Y. "CP Group: Balancing the Needs of a Family Business with the Needs of a Family of Businesses". HBS 9-312-059 (Boston: Harvard Business School Publishing, 2011).

[69] *Ibid.*

[70] Yuda, M. (2019). "Thai Magnate Grooms New Generation for $63bn CP Empire." *Nikkei Asia*, June 14, available at https://asia.nikkei.com/Spotlight/Asian-Family-Conglomerates/Thai-magnate-grooms-new-generation-for-63bn-CP-empire.

[71] Gray, D. (2017). "Thailand's Buddhist Nuns Fight for Equality." *Nikkei Asia*, August 24. https://asia.nikkei.com/NAR/Articles/Thailand-s-Buddhist-nuns-fight-for-equality.

Sri Lanka to be ordained; whereas such ordination is allowed in all the other countries covered in this book.[72]

If you are a woman negotiating in Thailand, you may find that you are frequently in a male-dominated setting. And when dealing with an SOE, some of your counterparts may be military personnel. Nevertheless, because the Thai negotiation style is generally integrative and the communication style is gentle and indirect, you are not expected to be aggressive or behave in a masculine manner. Of course, if you happen to have any military experience, you should definitely highlight that for added credibility, above your job title and credentials. If you hire a Thai interpreter, he/she may use specific first person or second person pronouns to convey what he/she regards as being the appropriate level of respect to be shown to your counterpart. You should check with your interpreter what type of pronouns are being used on your behalf to ensure that the level of formality or respect is appropriate and not excessively polite.

7. Intermediary/Interpreter

Interpreters are frequently engaged when negotiating in Thailand due to its language barrier. Thai is the official language and English proficiency is not high.[73] The 2022 English Proficiency Index ranked Thailand 97th out of 111 countries.[74] This is lower than other ASEAN countries covered in this book such as Singapore (2nd), the Philippines (22nd), Malaysia (24th), Vietnam (60th) and Indonesia (81st).[75] Moreover, because of their *Kreng jai* culture, Thai speakers sometimes adopt techniques which affect the accuracy of the communication. Thus, the Thai interpreter may want to avert confrontation or avoid hurting the Thai listener's ego. If you want to communicate something negative or aggressive, the interpreters may

---

[72] In fact, fully ordained female monks must observe 311 precepts whereas that number is 227 for male monks: Gray, D. (2017). "Thailand's Buddhist Nuns Fight for Equality." *Nikkei Asia*, August 24. https://asia.nikkei.com/NAR/Articles/Thailand-s-Buddhist-nuns-fight-for-equality.

[73] *Bangkok Post*. (2020). "English Skills Drop Again," November 27, https://www.bangkokpost.com/thailand/general/2026031/english-skills-drop-again.

[74] EF EPI 2022 — EF English Proficiency Index. Available at https://www.ef.com/wwen/epi/. (Accessed February 8, 2023).

[75] *Ibid.*

replace your complaint with a softer expression, or not translate any utterance that they feel is too sensitive and, in some exceptional cases, may even add positive remarks of their own.[76] So, if you intend to say that the negotiation has to end, this may instead be conveyed as the negotiation is experiencing some glitches or difficulties. Sometimes, your demands are translated as preferences. These nuances or inaccuracies are more common if the intermediary also has a close relationship with your Thai counterpart.

If you engage an intermediary or a middleman who has business dealing or connection with your Thai counterpart, you should be mindful of the issues such appointment brings. Because relationships always take centerstage, the Thai negotiator will have to be sensitive in their communication with you, as well as with the middleman. This adds a further layer to your negotiation which you need to weigh against its benefit.

Thailand is ranked 101 out of 180 countries by the Transparency International's Corruption Perception Index 2022.[77] This is the third lowest ranking among the countries covered in this book, beating both Indonesia (at 110th place) and the Philippines (at 117th place).[78] According to Komin, the flexibility trait in the Thai people and their adaptability to fit situations make them prone to corruption.[79] To be fair, the Thai situation and circumstances have been in a constant state of flux, with its many coups, change of governments and rewriting of constitutions. Moreover, the concept of *bun khun* (grateful reciprocal relations) can be misused to create a network of connections with officials, politicians and ministers in order to give and for favors to create patronage. Even though there are government agencies set up to counter corruption such as the National Anti-Corruption Commission (NACC) and the Royal Thai Police, corruption

---

[76] Hyun, Y. (2017). Preserving harmony first, then conveying information: Asian ways of interpreting as maintaining rapport at a Korean trans-national corporation in Thailand. *Manusya: Journal of Humanities,* 20(3), 61–84, doi: https://doi.org/10.1163/26659077-02003004.

[77] Transparency.org. (January 31, 2023). "2022 Corruption Perceptions Index — Explore Thailand's Results." Available at https://www.transparency.org/en/cpi/2022.

[78] North Korea is also assigned a separate ranking, at 171. See the Theoretical Chapter which compares the scores of the countries covered in this book.

[79] Komin, S. (1991). *Psychology of the Thai People: Values and Behavioral Patterns.* Bangkok: Magenta.

prevention and enforcement mechanisms are not strong.[80] Based on Assumption University's ABAC poll from 2011 to 2013, two-thirds of the populace were prepared to engage in corruption if they expected to derive some form of benefit.[81] Additionally, Thailand's laws and regulations pose another minefield when doing business. Its laws are rarely repealed, so new ones merely add on to the existing and sometime outdated provisions. Although the government launched a "Regulatory Guillotine" in 2017[82] to update its laws to encourage business and foreign investment, knowing the type of licenses and permits that are required, if any, is still a hot topic that surfaces in many negotiations.

All the above supply strong motivation for hiring lawyers when negotiating in Thailand, especially if the venture requires government approvals or permits. And since many of the leading Thai and International law firms can also help bridge the language barrier, their involvement is becoming more common. However, you should make sure that the necessary conflict of interests checks are carried out before you engage them as they may have pre-existing relationships with your Thai counterparts.

8. Time, Timelines and Timeliness

You should not be surprised that meetings, especially in Bangkok, rarely start on time. The traffic in the capital city during its long peak hours is a challenge even to its long-time residents. And since the relationship trumps most things, you should not be upset simply because your Thai counterpart is late. The Thai reaction to impunctuality and even no-show is to remind one to *jai yen* (have a cool heart, i.e do not get worked up) and *mai pen rai* (it's OK, let it go). This also means that deadlines and timeliness are usually not of the essence unless you make it extremely imperative to follow agreed schedules.

---

[80] OECD. "Economic Surveys: Thailand 2020 : Economic Assessment." Available at https://www.oecd-ilibrary.org/economics/oecd-economic-surveys-thailand-2020_ad2e50fa-en.

[81] *Bangkok Post*. "65% 'okay with Corruption' If They Gain." Available at https://www.bangkokpost.com/thailand/politics/358645/poll-65-of-thais-can-accept-corruption. (Accessed January 10, 2023).

[82] OECD. "Economic Surveys: Thailand 2020 : Economic Assessment." Available at https://www.oecd-ilibrary.org/economics/oecd-economic-surveys-thailand-2020_ad2e50fa-en.

The pace of negotiation, especially during the pre-negotiation and on-going phase, is generally slow. The Thai negotiators will undertake their own due diligence and check with their own network of associates and connections to find out about you, your company and your proposals. A lot of time and effort will be spent by them at this stage in order to decide whether there are opportunities for mutual benefits and what type of relationship they might have with your side. To the Thai negotiators, most of the work and time will be focused here because it sets the footing for the negotiation. You therefore have to be very patient in the beginning. During the on-going phase, in addition to discussing about tangibles of the negotiation, the Thai negotiator will commit time to building the *bun khun* relationship directly with you in order to map out the reciprocity. Typically, key decision-makers do not need to build consensus within their organizations, but they will want to ensure that all stakeholders and parties that will be affected by the negotiation outcome are generally happy and satisfied. This means added deliberation. Overall, you need to be extremely patient when negotiating in Thailand.

Bibliography

Andrews, T. G. & Chompusri, N. (2013). "Understanding organizational practice adoption at the Thai subsidiary corporation: Antecedents and consequences of Kreng Jai. *Management International Review*, 53(1), 61–82.

Association of Southeast Asian Nations. (2020). "The Founding of ASEAN." Asean.org. 2020. https://asean.org/the-founding-of-asean/. Indonesia, Malaysia, Philippines, Singapore and Thailand are the 5 founding member nations of ASEAN which now includes Brunei, Cambodia, Laos, Myanmar and Vietnam.

Bangkok Post. (November 27, 2020). "English Skills Drop Again." Available at https://www.bangkokpost.com/thailand/general/2026031/english-skills-drop-again.

Bangkok Post. (November 18, 2022). "Japan, Thailand Ink New Economic Partnership Plan." Available at https://www.bangkokpost.com, https://www.bangkokpost.com/business/2440742/japan-thailand-ink-new-economic-partnership-plan.

Bangkok Post. "65% 'okay with Corruption' If They Gain." Available at https://www.bangkokpost.com. https://www.bangkokpost.com/thailand/politics/358645/poll-65-of-thais-can-accept-corruption. (Accessed January 10, 2023).

Chia, J. (2021). "Remembering October 6 in Words and Pictures — Thai Enquirer Current Affairs." *Thai Enquirer*, October 6, available at https://www.thaien quirer.com/19329/remembering-october-6-in-words-and-pictures/.

Constituion of Kingdom of Thailand. (n.d.). "Official Translation CONSTI-TUTION of the KINGDOM of THAILAND*." Available at https://www.krisdika.go.th/documents/67673/181643/837163_0001.pdf/3d0aab10-e61f-03a4-136a-75003ce4c625.

CP Group. (n.d.). "Milestones." Available at www.cpgroupglobal.com. https://www.cpgroupglobal.com/en/about-cp/milestones. (Accessed January 1, 2023).

CP-Meiji. "CP-Meiji." Available at https://www.cpmeiji.com/sg/about-us. (Accessed January 5, 2023).

Draper, J. & Selway, J. S. (2019). A new dataset on horizontal structural ethnic inequalities in Thailand in order to address sustainable development goal 10. *Social Indicators Research,* 141(1), 275–297. https://doi.org/10.1007/s11205-019-02065-4.

EF English Proficiency Index. Available at https://www.ef.com/wwen/epi/. (Accessed February 8, 2023).

Fong, J. (2009). Sacred nationalism: The Thai monarchy and primordial nation construction. *Journal of Contemporary Asia,* 39(4), 673–696.

Ginsburg, T. (2009). "Constitutional afterlife: The continuing impact of Thailand's postpolitical constitution. *International Journal of Constitutional Law,* 7(1), 83–105.

Gray, D. (2017). "Thailand's Buddhist Nuns Fight for Equality." *Nikkei Asia,* August 24, https://asia.nikkei.com/NAR/Articles/Thailand-s-Buddhist-nuns-fight-for-equality.

Harding, A. (2007). Buddhism, human rights and constitutional reform in Thailand. *Asian Journal of Comparative Law,* 2(1). https://doi.org/10.2202/1932-0205.1045.

Hofstede Insights. "Country Comparison — Hofstede Insights." Available at https://www.hofstede-insights.com/country-comparison/. (Accessed February 6, 2023).

Hyun, Y. (2017). Preserving harmony first, then conveying information: Asian ways of interpreting as maintaining rapport at a Korean trans-national corporation in Thailand. *Manusya: Journal of Humanities* 20(3), 61–84. https://doi.org/10.1163/26659077-02003004.

Jackson, P. A. (1990). *Buddhism, Legitimation and Conflict: The Political Functions of Urban Thai Buddhism.* Singapore: Institute of Southeast Asian Studies.

Kirby, W. C. & Manty, T. Y. "CP Group: Balancing the Needs of a Family Business with the Needs of a Family of Businesses." HBS 9-312-059 (Boston: Harvard Business School Publishing, 2011).

Komin, S. (1991). *Psychology of the Thai people: Values and behavioral patterns.* Bangkok: Magenta.

Koning, J. & Verver, M. (2013). "Historicizing the 'ethnic' in ethnic entrepreneurship: The case of the ethnic Chinese in Bangkok." *Entrepreneurship and Regional Development*, 25(5–6), 325–348.

Englehart, N. A. (2001). *Culture and Power in Traditional Siamese Government.* Southeast Asia Program Series. Ithaca, NY: Southeast Asia Program Publications.

OECD. "Economic Surveys: Thailand 2020 : Economic Assessment." Available at https://www.oecd-ilibrary.org/economics/oecd-economic-surveys-thailand-2020_ad2e50fa-en.

Wongcha-um, P. & Johnson, K. (2020). "Timeline: Thailand's Coups, Kings and Protests." *Reuters*, December 18, available at https://www.reuters.com/article/thailand-protests-youth-history-int-idUSKBN28S1BZ.

Punturaumporn, B. & Hale, C. L. (2003). "Business Negotiations in Thailand: Navigating the Challenges of Traditions vs. Change." Available at SSRN: https://ssrn.com/abstract=400520.

Punyapiroje, C. & Morrison, M. A. (2007). Behind the smile: Reading cultural values in Thai advertising. *Asian Journal of Communication,* 17(3), 318–336.

Wongcha-um, R. & Johnson, K. (December 18, 2020). "Timeline: Thailand's Coups, Kings and Protests." Available at https://www.reuters.com/article/thailand-protests-youth-history-int-idUSKBN28S1BZ.

Reuters. (May 3, 2019). "'I Shall Reign with Righteousness': Thailand Crowns King in Ornate Ceremonies." sec. Emerging Markets. https://www.reuters.com/article/us-thailand-king-coronation-idUSKCN1S924H.

Reynolds, C. J. (1976). Buddhist Cosmography in Thai History, with Special Reference to Nineteenth-Century Culture Change. *The Journal of Asian Studies,* 35(2), 203–220.

Ricks, J. I. (2019). Proud to be Thai: The puzzling absence of ethnicity-based political cleavages in Northeastern Thailand. *Pacific Affairs*, 92(2), 257–285.

Robinson, G. (2022). "In Thailand, Hold the Drinks and Pass the Cannabis." *Nikkei Asia*, October 26, available at https://asia.nikkei.com/Editor-s-Picks/Tea-Leaves/In-Thailand-hold-the-drinks-and-pass-the-cannabis.

South China Morning Post. (November 27, 2019). "Thailand's 31 Richest Entrepreneurs Revealed." Available at https://www.scmp.com/magazines/style/news-trends/article/3039512/king-maha-vajiralongkorn-may-be-richest-person-thailand.

Susanto, A. B. & Susanto, P. (2013). *The Dragon Network: Inside Stories of the Most Successful Chinese Family Businesses.* Singapore: John Wiley & Sons.

Swierczek, F. W. & Onishi, J. (2003). Culture and conflict: Japanese managers and Thai subordinates. *Personnel Review,* 32(2), 187–210.

Tanzer, A. (1994). The bamboo network. *Forbes,* 154(2), 138–144.

Thai National Census 2015. Available at https://www.cia.gov/the-world-factbook/countries/thailand/#people-and-society.

"Thailand Criminal Law Text (Translation) | Laws in Thailand." (n.d.). Www.thailandlawonline.com, available at https://www.thailandlawonline.com/laws-in-thailand/thailand-criminal-law-text-translation. Section 112. (Accessed December 10, 2022).

"Thailand: Military, Monarchy and the Masses." (n.d.). www.lowyinstitute.org, available at https://www.lowyinstitute.org/the-interpreter/thailand-military-monarchy-masses. (Accessed December 10, 2022).

The Board of Investment of Thailand. July 1, 2022. Available at https://www.boi.go.th/.

Thipakorn, S. (2015). Japan's cultural diplomacy: Influence on Thai society. *Rian Thai: International Journal of Thai Studies*, 8, 209–226.

Transparency.org. (January 31, 2023). "2022 Corruption Perceptions Index — Explore Thailand's Results." Available at https://www.transparency.org/en/cpi/2022.

Wise, J. (2020). *Thailand: History, Politics and the Rule of Law*. Singapore: Marshall Cavendish International (Asia) Private Limited.

World Bank. (October 20, 2022). "Thailand Rural Income Diagnostic: Challenges and Opportunities for Rural Farmers." Available at https://www.worldbank.org/en/country/thailand/publication/thailand-rural-income-diagnostic-challenges-and-opportunities-for-rural-farmers.

World Economic Forum. (2022). "Global Gender Gap Report 2022." World Economic Forum, July 13, available at https://www.weforum.org/reports/global-gender-gap-report-2022/digest.

World Economic Forum. *Where Are the Largest Chinese Populations Outside of China? | Thailand or Indonesia: Which Country Has the Largest Chinese Population? | By World Economic Forum | Facebook.*" Available at https://www.facebook.com/worldeconomicforum/videos/where-are-the-largest-chinese-populations-outside-of-china/10153549858561479/. (Accessed November 8, 2022).

Yuda, M. (2019). "Thai Magnate Grooms New Generation for $63bn CP Empire." *Nikkei Asia*, June 14, available at https://asia.nikkei.com/Spotlight/Asian-Family-Conglomerates/Thai-magnate-grooms-new-generation-for-63bn-CP-empire.

Thailand Quiz

1. "Thailand 4.0" is the government's strategy to move towards a technology-oriented economy. To pursue this objective, a special economic zone made up of three provinces in eastern Thailand, called _____ has been set up. Fill in the blank.
   A. Thai Silicon Valley
   B. Eastern Innovation Zone
   C. Eastern Economic Corridor
   D. Special Technology Zone

2. Thai culture is informed by two key institutions in their society, namely _____ and _____. Fill in the blanks.
   A. Buddhism and the monarchy
   B. Buddhism and rice cultivation
   C. Confucianism and the monarchy
   D. Confucianism and rice cultivation

3. Thai Chinese are heavily influenced by Confucianism, which explains why they embrace values such as loyalty and filial piety, which in turn help build foundations for key *guanxi* (connections) when doing business. Is this general characterization true or false?
   A. True
   B. False

4. Despite their calm and gentle demeanor, the Thai negotiators may be easily provoked and react with sudden emotions if they feel insulted or belittled. This is because Thai people are ego-oriented and have a deep sense of pride and dignity. Is this general characterization true or false?
   A. True
   B. False

5. What makes the Thai negotiator difficult to decipher is their _____ belief system, which is overt consideration for the other person's feelings and requires self-sacrifice in order to keep intact the other person's ego. Fill in the blank.
   A. karma
   B. bun khun
   C. kreng jai
   D. sanuk

6. One trait that sets the Thai negotiator apart from those from other East Asian countries is their inclination for "fun-pleasure" also described as _____ (having fun or enjoying oneself) which explains why they prefer to keep social interactions pleasant and appreciate humor. Fill in the blank.
   A. karma
   B. bun khun
   C. kreng jai
   D. sanuk

7. The goal of the Thai negotiator would be to establish with you a reciprocal relationship underpinned by an element of gratitude, commonly translated as _____. With such a relationship, each party will seek to repay an act from the other with an equivalent or larger gesture to sustain the relationship. Fill in the blank.
   A. karma
   B. bun khun
   C. kreng jai
   D. sanuk

8. As Thailand is a homogeneous society that has never been colonized, the Thai negotiator is generally not familiar with foreign cultures with the exception of _____ culture. This is the result of institutionalized efforts undertaken by this foreign government to promote understanding and knowledge of their culture. Fill in the blank.
   A. China
   B. Singapore
   C. Korea
   D. Japan

9. Business people in Thailand have a complex network of external parties that may include their business associates, government officials and even the military, so decision-making takes time and involves many rounds of concession-making. Is this general characterization true or false?
   A. True
   B. False

10. Thai interpreters engaged for business negotiations sometimes adopt
    techniques which affect the accuracy of the communication because
    they want to avert confrontation or avoid hurting the Thai listener's
    ego. Is this general characterization true or false?
    A. True
    B. False

Answer Bank

1. C
2. A
3. B
4. A
5. C
6. D
7. B
8. D
9. A
10. A

Chapter 9

The Vietnamese Negotiator

1. The Environment

Vietnam is one of the few countries in the world to record a positive Gross Domestic Product (GDP) during the COVID-19 pandemic.[1] In 2022, the war in Ukraine and drastic measures taken by China to control the spread of the Omicron variant disrupted the global supply chain and blunted economic recovery around the world. Despite these challenges, Vietnam with a population of around 100 million, continued to buck the trend and achieved stellar GDP growth. According to the country's General Statistics Office, the growth rate of 8% achieved that year was in fact a record for the decade.[2]

This economic success story is remarkable considering the socialist state only embarked on economic reform of its centrally planned economy (known as *Doi Moi*) in 1986.[3] Moreover, this pivot to an 'open door' policy

---

[1] Dabla-Norris, Era, Yuanyan Sophia Zhang IMF Asia, & Pacific Department. (March 10, 2021). "Vietnam: Successfully Navigating the Pandemic." IMF. Available at https://www.imf.org/en/News/Articles/2021/03/09/na031021-vietnam-successfully-navigating-the-pandemic. Vietnam achieved a GDP growth of about 2.91% in 2020.

[2] VietnamPlus. (December 29, 2022). "Vietnam's GDP Expands by 8.02% in 2022 | Business | Vietnam+ (VietnamPlus)." Available at https://en.vietnamplus.vn/vietnams-gdp-expands-by-802-in-2022/246296.vnp.

[3] The 6th National Congress of the Communist Party of Vietnam (CPV) announced these reforms which initiated key changes such as price liberation, de-collectivization (property rights given to individual households) and privatization of State-owned Enterprises (also described as "Equitization") Riedel J, Turley W (1999) "The politics and economics of transition to an open market economy."

and multi-sector market economy took place in the midst of a 20-year trade embargo imposed by the US after the Vietnam War, which was lifted only in 1994. The feisty country proceeded to achieve several major milestones at a dizzying pace. Vietnam became a full member of the Association of Southeast Asian Nations (ASEAN) in 1995, joined the World Trade Organization in 2007 and became a middle-income country in 2010. From 2000, the country recorded strong positive growth every year for two decades and saw its GDP grow tenfold to US$ 362.64 billion.[4] As a result of the US–China trade war, many countries and corporations increased their existing investments or shifted them to Vietnam as part of the "China plus one" strategy to reduce dependence on the Chinese market. This resulted in record Foreign Direct Investment (FDI) into Vietnam.[5] Post pandemic, one of the top investors is the Danish LEGO group, which has committed to build a US$1 billion factory[6] in the country, the first in Southeast Asia. In economic terms, Vietnam is doubtless a success story.

Despite the *Doi Moi* reforms to privatize, state-owned enterprises (SOEs)[7] are still key players today. Although their numbers have decreased drastically and SOEs account for merely 0.28% of the total number of enterprises in the whole economy, they contribute approximately a fifth of the country's GDP.[8] These enterprises hold significant market share in a variety of key industries such as banking, telecommunications and energy. Alongside the SOEs, private entrepreneurship is thriving in Vietnam. Part of this is attributed to returning overseas Vietnamese (*Viet Kieu*), especially the ones formerly based in US; and in particular in the IT sector. The tech

---

[4] https://data.worldbank.org/country/vietnam.

[5] "Disbursement of Public Investment Capital, Foreign Direct Investment, Expecting the Last Months of 2022." General Statistics Office of Vietnam. (2022). Available at https://www.gso.gov.vn/en/data-and-statistics/2022/10/disbursement-of-public-investment-capital-foreign-direct-investment-expecting-the-last-months-of-2022/#:~:text=Realized%20FDI%20investment%20in%20Vietnam.

[6] Lien, H. (2022). "Lego Breaks Ground on $1bn Carbon-Neutral Factory in Vietnam." *Nikkei Asia*, November 3, https://asia.nikkei.com/Spotlight/Supply-Chain/Lego-breaks-ground-on-1bn-carbon-neutral-factory-in-Vietnam.

[7] SOE is defined as a company in which more than 50% of its charter capital or voting shares is held by the state (Law on Enterprises 2021, articles 4.11 and 88). SOEs are subject to more regulations than private enterprises.

[8] "Statistical Yearbook of 2021." General Statistics Office of Vietnam. (2021). Available at https://www.gso.gov.vn/en/data-and-statistics/2022/08/statistical-yearbook-of-2021/.

and startup scene in Vietnam received much attention over the past few years. In May 2020, three districts of Ho Chi Minh City were merged to create an innovation hub to become "Vietnam's Silicon Valley". One of the country's most prominent technology unicorns, VNG, is a source of national pride and has open ambitions to list in the US. Among the various tech products and services, VNG's social media application, Zalo, is the most popular social media network among Vietnamese, beating Facebook and Messenger.[9]

2. Culture

Though Vietnam is situated in Southeast Asia, it is culturally closer to Northeast Asian countries such as China, Japan and Korea.

Vietnam was under Chinese rule for more than a thousand years until the 10th century.[10] The Chinese introduced large-scale rice agriculture, as well as Confucianism, Buddhism and Taoism. After the Chinese were driven out, sucessive Vietnamese dynasties that took over administration of the country till the middle of the 16th century also adopted Confucianism as a key basis for governance and social relations. When the country built its first university (Quoc Tu Giam,) in Hanoi in 1070, its students were trained in Confucian classics and commentaries. The Vietnamese were influenced by the Mahayana Buddhism, which is different from the Theravada form practiced in Thailand. The Mahayana form blended with Confucianism and, in the case of Vietnam, also mixed with local folklore and beliefs.[11] The country was plunged into a series of civil wars from the 16th to the 18th centuries and was divided into two regions, namely, the Trinh in the North and the Nguyen in the South. It was unified at the start of the 19th century under the Nguyen dynasty, which retained the influence of Confucianism on the country's culture. The Nguyen emperors even built a scaled-down replica of Beijing's Forbidden City and adopted Chinese

---

[9] Alpuerto, A. (2023). "Tech Giant VNG Tests Stock Market Potential with UPCoM Listing." *Vietcetera*, January 4, available at https://vietcetera.com/en/tech-giant-vng-tests-stock-market-potential-with-upcom-listing.

[10] CIA. (September 15, 2022). "The World Factbook." CIA website [downloaded on 15 September 2022], available at https://www.cia.gov/the-world-factbook/countries/vietnam/.

[11] Church, P. (2017). *Short History of South-East Asia*. Singapore: John Wiley & Sons Inc.

administrative methods. Thus, over the long course of the country's history, Chinese culture and Confucianism asserted tremendous influence on its people.

Western influences such as Catholicism, French administration and legal systems were introduced during the French occupation (1883–1945). During this period, a line of puppet Nguyen emperors were retained. By the 1920s, a simple Romanized written form of Vietnamese (*Quoc Ngu*) was invented by French missionaries and adopted in place of traditional Chinese-style characters.[12] During World War II, Japan agreed to let Vietnam remain a French-administered region. After the war, the Communist Party of Vietnam (CPV) fought the French for independence and came to power in the North. A long period of civil wars was fought between North and South Vietnam (1955–1975) with heavy US involvement. The North prevailed and Vietnam remains a one-party system led by the CPV since 1975.

Though there are several ethnic groups in Vietnam, more than 85% of the population are Kinhs (Viets).[13] Ethnic or pure Chinese, known as *Hoa*, comprise a further 1.26 million (about 1% of Vietnam's population), which according to the World Economic Forum (2016) is the eighth largest Chinese population in the world residing outside of China.[14] However, the deep influence of Confucianism and Chinese culture permeates the entire society. For instance, the Vietnamese New Year starts on the first day of the lunar calendar, which is also the Chinese New Year. Known commonly as *Tet* (short for *Tet Nguyen Dan*) and celebrated over three days, this is a national holiday and the most important one in Vietnam. Most Vietnamese display characteristic Confucian traits such as respect for hierarchy, loyalty to family and emphasis on individual's social obligations.[15] Like China, Vietnam is a socialist state with a market economy featuring SOEs.

---

[12] Church, P. (2017). *Short History of South-East Asia*. Singapore: John Wiley & Sons Inc.
[13] "Vietnam — The World Factbook." (n.d.). www.cia.gov. Available at https://www.cia.gov/the-world-factbook/countries/vietnam/#people-and-society.
[14] "Where Are the Largest Chinese Populations Outside of China? | Thailand or Indonesia: Which Country Has the Largest Chinese Population? | By World Economic Forum | Facebook." Available at https://www.facebook.com/worldeconomicforum/videos/where-are-the-largest-chinese-populations-outside-of-china/10153549858561479/. (Accessed November 8, 2022).
[15] Church, P. (2017). *Short History of South-East Asia*. Singapore: John Wiley & Sons Inc.

You may have the impression that business dealings in Vietnam and China are similar, but this is not the case.[16] In some ways, the Vietnamese may come across as being more "Chinese" than the Chinese negotiators because more traditional familial bonds are retained. Vietnam also experienced influences from Western values adapted from its French colonial days and from fighting the Americans. Its own communist ideology and its modernization path post-*Doi Moi* — results in a unique mix of cultural values in contemporary Vietnamese society.[17]

Hofstede's Cultural Dimensions

• Power Distance
Vietnam scores 70 on this index, higher than Japan (54) and South Korea (60), but lower than China (80).[18] In both SOEs and privately owned companies, the Vietnamese corporation is hierarchical and seniority is important. Regardless of qualification or financial status, an older person is generally accorded respect and shown deference.[19] Especially within SOEs, employees expect their supervisors to give instructions and bosses see themselves as benevolent autocrats. Even in private enterprises, employees tend to look for guidance from their managers even for decisions that are well within their scope of responsibility.[20] Some foreign-owned enterprises find it frustrating that their Vietnamese hires do not

[16] Katz, L. (2017). "Negotiating International Business — Vietnam." *Negotiating International Business — The Negotiator's Reference Guide to 50 Countries Around the World* [downloaded on 1 January 2022], available at http://www.leadershipcrossroads.com/mat/cou/Vietnam.pdf.

[17] Nguyen, Q. T. N. (2016). The Vietnamese values system: A blend of oriental, western and socialist values. *International Education Studies*, 9(12), 32–40. Available at https://files.eric.ed.gov/fulltext/EJ1121509.pdf.

[18] Hofstede Insights. "Country Comparison — Hofstede Insights." Available at https://www.hofstede-insights.com/country-comparison/. (Accessed February 6, 2023).

[19] Nguyen, Q. T. N. (2016). The Vietnamese values system: A blend of oriental, western and socialist values. *International Education Studies*, 9(12), 32–40. Available at https://files.eric.ed.gov/fulltext/EJ1121509.pdf.

[20] Le, T. C., Rowley, C., Truong, Q., & Warner, M. (2007). To what extent can management practices be transferred between countries? The case of human resource management in Vietnam. *Journal of World Business*, 42, 113–127.

exercise much autonomy even when this is given.[21] There is constant checking for confirmation even after the decision is taken. The superior–subordinate line is drawn very clearly. Even for those who have studied or worked overseas, disagreeing with their bosses or supervisors is rare. You may soon realize that junior members of the Vietnamese negotiating team are expected to work beyond office hours and even run personal errands for their managers.

During negotiations, you should initiate any new discussion or proposal through junior members of the Vietnamese team for them to forward your proposal to someone more senior in the organization. This acknowledges their hierarchy and way of doing things. Frequently, this has to be put in writing to facilitate communication. Junior team members will not offer any comment at all as their task is merely to pass on the message. Especially in SOEs, junior employees will not speak their mind because they fear being seen as "too competent" or worse, arrogant or disrespectful. Although in cities such as Ho Chi Minh and in IT sectors, many young employees seem outwardly Westernized, hierarchy is still important. Nevertheless, decisions are made in groups after reaching consensus even though the junior members rarely express dissenting views. The final say typically comes from someone with the appropriate authority and rank, with the support of the entire team.

- **Individualism–Collectivism**

Despite the geographical proximity to China and limitations of its national healthcare system, Vietnam achieved impressive results in its battle against the COVID-19 pandemic and was one of the first countries to open its borders. Many Vietnamese will attribute such success to the collectivistic feature of their society.[22] There was a clear awareness that individual well-being was dependent on society's well-being. This collectivism can trace its roots to the group agricultural life in the society. Vietnam's long history of rice cultivation originated even before the Chinese rule.

---

[21] Tran, T., Admiraal, W., & Saab, N. (2020). Work-related values in international workplaces in Vietnam: Cross-cultural differences between employers and employees. *Open Journal of Business and Management*, 8, 1567–1586. doi: 10.4236/ojbm.2020.84100.

[22] Dinh, P. L. & Ho, T. T. (2020). "How a collectivistic society won the first battle against COVID-19: Vietnam and their "weapons."" *Inter-Asia Cultural Studies*, 21(4), 506–520, doi: 10.1080/14649373.2020.1831811.

In the Individualism index, Vietnam's low score of 20 is the same as that of China (20), Singapore (20) and Thailand (20).[23] It is slightly higher than South Korea's (18), but far lower than Japan's (46).[24] Thus, it can be seen that Vietnam is almost equal in terms of its "collectivism" score to China and Korea. As is the case in many collectivist cultures, Vietnamese regard themselves as members of a group and will subordinate their own individual interests to that of the group's.[25] They will share and promote the beliefs and goals of the group, are accepting of the roles assigned to them and will comply with instructions from leaders within the group. Traditionally, the Vietnamese see themselves as a unit of a family, a village and a country and regard anyone who prioritizes individual self-interests as selfish. Individualism is therefore not a strong feature in either its culture or language.[26] Notwithstanding, a popular view is that there is a north–south cultural difference along this particular dimension in Vietnam.[27] Northerners are reserved and more conservative, showing more deference to the group. People in the South are seen as being more individualistic — less constrained by rules and regulations and more innovative. This might explain why the Silicon Valley of Vietnam is located in the southern city of Ho Chi Minh.

When negotiating with a Vietnamese counterpart, efforts must be undertaken to engage the group and socialize with all members of the team. Meetings are invariably preceded by small talk, which is not merely perfunctory. There is a genuine desire on their part to get to know you better. Do not be too quick to decline invitations to have copious amounts of (egg) coffee, lunches and dinners — even if the venue seems too casual for the always formally attired Vietnamese. Though the younger

---

[23] Hofstede Insights. "Country Comparison — Hofstede Insights." Available at https://www.hofstede-insights.com/country-comparison/. (Accessed February 6, 2023).

[24] *Ibid.*

[25] Nguyen, L. D., Mujtaba, B. G., & Boehmer, T. (2012). Stress, task, and relationship orientations across German and Vietnamese cultures. *International Business and Management*, 5 (1), 10–20. doi: http://dx.doi.org/10.3968/j.ibm.1923842820120501.1060.

[26] Huong, Ngo Thi Minh, Vu, Giao Cong, & Nguyen, Tam Minh. (2018). Asian values and human rights: A Vietnamese perspective. *Journal of Southeast Asian Human Rights*, 2(1), 302. https://doi.org/10.19184/jseahr.v2i1.7541.

[27] Ho, H.-A., Martinsson, P., & Olsson, Ola. (August 2021). "The origins of cultural divergence: Evidence from Vietnam." *Journal of Economic Growth*, https://doi.org/10.1007/s10887-021-09194-x.

Vietnamese tend to be more open and individualistic, the work culture is still predominantly collectivist.

Therefore, expect to conduct your negotiation with a team rather than with an individual. One fun fact is that you will certainly meet someone who has Nguyen as their family name or surname, which is shared by approximately 40% of the population.[28]

- **Uncertainty Avoidance**

Vietnam has a complex regulatory environment constantly being revised and updated by its one-party state. Business people know that there may be laws and regulations, but compliance (and circumvention) can come in many forms. Then there is also government bureaucracy and even corruption.

At the same time, the "can do" spirit of the Vietnamese people makes them very adaptable. They in fact take some pride in being able to overcome hurdles and barriers put in their way. When getting things done, there is a wide latitude for individual discretion and autonomy. So long as objectives are met, Vietnamese typically do not mind what measures are taken. The environment, coupled with their "can do" spirit, translates to a relatively low uncertainty avoidance index (UAI). As can be seen from the Hofstede Dimensions table, Vietnam scores 30 for this index for which Singapore's score (8) is the lowest and Japan's score (92) is the highest among the countries covered in this book.[29]

Japan takes a diametrically opposite approach when faced with uncertainty. As explained in the country-specific chapter on Japan, the Japanese have a strong preference for predictability and diligently follow prescribed protocols. Moreover, the country faces constant threats from natural disasters such as earthquakes and typhoons. Being prepared and following instructions are part of their national identity. It is thus no surprise that Japan has one of the highest scores for this index. Singapore is at the other end of this spectrum. Generally, Singaporeans diligently abide by rules and regulations. There is high predictability and thus low levels of uncertainty

---

[28] Nosowitz, D. (2017). "Why 40% of Vietnamese People Have the Same Last Name." *Atlas Obscura*, March 28. Available at https://www.atlasobscura.com/articles/pronounce-nguyen-common-vietnam.

[29] Hofstede Insights. "Country Comparison — Hofstede Insights." Available at https://www.hofstede-insights.com/country-comparison/. (Accessed February 6, 2023).

in the society. In short, the Japanese dislike uncertainty (hence high score) whereas the Singaporeans are unaccustomed to thinking of uncertainty (hence low score). Interestingly, both Japan and Singapore are two of the biggest investors in Vietnam since 2020.[30]

Whether you come from culture that dislikes uncertainty (high UAI) or is unfamiliar with unpredictability (low UAI), one useful approach is to get some granularity and clarity as to the Vietnamese party's key obligations. What are their promises on tangible items such as prices, schedules and meeting regulatory requirements? You do not have to capture all the details in writing, but it is necessary to have many discussions and conversations about this to ensure that both sides are generally on the same page. When negotiating with a Vietnamese party, we should not assume that outcomes have been finalized, or that agreements or contracts signed are the last word on the matter. If they do not share your understanding, there are many administrative rules or regulations that can be invoked to scuttle the deal.

3. Communication

Henry Kissinger, former National Security Advisor to the US, negotiated with North Vietnamese politburo member Le Duc Tho for a cease fire of the Vietnam War. The negotiations went on for many rounds and lasted for more than three years, culminating in the Paris Peace Accord in 1973. For their efforts, both were awarded the Nobel Peace Prize.[31] In the article "The Viet Nam Negotiations", Kissinger gave an insightful account as to the communication style of his opponent in what he called "The Environment of Negotiations":

> ... the *way* the negotiations are carried out is almost as important as *what* is negotiated. The choreography of how one enters negotiations, what is settled first and in what manner is inseparable from the substance of the

---

[30] "Ministry of Planning and Investment Portal." (n.d.) Www.mpi.gov.vn. Available at https://www.mpi.gov.vn/en/Pages/tinbai.aspx?idTin=54532&idcm=122. For the first 6 months of 2022, Singapore was Vietnam's top source of FDI (USD 4 billion accounting for almost 30%) and Japan ranked fifth.

[31] "Foreign Relations, 1969–1976, Volume XLII, Vietnam: The Kissinger-Le Duc Tho Negotiations — Office of the Historian." (n.d.) History.state.gov. Available at https://history.state.gov/historicaldocuments/frus1969-76v42/preface. (Accessed October 24, 2022).

issues ... The incompatibility of the American and North Vietnamese style of diplomacy produced a massive breakdown in communication — especially in the preliminary phases of negotiation. Hanoi was feeling its way toward negotiations, it bent all its ingenuity to avoid clear-cut, formal commitments. Ambiguity permitted Hanoi to probe without giving much in return. Hanoi has no peers in slicing the salami very thin. It wanted the context of events rather than a formal document to define its obligations ... (emphasis by Kissinger).[32]

Though he was negotiating with a North Vietnamese party under circumstances that were intensely confrontational — his analysis as to the importance of context and how it can define the substance of the communication holds true for most negotiations in Vietnam. By and large, Vietnamese are indirect communicators and tend to understate their meanings. You must always pay attention to the form of the communication — their facial expression, tone of voice and posture. While their vocabulary is subtle, their body language usually conveys explicit cues about their intentions. You need to be more aware of this, especially at the start of the concurrent phase (ongoing process)[33] when both sides lay out their initial position regarding the tangibles of negotiation such as a price. As a result of their high-context culture, the Vietnamese negotiator may come across as being intentionally ambiguous or vague. However, you should not jump to unnecessary conclusions. Much of the indirectness is due to the Vietnamese language. It is nuanced and requires appropriate words to reflect the speaker and listener's social roles and statuses, which is expected in their collectivist society. As a result, they sometimes go in a roundabout way to say something in order to ensure that they accord proper respect to you. For instance, there are many ways to say "yes" in Vietnamese and this depends on the situation and whether you are speaking to someone more senior or to whom you should show respect.[34] An

---

[32] Kissinger, H. A. (1969). The Vietnam negotiations. *Foreign Affairs*, 47(2), 211. https://doi.org/10.2307/20039369.

[33] Negotiations are generally classifiable into three parts: Antecedent phase (pre-negotiation stage and preparations), the concurrent phase (ongoing process), and the consequent phase (post-negotiation stage) — see Theoretical Chapter under Negotiation Strategies: Distributive or Integrative.

[34] "31 Ways to Say Yes No in Vietnamese | Ling App." December 12, 2020. Available at https://ling-app.com/vi/yes-no-in-vietnamese/.

affirmative answer from an older person is different from the term used by and expected from a younger person. And in formal settings, the affirmative reply must also be formal. Further, Vietnamese have the habit of using proverbs and parables, even in written communication. Some may think these are mere fillers in conversation or are irrelevant, but foreigners familiar with their culture will understand that the context is being described and this indirectness is, in fact, a display of tact.[35] As Kissinger cautioned — if you do not attend to the context or decipher it, there will be miscommunication.

While on the topic of saying "yes", one other point to note is that the Vietnamese negotiator may say "yes" a lot to you and very often. Mostly, this is merely a polite acknowledgement that they are listening and not to be taken as an affirmative answer or agreement.[36] In this respect, it is similar to the Chinese habit of repeatedly saying "yes". On the other hand, the Vietnamese generally find it difficult to say "no" or to outrightly reject you because this might result in a loss of face for you. In its place, you may get a "this is difficult", "now is not the right time" or something along the lines of suggesting there is a problem to be solved.[37] Likewise, a smile from your Vietnamese negotiator can take on a wide range of meanings and significance. A smile can mean joy, a simple apology, an acknowledgement and even ill feelings.[38] Long periods of silence during meetings need to be investigated with sensitivity. Generally, when it comes to important points or feedback — the Vietnamese negotiator tends to take an indirect approach, so you need to read the room. It is their way of being tactful.

One possible approach is for you to check that your understanding is correct. You may suggest a few possible meanings and see which one resonates with them. In discussions, the Vietnamese tend to always ask you, at intervals, whether everything is OK, are you alright? You can do the same for them. This form of checking is a good way to signpost the direction you are heading in.

---

[35] Borton, L. (2000). Working in a Vietnamese voice [and Executive Commentary]. *Academy of Management Perspectives*, 14(4), 20–31.

[36] *Ibid.*

[37] *Ibid.*

[38] Nguyen, Quynh-Anh Ngoc. (2019). "Exploring Emotional Intelligence: A Study of Vietnamese Hotel Workers." Available at https://eprints.bournemouth.ac.uk/32580/1/NGUYEN,%20Quynh_Ph.D.2019.pdf.

The Vietnamese concept of face is made up of social roles as well as characteristics and achievements that are role-driven.[39] Loss of face means disapproval of the individual as well as the group he/she is associated with. Thus, in Vietnamese culture, face (*mặt*) is both an individual and collective possession.[40] The Vietnamese negotiators are very conscious of possible negative social judgment of their behavior as this will reflect badly on their entire team. If something you say or do towards one member causes him or her to lose face — the entire team will suffer the loss. This means that when you acknowledge and "give face" or show deference to a single member in front of the team, all of them will appreciate the gesture greatly.[41]

4. Negotiation Strategies: Distributive or Integrative

In the beginning, the Vietnamese team may come across as integrative because they are always asking what they can do for you and how they can help you. Constantly polite and seemingly eager to compromise is frequently the first impression given. Yet, this demeanor has more to do with the way they communicate than with their strategy. Overall, the Vietnamese Negotiator is clear and focused on the outcomes they want and at times, can be rather inflexible.

Bargaining is an integral part of their everyday life. Vietnamese have to constantly navigate a web of regulatory and administrative requirements and red tape. Corruption is still very much an issue faced by businesses, so they always need to flex their bargaining muscles to get things done. The instinct to fight for what they want is ingrained in their psyche due to the intermittent civil wars between the North and the South, their long history of fending off foreign aggression and struggle for self-rule. When you are negotiating in their offices, your Vietnamese counterpart will make you

[39] Pham, T. H. N. (2014). How do the Vietnamese lose face? Understanding the concept of face through self-reported face loss incidents. *International Journal of Language and Linguistics*, 2(3), 223. https://doi.org/10.11648/j.ijll.20140203.21.

[40] Pham, T. H. N. (2007). Exploring the concept of "face" in Vietnamese: Evidence from its collocational abilities/Khám phá Khái niệm Thể diện trong Tiếng Việt: Bằng chứng từ Kết hợp Từ. *Electronic Journal of Foreign Language Teaching*, 4, 257–266.

[41] Pham, T. H. N. (2014). The impact of third party presence on the motivational concerns underlying linguistic politeness behavior in English-speaking intercultural contexts. *Journal for the Study of English Linguistics*, 2(1), 19. https://doi.org/10.5296/jsel.v2i1.5833.

feel very welcome as their guests. However, in the meeting rooms, you will usually be led to your designated seats and soon realize that the setup gives your host more control of the situation. Moreover, the Vietnamese negotiators are generally not forthcoming with information since they regard this an important advantage for bargaining purposes. Information tends to be provided in a piecemeal manner and you often get conflicting data from different persons (or even from the same person) at various times. Although the general atmosphere will be pleasant and amicable, during the negotiation your Vietnamese counterpart may engage in fierce and protracted bargaining for minor gains. Senior members of their team (usually seated in the middle) may even adopt aggressive stances now and then. If your negotiation involves multiple items, the Vietnamese negotiator may bargain and haggle over several aspects in parallel and re-open discussions over issues or items already agreed upon.[42] Overall, the Vietnamese are so accustomed to value claiming that they will come across as being distributive, even if they do not intend to do so.

Vietnam has a low-trust culture and its people generally express a low level of trust of people from another nationality or culture.[43] Even as the country modernizes rapidly after the initializing of the *Doi Moi*, studies have shown that the Vietnamese will only trust small circles of people close and known to them; and they have grown more distrusting of strangers (including their own countrymen).[44] When dealing with you, they will carefully gauge the amount of trust they can place on you. They will form various hypotheses about you and carry out step-by-step testing of these through interactions and observations.[45]

---

[42] Katz, L. (2017). "Negotiating International Business — Vietnam." *Negotiating International Business — The Negotiator's Reference Guide to 50 Countries Around the World* [downloaded on 1 January 2022], available at http://www.leadershipcrossroads.com/mat/cou/Vietnam.pdf.

[43] An, N. H. & Phuong, L. D. M. (2021). "Social capital in Vietnam: An analysis of social networks and social trust. *Journal of Mekong Societies*, 17(2), 1–27. Available at https://so03.tci-thaijo.org/index.php/mekongjournal/article/view/249714; This study is based on data of Vietnam from Waves 5 and 7 of the World Values Survey (WVS). Available at https://www.worldvaluessurvey.org/WVSContents.jsp.

[44] *Ibid.*

[45] Le, T. C., Rowley, C., Truong, Q., & Warner, M. (2007). To what extent can management practices be transferred between countries? The case of human resource management in Vietnam. *Journal of World Business*, 42, 113–127.

In sum, the combined effect of their bargaining style, their attitudes towards information-sharing and low trust in the beginning explains why the default strategy of the Vietnamese negotiator is distributive. Even so, the Vietnamese negotiators are open to integrative processes, because they value long-term commitment and are relationship-oriented.[46]

There is a strong national aspiration to achieve prosperity and upward social mobility, which supplies a deeper motivation to achieving win–win outcomes in business. At the Congress of the CPV in 2021, a 10-year socio-economic development strategy was adopted to achieve upper middle income status by 2030 and to achieve high-income status by 2045, which will mark the 100th anniversary of the establishment of the Socialist Republic of Vietnam.[47] If you can convince your Vietnamese counterpart that there are gains and wins for them, they will commit to cooperating and collaborating.

To achieve an integrative process, you have to work on earning their trust. One approach is for you show some transparency about your information and position. This is a common dilemma for negotiators called the dilemma of honesty — because telling the other party too much about your situation will allow them to take advantage of you.[48] However, the Vietnamese party is very appreciative of such honesty as they typically face secretive and corrupt public administration. Indeed, the transparent information-sharing and decision-making of its government during the pandemic crisis is credited as being a key reason for the high level of trust shown by the people.[49] The gesture of transparency on your part will be

---

[46] Katz, L. (2017). "Negotiating International Business — Vietnam." *Negotiating International Business — The Negotiator's Reference Guide to 50 Countries Around the World* [downloaded on 1 January 2022], available at http://www.leadershipcrossroads.com/mat/cou/Vietnam.pdf; Ready, Kathryn, J. & Van Dinh. (2006). Vietnams developing markets: How do perceptions and strategies in the negotiation process differ from the US? *Journal of Diversity Management (JDM)*, 1(1), 49–60. https://doi.org/10.19030/jdm.v1i1.5029.

[47] Do, T. T. (March 2022). Vietnam's emergence as a middle power in Asia: Unfolding the power–knowledge nexus. *Journal of Current Southeast Asian Affairs*, 186810342210811. https://doi.org/10.1177/18681034221081146.

[48] Lewicki, R. J., Saunders, D. M., & Barry, B. (2021). *Essentials of Negotiation*. New York: Mcgraw-Hill Education.

[49] Phạm, Q. P. (December 2020). Covid-19 in Vietnam: Social engagement, trust creation and political legitimacy. *Halshs.archives-Ouvertes,fr*, available at https://halshs.archives-ouvertes.fr/halshs-03151081.

reciprocated, and will be understood as building of *quan he* (same as *guanxi* in Chinese, meaning connection) for mutual benefit. Effective information sharing is a key building block for all win–win relationships. If at this point, negotiation appears to be slowing or stalling, assess whether they are in fact seeking alternatives or finding ways to meet both sides' interests. Do not rush them as they generally take their time to process important information from you and to make decisions as to next steps. Be patient and flexible. Showing patience and humility are traits they admire. Knowing who are the influential stakeholders and the role of the senior leaders on the Vietnamese side will also be useful because you can work on winning their support for an integrative outcome.

Deep down, there is a genuine desire on their part to build a relationship. If they are convinced that you are also seeking a long-term commitment, they will commit to a win–win strategy. The Vietnamese negotiator will then invoke their "can-do" spirit to think up all the ways and alternatives to accommodate both parties' interests. Sometimes, their proposals may come across as being unconventional and out of left field. This is their way of creating value. Do not be put off and assume that they are not being sincere. Take time to better understand their rationale and you may even be surprised with the ingenuity of their suggestions. One of the best opportunities to build rapport is when you share meals with them at the roadside pop-up restaurants with the ubiquitous tiny chairs and tables. This informal and cozy setting is a stark contrast to the rigid office meeting setup where you both sit on opposite sides of a wide table. Your Vietnamese counterpart will usually be relaxed and chatty in this casual setting as you huddle over a small table and sample some of the best dishes in the country. Business is rarely discussed over such meals, but if during or after the meal your Vietnamese dining companions ask you to call them by their first or given names, you'll know that you have taken the relationship to the next level.

When drawing up contracts in Vietnam, it is definitely useful to capture and circulate key points of the agreement; especially with SOEs. Until a final agreement is signed by key representatives from both sides; draft agreements can be repeatedly revised and revisited. This is more a reflection of their bargaining style rather than any underlying ill intention. Even if a final contract has been made; there may be requests for variation. It is a common practice for contracts to have multiple schedules and appendices especially where approvals or permits are needed from various regulatory bodies or authorities. However, you should carry out your own due

diligence to ensure that there is clear understanding about the main obligations and rights of both parties. What is important is for both sides to
remain committed to key obligations and agree on how to resolve any
issues if and when they arise.

5. Concession-making and Hardball Tactics

The Vietnamese are tenacious bargainers so you should be prepared for the
concession-making to be a drawn-out affair. Because they are very price
sensitive, the movement in their concessions at times seem miniscule. Even
after they say "okay, okay", their concession may sound suspiciously similar to their earlier offer. If they engage in rounds of haggling, it can be a
tiresome affair. It will also be challenging to gauge your counterpart's resistance levels from their initial offers because many of them prefer a generous
buffer. In some cases, prices can move by 50% between the initial and final
offers from your Vietnamese counterpart. The Vietnamese negotiator's
concession-making pattern can be quite random and it may be difficult to
see the pattern or know whether negotiations are coming to a close. They
may offer you unexpected concessions, e.g. by informing you of unforeseen
challenges and obstacles and offering to resolve them. Do not dismiss such
concessions as being irrelevant. Every offer should go into the bargaining
mix for consideration. Although people frequently expect large concessions
to be offered by the Vietnamese team only near the end of the negotiations,
this is not always the case. An important concession can arrive mid-way;
especially if the relationship building has been smooth. Of course, this is
more likely for small- and mid-sized enterprises (SMEs) than for SOEs.
This has to do with the approval processes and systems at these enterprises.
As consensus building is necessary, do not expect decisions to be taken by
your Vietnamese counterpart at meetings. Although the junior members
rarely voice any disagreement, and seniors usually lead the meetings, a lot
of internal discussion must still take place before significant concessions
will be offered by the Vietnamese negotiator.

The Vietnamese practice reciprocity — this is part of the Buddhist/Taoist
influence. So, if you are prepared to make major concessions, you should also
get ready a list of concessions you would like in exchange. The Vietnamese
negotiator is very likely to offer something in return. This reflects well on
them as it is a face-giving gesture on their part. Sometimes, their concessions

are packaged or are subject to conditionality. If so, you need to be clear about any contingencies that may negate or discount the concessions.

In terms of hardball tactics, you should be prepared for some degree or form of deception. In the course of negotiation, you may receive some misrepresentation or half-truths. The Vietnamese negotiator will always check information received from you so they will operate on the premise that you will do the same. You should therefore investigate and carry out your own due diligence exercises, as mentioned earlier. If you decide to practice some deception, you should be very careful. If poorly executed, you will lose a lot of credibility in their eyes. If you lose the respect of your Vietnamese counterpart, they might step up on their tenacious bargaining to wear you out. Interestingly, they may not regard this as an end to the relationship but will regard the current negotiation as a chapter or episode. Another hardball tactic you may encounter is the nibble (proportionately small concessions); especially if negotiations are protracted.[50] You may be asked to include an item or clause that was not previously discussed, just before conclusion of the negotiation. You should not react immediately to such requests since you are not expected to make decisions on the spot. One approach is to take notes; ask questions to find out more why this concession is needed. Keep a record of all requests and assure the other party that you are looking into them.

Intimidation is rare as the Vietnamese generally avoid conflict and prefer to keep discussions genial. They do not use "good cop, bad cop" routines because of their collectivist culture. They may also not appreciate or understand the purpose of this tactic if you were to use it. One important thing to note is that Vietnamese pride themselves on being tenacious — so there would be various attempts to wear you out to obtain concessions.

6. Role of Women

Though heavily influenced by Confucianism, women in Vietnam have a higher social status than their counterparts in China, Japan and Korea. According to its folklore, Vietnam was a matriarchal society and women

---

[50] Katz, L. (2017). "Negotiating International Business — Vietnam." *Negotiating International Business — The Negotiator's Reference Guide to 50 Countries Around the World* [downloaded on 1 January 2022], available at http://www.leadershipcrossroads.com/mat/cou/Vietnam.pdf.

were frequently depicted as strong, capable and heroic in its folklore literature.[51] Even in contemporary society, Vietnamese women are seen as capable, independent and powerful, both in public and the private domain.[52]

According to a 2021 report by the International Labour Office (ILO), Vietnamese women play an active role in its economy.[53] It showed that the participation gap between men and women in the labor market is just below 10%; against the whole-of-Asia rate of over 32%.[54] In fact, pre-pandemic, there was no significant difference in the unemployment rate between men and women. Moreover, Vietnamese women (comprising slightly less than half its labor force) occupy 24.7% of overall management roles.[55] Though this ILO report focused on Vietnam and did not provide comparisons with other countries, the percentage of women in managerial positions is still significantly higher than comparable scores for women in Japan (14.5%) and Indonesia (19.4%).[56] Based on the 2022 Global Gender Gap Report by the World Economic Forum, Vietnam is ranked ninth out of 19 countries in the East Asia and the Pacific region — ahead of several countries covered in this book.[57]

---

[51] Chiricosta, A. (2010). Following the trail of the fairy-bird: The search for a uniquely Vietnamese women's movement. In M. Roces & L. Edwards (Eds.), *Women's Movements In Asia: Feminisms And Transnational Activism* (pp. 124–43). London and New York: Routledge; Taylor & Francis Group.

[52] Do, V. H. T. & Brennan, M. (2015). Complexities of Vietnamese femininities: A resource for rethinking women's university leadership practices. *Gender and Education*, 27(3), 273–287.

[53] "Gender and the Labour Market in Viet Nam." (2021). Ilo.org. March 2, 2021. Available at https://ilo.org/hanoi/Whatwedo/Publications/WCMS_774434/lang--en/index.htm.

[54] Research Brief: Gender and the Labour Market in Viet Nam. "Gender and the Labour Market in Viet Nam," March 2, 2021. Available at http://www.ilo.org/hanoi/Whatwedo/Publications/WCMS_774434/lang--en/index.htm.

[55] *Ibid.*

[56] International Labour Office. (2021). "Women in Managerial and Leadership Positions in the G20." Available at https://www.ilo.org/wcmsp5/groups/public/---dgreports/---ddg_p/documents/publication/wcms_762098.pdf.

[57] "Global Gender Gap Report 2022." (July 13, 2022). World Economic Forum. Available at https://www.weforum.org/reports/global-gender-gap-report-2022/digest. The Global Gender Gap Index benchmarks the current state and evolution of gender parity across four key dimensions (Economic Participation and Opportunity, Educational Attainment, Health and Survival, and Political Empowerment). It is the longest-standing index which tracks progress towards closing these gaps over time since its inception in 2006.

Global Gender Gap Report 2022 INSIGHT REPORT JULY 2022

EAST ASIA & the PACIFIC	Rank		
Country	Regional (19)	Global (146)	Score
Philippines	2	19	0.783
Singapore	4	49	0.734
Thailand	8	79	0.709
Vietnam	**9**	**83**	**0.705**
Indonesia	10	92	0.697
Korea (South)	12	99	0.689
China	13	102	0.682
Malaysia	14	103	0.681
Japan	19	116	0.650

Source: "Global Gender Gap Report 2022." World Economic Forum. July 13, 2022. https://www.weforum.org/reports/global-gender-gap-report-2022/digest.

The Vietnamese government is also proactive in its effort to promote gender parity. Legislations such as Law on Gender Equality 2006[58] and a special section in its Labour Law 2012 provide equal rights in all fields and to employment. Of course, these may be the rules on paper and there are bound to be gaps in implementation. In addition, there will always be gender stereotyping and gender-related norms shaped by Confucianism.[59]

If you were a woman negotiating in Vietnam, you are unlikely to be perceived as being weak. In fact, being dominant and assertive might work against you; on the other hand, exercising empathy will be appreciated. Communicate your concerns and requests, if any, with politeness and confidence. It goes without saying that you would also accord respect to any female member of the Vietnamese team, whether they are junior or senior.

---

[58] Law on Gender Equality No. 73/2006/QH11 dated 29 November 2006.
[59] Grosse, I. (2015). "Gender values in Vietnam — Between confucianism, communism, and modernization. *Asian Journal of Peacebuilding*, 3(2), 253–272. https://doi.org/10.18588/201511.000045.

7. Intermediary/Interpreter

Vietnam's official language is Vietnamese. English is a compulsory subject from third grade onwards. In 2008, its government launched a US$446 million 12-year program (Project 2020) to help its students acquire proficiency in a foreign language, mostly English. The 2022 English Proficiency Index ranked the country at 60th place, out of 111 countries. This is lower than other ASEAN countries covered in this book such as Singapore (2nd), the Philippines (22nd) and Malaysia (24th), but higher than Indonesia (81st) and Thailand (97th). In cities such as Ho Chi Minh and Hanoi, spoken English proficiency at the workplace is not uncommon, especially among the younger generation. Even if some members of the Vietnamese team speak reasonably good English, discussions among themselves in front of you will be conducted in Vietnamese.

Post the *Doi Moi* economic reforms, the government has been working hard to reduce bureaucracy and red tape. Since then, the number of ministries and government agencies have been drastically reduced. The tech-savvy nation now has official email systems for most of its government departments and administrative documents are exchanged electronically at central and various local levels. Despite these changes, Vietnam is a one-party state, so accountability and transparency remain a challenge. Cumbersome and inconsistent administrative procedures still remain and are a constant source of frustration for its people and businesses. Your Vietnamese counterpart will tell you that informal payment to the government or public bodies are still considered a "must-have behavior" for businesses.[60] In 2022, Vietnam was ranked 77 out of 180 countries according to Transparency International's Corruption Perception Index.[61] Based on the latest Enterprise Survey by the World Bank, Vietnam performs poorly in the area of extortion of funds by public officials "in order to get things done" and in order to secure a government contract.[62] In fact, after

---

[60]Tran, N. M., Nguyen, T. T., Nguyen, T. P. L., Vu, A. T., Phan, T. T. H., Nguyen, T. H. T., Do, N. D., & Phan, A. T. (2022). Female managers and corruption in SMEs: A comparison between family and nonfamily SMEs in Vietnam. *SAGE Open*, 12(1). https://doi.org/10.1177/21582440221082131.

[61]Transparency.org. (January 31, 2023). "2022 Corruption Perceptions Index — Explore Vietnam's Results," Available at https://www.transparency.org/en/cpi/2022.

[62]"Explore Economies." (n.d.). World Bank. Available at https://www.enterprisesurveys.org/en/data/exploreeconomies/2015/vietnam#corruption. (Accessed October 26, 2022).

the pandemic, there was a palpable increase in corruption as its Ministry of Public Security reported a 40% increase in corruption and economic crimes.[63]

The red tape, corruption and language barrier together create a formidable barrier for the foreign negotiator. Especially for those of us who are negotiating in Vietnam for the first time, it is always advisable to seek the help of a Vietnamese intermediary or consultant. The appropriate intermediary can guide the newcomer, make appropriate introductions, maintain tangential involvement and, most importantly, facilitate the trust building with your negotiating counterpart.[64] Relationship building in this country requires working through layers so the right intermediary can avoid pitfalls and fast-track networking.

At the time of writing this chapter, Singapore was the largest investor in Vietnam in 2022 with over 1.45 billion USD, ahead of Japan (third largest), South Korea (fourth largest) and China (fifth largest).[65] Enterprise Singapore, a government agency which helps Singapore companies invest overseas, knows the importance of having the right intermediaries when negotiating deals in countries such as Vietnam. The agency provides a list of firms that can serve as consultants or help with networking.[66] The overarching message is still to build trust and relationships.

Some might consider that returning overseas Vietnamese (*Viet Kieu*) can make suitable intermediaries or interpreters as they have the necessary linguistic and ethnic background. However, this is not always the case. If the Viet Kieu exhibits behavior or communication style that is too

---

[63] VnExpress. (n.d.) "Corruption, Economic Crimes Increase by 40% in Vietnam — VnExpress International." VnExpress International — Latest News, Business, Travel and Analysis from Vietnam. Available at https://e.vnexpress.net/news/news/corruption-economic-crimes-increase-by-40-in-vietnam-4523468.html. (Accessed October 26, 2022).

[64] Borton, L. (2000). Working in a Vietnamese voice [and executive commentary]. *Academy of Management Perspectives*, 14(4), 20–31.

[65] Figures for the first 9 months of 2022. "Disbursement of Public Investment Capital, Foreign Direct Investment, Expecting the Last Months of 2022." General Statistics Office of Vietnam. (2022). Available at https://www.gso.gov.vn/en/data-and-statistics/2022/10/disbursement-of-public-investment-capital-foreign-direct-investment-expecting-the-last-months-of-2022/#:~:text=Among%2063%20countries%20and%20territories.

[66] "Vietnam | In-Market Consultants | Enterprise Singapore." (n.d.). www.enterprisesg.gov.sg. Available at https://www.enterprisesg.gov.sg/overseas-markets/asia-pacific/vietnam/doing-business-in-vietnam/in-market-consultants. (Accessed October 27, 2022).

Westernized, he or she may not be regarded as part of the "in-group" by your Vietnamese negotiator.[67] Even after engaging an intermediary, you should continue to observe for cues to ensure that the relationship-building efforts are not derailed.

8. Time, Timelines and Timeliness

Meetings and appointments typically start on time as the Vietnamese are punctual. You should nevertheless expect discussions to stretch out because there are always the informal chats and small talk before getting on with the agenda. More importantly, you must be prepared for deadlines to move as requests for extension of time are common.[68] Initially, you may be lulled into believing that decision-making can be quite expeditious because of the positive "yes, yes" responses. However, what is more operative are the assurances that follow, such as "I will try my best" or "Should be OK. Don't worry". This means that work is still very much in progress and that you have to wait for the next milestone. You can seek clarification by asking about the time frames involved. Even if decisions are made, they tend to be tentative and subject to change. There is a host of pretexts or reasons for this (regulatory, administrative, oversight, etc.).

However, the Vietnamese are a hardworking people with a "can-do" attitude that is fast becoming their hallmark.[69] They will generally try to get things done, with their own ways and means, and even if they do not have all the resources ready. When you are in Vietnam, you will find this energy in almost all walks of life, in the cities or the rural areas, from micro-businesses to startups to large businesses. So, if you have already put in the effort to build trust with the Vietnamese negotiator, be patient; as things will eventually work out.

---

[67] Borton, L. (2000). Working in a Vietnamese voice [and executive commentary]. *Academy of Management Perspectives*, 14(4), 20–31.

[68] Tran, T., Admiraal, W., & Saab, N. (2020). Work-related values in international workplaces in Vietnam: Cross-cultural differences between employers and employees. *Open Journal of Business and Management*, 8, 1567–1586. doi: 10.4236/ojbm.2020.84100.

[69] Macdonald, R. (2020). Vietnam, land of opportunity. In R. Macdonald (Eds), *The Economy and Business Environment of Vietnam*. Cham: Palgrave Macmillan. https://doi.org/10.1007/978-3-030-49974-7-1.

Bibliography

Alpuerto, A. (2023). "Tech Giant VNG Tests Stock Market Potential with UPCoM Listing." *Vietcetera*, January 4. Available at https://vietcetera.com/en/tech-giant-vng-tests-stock-market-potential-with-upcom-listing.

An, N. H. & Phuong, L. D. M. (2021). Social capital in Vietnam: An analysis of social networks and social trust. *Journal of Mekong Societies*, 17(2), 1–27.

Borton, L. (2000). Working in a Vietnamese voice [and executive commentary]. *Academy of Management Perspectives*, 14(4), 20–31.

Chiricosta, A. (2010). Following the trail of the fairy-bird: The search for a uniquely Vietnamese women's movement. In M. Roces & L. Edwards (Eds.), *Women's Movements in Asia: Feminisms and Transnational Activism* (pp. 124–143). London and New York: Routledge: Taylor & Francis Group.

Church, P. (2017). *Short History of South-East Asia*. Singapore: John Wiley & Sons Inc.

CIA. (September 15, 2022). "The World Factbook." CIA website [downloaded on 15 September 2022], Available at https://www.cia.gov/the-world-factbook/countries/vietnam/.

Dabla-Norris, E., Zhang, Yuanyan Sophia, IMF Asia, & Pacific Department. (March 10, 2021). "Vietnam: Successfully Navigating the Pandemic." IMF. Available at https://www.imf.org/en/News/Articles/2021/03/09/na031021-vietnam-successfully-navigating-the-pandemic. Vietnam achieved a GDP growth of about 2.91% in 2020.

Dinh, P. L. & Ho, T. T. (2020). "How a collectivistic society won the first battle against COVID-19: Vietnam and their "weapons." *Inter-Asia Cultural Studies*, 21(4), 506–520. doi: 10.1080/14649373.2020.1831811.

Do, T. T. (March 2022). "Vietnam's emergence as a middle power in Asia: Unfolding the power–knowledge nexus. *Journal of Current Southeast Asian Affairs*, 186810342210811. https://doi.org/10.1177/18681034221081146.

Do, V. H. T. & Brennan, M. (2015). Complexities of Vietnamese femininities: A resource for rethinking women's university leadership practices. *Gender and Education*, 27(3), 273–287.

Enterprise Singapore. "Vietnam I In-Market Consultants I Enterprise Singapore." (n.d.). www.enterprisesg.gov.sg. Available at https://www.enterprisesg.gov.sg/overseas-markets/asia-pacific/vietnam/doing-business-in-vietnam/in-market-consultants. (Accessed October 27, 2022).

"Foreign Relations, 1969–1976, Volume XLII, Vietnam: The Kissinger-Le Duc Tho Negotiations — Office of the Historian." (n.d.) History.state.gov.

Available at https://history.state.gov/historicaldocuments/frus1969-76v42/preface. (Accessed October 24, 2022).

General Statistics Office of Vietnam. (2021). "Statistical Yearbook of 2021." General Statistics Office of Vietnam. Available at https://www.gso.gov.vn/en/data-and-statistics/2022/08/statistical-yearbook-of-2021/.

General Statistics Office of Vietnam. "Disbursement of Public Investment Capital, Foreign Direct Investment, Expecting the Last Months of 2022." Available at https://www.gso.gov.vn/en/data-and-statistics/2022/10/disbursement-of-public-investment-capital-foreign-direct-investment-expecting-the-last-months-of-2022/#:~:text=Realized%20FDI%20investment%20in%20Vietnam.

Grosse, Ingrid. (2015). Gender values in Vietnam — Between confucianism, communism, and modernization. *Asian Journal of Peacebuilding*, 3(2), 253–272. https://doi.org/10.18588/201511.000045.

Ho, H.-A., Martinsson, P., & Olsson, O. (August 2021). The origins of cultural divergence: Evidence from Vietnam. *Journal of Economic Growth*. https://doi.org/10.1007/s10887-021-09194-x.

Hofstede Insights. "Country Comparison — Hofstede Insights." Available at https://www.hofstede-insights.com/country-comparison/. (Accessed February 6, 2023).

Huong, Ngo Thi Minh, Vu, Giao Cong, & Nguyen, Tam Minh. (2018). Asian values and human rights: A Vietnamese perspective. *Journal of Southeast Asian Human Rights*, 2(1), 302. https://doi.org/10.19184/jseahr.v2i1.7541.

International Labour Office. (2021). "Women in Managerial and Leadership Positions in the G20." Available at https://www.ilo.org/wcmsp5/groups/public/---dgreports/---ddg_p/documents/publication/wcms_762098.pdf.

International Labour Office. (March 2, 2021). "Gender and the Labour Market in Viet Nam." Ilo.org. Available at https://ilo.org/hanoi/Whatwedo/Publications/WCMS_774434/lang--en/index.htm.

Katz, L. (2017). "Negotiating International Business — Vietnam." Negotiating International Business — The Negotiator's Reference Guide to 50 Countries around the World [downloaded on 1 January 2022], available at http://www.leadershipcrossroads.com/mat/cou/Vietnam.pdf.

Kissinger, H. A. (1969). The Viet Nam negotiations. *Foreign Affairs*, 47(2), 211. https://doi.org/10.2307/20039369.

Vietnam. *Law on Gender Equality No. 73/2006/QH11 dated 29 November 2006.* https://thuvienphapluat.vn/van-ban/Quyen-dan-su/Law-No-73-2006-QH11-of-November-29-2006-on-gender-equality-91540.aspx

Le, T. C., Rowley, C., Truong, Q., & Warner, M. (2007). To what extent can management practices be transferred between countries? The case of human resource management in Vietnam. *Journal of World Business*, 42, 113–127.

Lewicki, R. J., Saunders, D. M., & Barry, B. (2021). *Essentials of Negotiation.* New York: Mcgraw-Hill Education.

Lien, H. (2022). "Lego Breaks Ground on $1bn Carbon-Neutral Factory in Vietnam." *Nikkei Asia*, November 3. Available at https://asia.nikkei.com/Spotlight/Supply-Chain/Lego-breaks-ground-on-1bn-carbon-neutral-factory-in-Vietnam.

Macdonald, R. (2020). Vietnam, land of opportunity. In R. Macdonald (Eds.), *The Economy and Business Environment of Vietnam.* Cham: Palgrave Macmillan. https://doi.org/10.1007/978-3-030-49974-7_1.

Ministry of Planning and Investment. (n.d.). "Ministry of Planning and Investment Portal." www.mpi.gov.vn. Available at https://www.mpi.gov.vn/en/Pages/tinbai.aspx?idTin=54532&idcm=122.

Nguyen, L. D., Mujtaba, B. G., & Boehmer, T. (2012). Stress, task, and relationship orientations across German and Vietnamese cultures. *International Business and Management*, 5(1), 10–20. http://dx.doi.org/10.3968/j.ibm.1923842820120501.1060.

Nguyen, Q. T. N. (2016). The Vietnamese values system: A blend of oriental, Western and Socialist values. *International Education Studies*, 9(12), 32–40. Available at https://files.eric.ed.gov/fulltext/EJ1121509.pdf.

Nguyen, Quynh-Anh Ngoc. (2019). "Exploring Emotional Intelligence: A Study of Vietnamese Hotel Workers." Available at https://eprints.bournemouth.ac.uk/32580/1/NGUYEN,%20Quynh_Ph.D._2019.pdf.

Nosowitz, D. (March 28, 2017). "Why 40% of Vietnamese People Have the Same Last Name." *Atlas Obscura*, March 28. Available at https://www.atlasobscura.com/articles/pronounce-nguyen-common-vietnam.

Phạm, Q. P. (December 2020). "Covid-19 in Vietnam: Social Engagement, Trust Creation and Political Legitimacy." *Halshs.archives-Ouvertes.fr*. Available at https://halshs.archives-ouvertes.fr/halshs-03151081.

Pham, T. H. N. (2007). Exploring the concept of "face" in Vietnamese: Evidence from its collocational abilities/Khám phá Khái niệm Thể diện trong Tiếng Việt: Bằng chứng từ Kết hợp Từ. *Electronic Journal of Foreign Language Teaching*, 4, 257–266.

Pham, T. H. N. (2014). How do the Vietnamese lose face? Understanding the concept of face through self-reported, face loss incidents. *International Journal of Language and Linguistics*, 2(3), 223. https://doi.org/10.11648/j.ijll.20140203.21.

Pham, T. H. N. (2014). The impact of third party presence on the motivational concerns underlying linguistic politeness behavior in English-speaking intercultural contexts. *Journal for the Study of English Linguistics*, 2(1), 19. https://doi.org/10.5296/jsel.v2i1.5833.

Ready, K. J. & Van Dinh. (2006). Vietnams developing markets: How do perceptions and strategies in the negotiation process differ from The US? *Journal of Diversity Management (JDM)*, 1(1), 49–60. https://doi.org/10.19030/jdm.v1i1.5029.

Tran, N. M., Nguyen, T. T., Nguyen, T. P. L., Vu, A. T., Phan, T. T. H., Nguyen, T. H. T., Do, N. D., & Phan, A. T. (2022). Female managers and corruption in SMEs: A comparison between family and nonfamily SMEs in Vietnam. *SAGE Open*, 12(1). https://doi.org/10.1177/21582440221082131.

Tran, T., Admiraal, W., & Saab, N. (2020). Work-related values in international workplaces in Vietnam: cross-cultural differences between employers and employees. *Open Journal of Business and Management*, 8, 1567–1586. doi: 10.4236/ojbm.2020.84100.

Transparency.org. (January 31, 2023). "2022 Corruption Perceptions Index — Explore Vietnam's Results." Available at https://www.transparency.org/en/cpi/2022.

VietnamPlus. (December 29, 2022). "Vietnam's GDP Expands by 8.02% in 2022 | Business | Vietnam+ (VietnamPlus)." Available at https://en.vietnamplus.vn/vietnams-gdp-expands-by-802-in-2022/246296.vnp.

VnExpress. (n.d.). "Corruption, Economic Crimes Increase by 40% in Vietnam — VnExpress International." VnExpress International — Latest News, Business, Travel and Analysis from Vietnam. Available at https://e.vnexpress.net/news/news/corruption-economic-crimes-increase-by-40-in-vietnam-4523468.html. (Accessed October 26, 2022).

"31 Ways to Say Yes No in Vietnamese | Ling App." December 12, 2020. Available at https://ling-app.com/vi/yes-no-in-vietnamese/.

World Bank. (n.d.). "Explore Economies." World Bank. Available at https://www.enterprisesurveys.org/en/data/exploreeconomies/2015/vietnam#corruption. (Accessed October 26, 2022).

World Economic Forum. (July 13, 2022). "Global Gender Gap Report 2022." World Economic Forum. Available at https://www.weforum.org/reports/global-gender-gap-report-2022/digest.

World Economic Forum. "Where Are the Largest Chinese Populations Outside of China? | Thailand or Indonesia: Which Country Has the Largest Chinese Population? | By World Economic Forum | Facebook." Available at https://www.facebook.com/worldeconomicforum/videos/where-are-the-largest-chinese-populations-outside-of-china/10153549858561479/. (Accessed November 8, 2022).

Vietnam Quiz

1. In 1986, Vietnam embarked on an economic reform to transform its
   centrally planned economy to a socialist-oriented multi-sector market
   economy known as _____. Fill in the blank.
   A. Quoc Ngu
   B. Viet Kieu
   C. Quan He
   D. Doi Moi

2. The Vietnamese society is deeply influenced by Confucianism and
   Chinese culture and most Vietnamese display characteristic Confucian
   traits such as respect for hierarchy, loyalty to family and emphasis on
   individual's social obligation. Is this general characterization true or
   false?
   A. True
   B. False

3. Like China, Vietnam is a socialist state with a market economy. The
   Vietnamese society is also deeply influenced by Confucianism.
   Therefore, business dealing in Vietnam is the same as in China. Is this
   general characterization true or false?
   A. True
   B. False

4. It is popularly believed that there is a north–south cultural difference
   along which one of Hofstede's cultural dimensions?
   A. Power Distance
   B. Individualism–Collectivism
   C. Uncertainty Avoidance
   D. None of the above

5. Vietnam has a complex regulatory environment constantly being
   revised and updated by its one-party state. Business people know that
   there may be laws and regulations, but compliance and circumvention
   can come in many forms. Is this general characterization true or false?
   A. True
   B. False

6. The Vietnamese concept of face ("mặt") is both an individual and collective possession. Loss of face thus means disapproval of the individual as well as the group he/she is associated with. Is this general characterization true or false?
   A. True
   B. False

7. The Vietnamese are constantly polite and appear eager to compromise. They commonly begin the negotiation by asking you what they can offer and how they can help. What is the fundamental or default strategy for the Vietnamese negotiator?
   A. Integrative
   B. Conciliatory
   C. Distributive
   D. Accommodating

8. In order to achieve integrative negotiation with the Vietnamese, you have to work on earning their trust. One approach you can take is to _____. Fill in the blank.
   A. make large concessions at the start of the negotiation
   B. engage a Vietnamese intermediary
   C. disclose some relevant information about your position and interest
   D. be punctual for all meetings and appointments

9. As a result of the deep influence of Confucianism and hierarchical structures in the society, Vietnamese women have a low social status, similar to their counterparts in China, Japan and Korea. Is this general characterization true or false?
   A. True
   B. False

10. Business meetings in Vietnam rarely start on time. The Vietnamese are always pleasant and amicable and are rarely worked up when you are late or even when you fail to show up. Is this general characterization true or false?
    A. True
    B. False

Answer Bank

1. D
2. A
3. B
4. B
5. A
6. A
7. C
8. C
9. B
10. B

Conclusion

In 2014, Harvard Law School's Program on Negotiation and Harvard Kennedy School's Future of Diplomacy Project jointly named former Singapore diplomat, Professor Tommy Koh, the winner of the Great Negotiator Award.[1] The award is in recognition of Koh's illustrious work including serving as chief negotiator for the US–Singapore Free Trade Agreement, as the chair for negotiations that produced the ASEAN charter and for leading two global mega-conferences, namely, the Third UN Conference on the Law of the Sea and the UN Conference on the Environment and Development, also known as the Rio Earth Summit. The veteran negotiator was Singapore's Permanent Representative to the United Nations, New York, for over a decade and served as ambassador to the US (1984–1990). One of Professor Koh's top tips for successful negotiation is this: "The beginning of wisdom is to understand that we all live in our own cultural box. We should therefore make an attempt to understand the content of the cultural box of our negotiating counterparts. This will help move the negotiation forward."[2]

---

[1] PON. (September 16, 2013). "Ambassador Tommy Koh of Singapore Named the Great Negotiator by the Program on Negotiation and the Future of Diplomacy Project." PON — Program on Negotiation at Harvard Law School. Available at https://www.pon.harvard.edu/daily/international-negotiation-daily/the-program-on-negotiation-and-the-future-of-diplomacy-project-name-tommy-koh-of-singapore-great-negotiator-of-2014/.

[2] Leadership Institute. (August 7, 2019). "Tommy Koh's Top Tips for Successful Negotiation." Available at https://www.leadershipinstitute.sg/post/tommykohtips.

Cultural differences can be a huge barrier, so appropriate understanding is definitely needed to yield results. Yet, unpacking cultural boxes — yours as well as those of others — is one of the greatest rewards of international negotiations. East Asia offers fertile grounds for you to claim this prize. Far from being homogeneous, Asian culture is richly pluralistic. Each East Asian negotiator covered in this book brings to the table their own unique communication pattern, negotiation style and distinct brand of collectivistic behavior.

The Javanese negotiator in Indonesia, as well as their *Tionghua* (ethnic Chinese) countrymen are both skilled in projecting a calm demeanor to mask their adroit distributive bargaining skills. The Indonesian collectivist trait is reinforced by their state ideology of *gotong royong* (mutual assistance) so everyone must work together for the interest of the group. The Malaysian negotiation style tends to be more integrative because they prefer longer-term business relationships. Poor delivery of negative feedback can cause loss of face to them and result in unintended distributive outcomes; thus, using an intermediary or third party to convey disagreement or rejection is particularly useful in this high power-distance society. The Filipinos also have a strong preference for integrative negotiation as they are guided by their concept of *kapwa* (meaning: "seeing you as their fellow being"). Their indirect communication pattern stems from a deep desire to avoid causing you (the negotiator) embarrassment or shame. This is their way of "giving face" to you and not jeopardizing your social standing, which is very important to them. The pragmatic but competitive Singaporean negotiator tends to claim utilitarian value first, especially when negotiating over tangibles such as prices and time schedules. Their multicultural background coupled with the fact that English is their first and working language make Singaporeans more direct in their communicative style compared to their fellow East Asians. Nevertheless, they are group-oriented and "face" is still important, which means they do not like to overstep their authority or make mistakes in front of others. The Thai negotiators have both the personality and the propensity to be integrative. Their goal is to build a reciprocal relationship with you as their fellow negotiator, underpinned and serviced by an element of gratitude. However, you may find it difficult to decipher the indirect Thai communicator because of their *krengjai* culture that will readily sacrifice honesty to observe hierarchy and preserve your ego. Distributive bargaining is the default style of the tenacious Vietnamese negotiator. When motivated to build long-term win–win relationships, their "can-do" attitude will help find ways and means to accommodate your and their interests. In this collectivist society, Southerners are perceived as being more individualistic than the Northerners, but both will understate their meanings and rely on nonverbal cues to communicate with you. Though situated in Southeast Asia, Vietnam is culturally closer to its Northeast Asian neighbors — China, Japan and Korea — all of whom have their own distinctive negotiation styles.

Chinese negotiators prefer the distributive approach because business dealings are generally perceived as being low-trust endeavors. And if you have not established the necessary *guanxi* (connections), you have very slim chances of achieving an integrative process. Their subtle and even ambivalent communication style adds another challenge as the Chinese have an array of tactics and techniques at their disposal to convey rejection and disagreement. In contrast, you can expect the Japanese negotiators to pursue integrative strategies. They will meticulously prepare all information necessary for negotiation and are willing to share these with you. Of course, there will be instances where you will face distributive behavior. In this case, the Japanese negotiators will try their utmost to conceal their true positions and put up a *tatemae* (façade). Inferential skills are definitely required to understand this high-context culture that may even express rejection in polite terms when the deal falls through. Establishing the appropriate *kibun* (feeling/atmosphere) with the South Korean negotiator will set the stage for an integrative negotiation. Because they are emotionally more expressive, the South Koreans are comparatively more direct and forthcoming than their other Northeast Asian counterparts, including the North Koreans.

The authors hope that you will look forward to your next negotiation encounter with one of the East Asian negotiators profiled in this book. And to build on Professor Tommy Koh's advice — "Think out of the box and have a great adventure!"[3]

---

[3] *Ibid.*

Printed in the USA
CPSIA information can be obtained
at www.ICGtesting.com
LVHW012205081223
765507LV00003B/10